LEGENDARY LOCALS OF WHEATON ILLINOIS

KEITH CALL

LEGENDARY LOCALS

ISBN 978-1-4671-0011-3

Published by Legendary Locals, an imprint of Arcadia Publishing
Charleston, South Carolina

Printed in the United States of America

Library of Congress Control Number: 2011944079

For all general information, please contact Arcadia Publishing:
Telephone 843-853-2070
Fax 843-853-0044
E-mail sales@arcadiapublishing.com
For customer service and orders:
Toll-Free 1-888-313-2665

Visit us on the Internet at www.arcadiapublishing.com

Dedication

To Seth, Amy, Caleb, Colin, Callie and Carson, not local but surely legendary.

On the Cover: From left to right:
(TOP ROW) Shannon Lucid, astronaut (Courtesy of NASA; see page 114), Louise Stoddard Wheaton, distinguished citizen (Courtesy of Wheaton College Archives and Special Collections; see page 51), Jordan Kemper, health enthusiast (Courtesy of Jordan Kemper; see page 15), Paul Gast, scientist (Courtesy of Walter Gast; see page 118), Muriel Fuller, editor (Courtesy of Wheaton College Archives and Special Collections; see page 30).
(MIDDLE ROW) Frances Carothers Blanchard, physician (Courtesy of Wheaton College Archives and Special Collections; see page 65), Catherine Marshall, author (Courtesy of Wheaton College Archives and Special Collections; see page 49), Lt. Archibald Campbell, fallen World War II veteran (Courtesy of Wheaton College Archives and Special Collections; see page 68), Edgar C. Bundy, patriot (Courtesy of Wheaton College Archives and Special Collections; see page 80), Robert E. Webber, professor (Courtesy of Wheaton College Archives and Special Collections; see page 124).
(BOTTOM ROW) Joseph M. Stowell, college president (Courtesy of Cornerstone University; see page 55), David Maas, historian (Courtesy of Wheaton College Archives and Special Collections; see page 126), Coleman Luck, screenwriter (Courtesy of Wheaton College Archives and Special Collections; see page 32), David Lyon, outstanding father (Courtesy of College Church; see page 87), William Osborne, ex-slave and pastor (Courtesy of Wheaton College Archives and Special Collections; see page 95).

CONTENTS

ACKNOWLEDGMENTS

Unless otherwise noted, most images appearing without credit were graciously provided by Wheaton College (IL) Archives and Special Collections. I scanned one non-archival image from a book by a deceased author (David Fasold) published by a defunct publishing house (Knightsbridge). I did not find contact information.These kind folk deserve a steak dinner or a serenade: Augie Fackler, Jeff Jeffers, Marcia Gray Martin, Barbara Hall, Walter Gast, Bill Pollard, Rick McKinley, Bob Dresser, Josh Okerman, Bob Adams, Shauna Berman, Sergio Villanueva, Kevin Jones, Keaton Halley, Audra Bonnet, Bob Maher, Bill and Mary Anne Phemister, Aaron Fisher, Margie Wilhelmi, Ron Stewart, Tim Botts, Ray Wu, Jordan Kemper, Mike Lee, Hannah Maletich, Mike Pellegrini, Janis Herbert, David Maas, Dean Arnold, Jason and Charisa Krieg, John Belle, Vonny Albert, Greg Aagaard, Dawn Clark, Carolyn DeAre, Joseph Stowell, Sara Arnas, Josh McDowell, Pete Leonard, Bernie Ishmael, Tim Peters, Stefan Bechtel, Lawrence Reid Bechtel, Phil Taschetta, Don Toht, Chuck and Vicki Kinnaman, Leanne Payne, Shannon Lucid, Kay McKeen, Richard Gieser, Dick and Florence Nogaj, Norma Whitt, and Ron Moore. Gift-wrapped gratitude is extended to David Malone, head of Wheaton College Archives and Special Collections, Barbara Fackler, Ray Smith, and Chip Krueger for hot tips and a gentle push. And lastly, I bow at the waist and kiss the hand of Tiffany Frary, the Lady Editor. If I've forgotten anybody, please accept my apologies. Acknowledged or not, you are a hero too.

LEGENDARY LOCALS OF WHEATON ILLINOIS

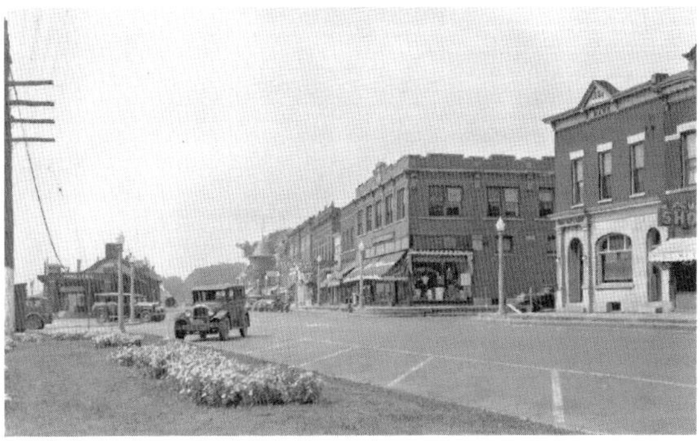

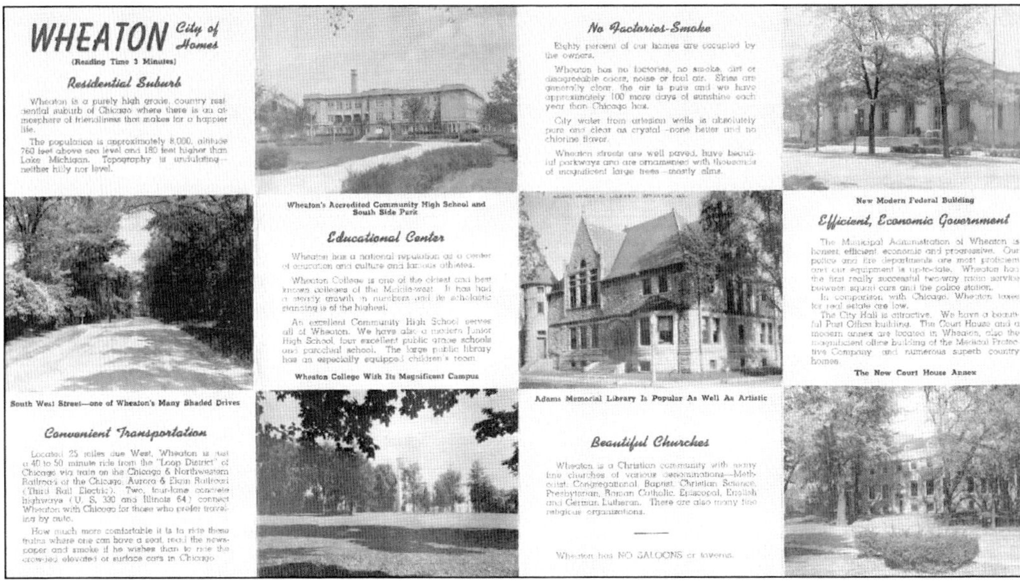

WHEATON *City of Homes*

(Reading Time 3 Minutes)

Residential Suburb

Wheaton is a purely high grade, country residential suburb of Chicago where there is an atmosphere of friendliness that makes for a happier life.

The population is approximately 8,000, altitude 760 feet above sea level and 180 feet higher than Lake Michigan. Topography is undulating—neither hilly nor level.

Wheaton's Accredited Community High School and South Side Park

Educational Center

Wheaton has a national reputation as a center of education and culture and famous athletes.

Wheaton College is one of the oldest and best known colleges of the Middle-west. It has had a steady growth in numbers and its scholastic standing is of the highest.

An excellent Community High School serves all of Wheaton. We have also a modern Junior High School, four excellent public grade schools and parochial school. The large public library has an especially equipped children's room.

Wheaton College With Its Magnificent Campus

No Factories-Smoke

Eighty percent of our homes are occupied by the owners.

Wheaton has no factories, no smoke, dirt or disagreeable odors, noise or foul air. Skies are generally clear, the air is pure and we have approximately 100 more days of sunshine each year than Chicago has.

City water from artesian wells is absolutely pure and clear as crystal—none better and no chlorine flavor.

Wheaton streets are well paved, have beautiful parkways and are ornamented with thousands of magnificent large trees—mostly elms.

Adams Memorial Library Is Popular As Well As Artistic

New Modern Federal Building

Efficient, Economic Government

The Municipal Administration of Wheaton is honest, efficient, economic and progressive. Our police and fire departments are most proficient and our equipment is up-to-date. Wheaton has the first really successful two-way radio service between squad cars and the police station.

In comparison with Chicago, Wheaton taxes for real estate are low.

The City Hall is attractive. We have a beautiful Post Office building. The Court House and a modern annex are located in Wheaton, also the magnificent office building of the Medical Protective Company and numerous superb country homes.

The New Court House Annex

South West Street—one of Wheaton's Many Shaded Drives

Convenient Transportation

Located 25 miles due West, Wheaton is just a 40 to 50 minute ride from the "Loop District" of Chicago via train on the Chicago & Northwestern Railroad or the Chicago, Aurora & Elgin Railroad (Third Rail Electric). Two, four-lane concrete highways (U. S. 330 and Illinois 64) connect Wheaton with Chicago for those who prefer traveling by auto.

How much more comfortable it is to ride these trains where one can have a seat, read the newspaper and smoke if he wishes than to ride the crowded elevated or surface cars in Chicago.

Beautiful Churches

Wheaton is a Christian community with many fine churches of various denominations—Methodist, Congregational, Baptist, Christian Science, Presbyterian, Roman Catholic, Episcopal, English and German Lutheran. There are also many fine religious organizations.

Wheaton has NO SALOONS or taverns.

Page 1: Front Street

Everything changes, everything stays the same. In this view looking from Cross St. to the shops along Front St. in the 1930s, the buildings remain, as do the diagonal parking slots facing the train tracks, but all of these businesses are gone. Of course, a Starbucks now occupies the corner bank building with the stone façade. The train station on the far left houses a frozen yogurt shop, and the building with the cupola has an upscale Italian restaurant on the second floor. During the summer, Front Street is closed on Friday evenings for a car show featuring many of the models seen here, in addition to vehicles from successive decades.

Page 2: Wheaton, City of Homes

A late 1950s booklet, *Wheaton, City of Homes*, published by the Chamber of Commerce, describes the residential suburb of 8,000 as "purely high grade," with "no factories, no smoke, dirt or disagreeable odors, noise or foul air." The text, confidently stating that "Wheaton has never had or wanted a real estate boom," surely evokes bygone days as it goes on about "city water from artesian wells…absolutely clear as crystal – none better and no chlorine flavor." Since those words were written, Wheaton has been totally absorbed into the monstrous urban blob called "Chicagoland," surrendering its spacious horse ranches, orchards, and shaded country drives to tight tract housing and shopping malls. A terse statement near the bottom of the page declares, "Wheaton has NO SALOONS or taverns." That, too, has changed. Today, Wheaton's population is 55,000.

INTRODUCTION

January 20, 1981. Sixth grade at Central School. Cold. The gunmetal-gray weeks stretching beyond Christmas.

Around noon our teacher told us to lay aside our pencils, sit still, and watch the televised inauguration of Ronald Reagan. This is history, she insisted. Indeed, two impressions from that day remain. Firstly, as a loyal Boy Scout, I was the only student in that fidgety, overheated classroom who stood and placed his hand on his heart during the national anthem, a lonely act of patriotism both embarrassing and exhilarating. The second memory is Reagan's speech. Duly sworn in, he stepped to the microphone, eyes twinkling, to address the nation. Of course, his politics meant nothing to us. Eventually, however, he started talking about heroes. Heroes? We had them. Batman. G.I. Joe. The Six Million Dollar Man.

Suddenly he had my ear.

"We have every right to dream heroic dreams," said the Great Communicator. "Those who say that we are in a time when there are no heroes just don't know where to look. You can see heroes every day going in and out of factory gates . . .You meet heroes across a counter—and they are on both sides of that counter. There are entrepreneurs with faith in themselves and faith in an idea who create new jobs, new wealth, and opportunity. They are individuals and families whose taxes support the government and whose voluntary gifts support church, charity, culture, art, and education. Their patriotism is quiet but deep. Their values sustain our national life. I have used the words 'they' and 'their' in speaking of these heroes. I could say 'you' and 'your' because I am addressing the heroes of whom I speak—you, the citizens of this blessed land."

But Reagan seemed to have in mind another sort of hero, not those ostentatious chaps wearing capes or driving sexy cars, but people like my teacher, doctor, or scoutmaster. In the years following his speech, the idea stuck firmly in my head that heroism does not always wear glitter. In fact, it often walks softly and carries a weary world on its shoulders. Heroism works hard and shares its cookies without coercion. It says "please" and "thank you" and shows up on time.

With this notion tucked away with other facts of life picked up along the way, I eventually secured employment in the Wheaton College Archives and Special Collections. Spelunking among rusty artifacts and crumbling scrapbooks, I frequently stumbled across the poems of Judge Frank Herrick, longtime magistrate and arch-Prohibitionist.

An 1899 graduate of Wheaton College (which he described as "a hotbed of Prohibition and a darn nice place"), Herrick then graduated from Illinois College of Law and was admitted to the bar in 1902. That year he was elected justice of the peace, and in 1905 he was elected police magistrate and remained so for the next 50 years, maintaining an office in the Gary-Wheaton Bank Building. Struck by the muse, Herrick wrote poetry. Lots of it. When he was not tending to official business, he seemed to spend every moment roaming shops and byways, observing mundane tasks, listening, studying faces. And then, bursting, he wrote—of professors and preachers and grocers and housewives and politicians and veterans, poems stacked on poems tucked away in countless saddle-stitched chapbooks. Endlessly fascinated with the lifeblood of his hometown, Herrick wrote in 1936:

Wheaton is the city of many beauties,
It is replete with Christian temples
And great towers of learning adorn it!

Its streets are lined with living pillars
And its avenues with verdant columns,
The people pass beneath leafy arches!

Brave forbears laid its foundations
And true hearts established its borders,
From strong souls came this inheritance!

I have written its praises in rhythm,
In meter have I measured its greatness
And crowned its fine people with poems!

It is full of the daughters of music,
Divines and teachers have graced it,
Its children are like fields of flowers!

I love this place with great passion,
The cords of the past bind me to it,
I have anchored my ship in this haven!

When he died at 92 in 1967, Wheaton's best-known citizen and official poet laureate had hammered out 2,000 poems on his Oliver typewriter. Undisturbed by the earth-shaking alterations wrought upon literature by Ezra Pound, T.S. Eliot, and Wallace Stevens, Herrick's poetry is, however, supercharged with a profound respect and fascination for good neighbors reliably performing their daily activities. Less talented, perhaps, than his better-known contemporaries, he nonetheless captured otherwise irretrievable moments with his notepad rather than a camera, offering a unique historical perspective spanning decades. Another Illinois poet, Edgar Lee Masters, portrays the characters of *Spoon River Anthology* as lost, brittle ghosts, cold and hopeless in the ground; but Herrick's "true hearts" and "daughters of music" are touchable, gallant, warm-blooded, alive in the light. With Reagan's royal words about "heroes across the counter" echoing in my psyche, discovering Herrick's corpus, soaked with joy, praise, and celebration, is pleasing indeed. This book should be considered a continuation of his desire to "crown [Wheaton's] fine people with poems." While not employing verse, I have attempted, as he did, to look and listen and sensitively absorb the ripest fragrances and the sweetest music of this place and pass it all along, discreetly whispering to the ear of posterity, "See that man over there? That woman? Heroes. Leave your mark, too."

As the legend has it, Diogenes the philosopher roamed the streets of Athens, holding forth his lantern, searching for an honest man. Similarly, compiling this book, I walked the streets of Wheaton, searching for men and women of honesty, productivity, creativity, and dedication. I found them. In nearly every instance when a subject was approached about possible inclusion, the quiet response was, "I'm honored. But I'm really not worthy." Then I would offer the truthful assurance that I am the one who is honored. To ask a man or woman of extraordinary character, ability, or sacrifice to pause for a moment and consider sharing something of these qualities through word and image, trusting me with the responsibility . . . ?

No. I am the one who is honored.

Choosing the faces represented, I have purposely avoided, with a few notable exceptions, covering those who have been featured elsewhere. You will find excellent profiles of comedians John and Jim Belushi, football superstar Red Grange, historian Glennette Tilley Turner, and filmmaker Wes Craven in Mary Anne Phemister's charming *32 Wheaton Notables: Their Stories and Where They Lived.* Jean Moore's *Wheaton: A Pictorial History* is a detailed, beautifully produced history. Jeanne Guilfoyle has already discussed a portion of the Catholic community in *The Wheaton Franciscan Heritage* (Arcadia); and *Veggie Tales* creator Phil Vischer, crime novelist Robert Goldsborough, and The Theosophical Society are covered in *Wheaton* (Arcadia).

A few discussed herein are dead. Some no longer reside in Illinois. But each has driven a nail, so to speak, into this big house on the prairie. The profiles cover a broad range of experiences and eras, but one aspect each subject shares is the unshakeable pleasure of *life*—and these lives are spacious enough to accommodate friendly visits from curious neighbors. If your flame flickers in the cold and requires a bit of fanning, enter the chapters ahead where the fires of life dance in the night.

CHAPTER ONE

The Athletes

A biographer of Harold "Red" Grange, the legendary football player from Wheaton, was asked why anybody should still care about the Galloping Ghost. Though Grange's athletic career is impressive, his persistent presence in the contemporary sports pantheon seems somewhat misplaced. He was not particularly charismatic, spoke quietly, and did not boast a steroid-marinated musculature. In fact, he is nondescript. After considering the question, the biographer responded that Grange was a stand-up boy from a small, wholesome Midwestern town, performing in what was considered a sleazy sport. He threw himself into battle and won, won, won—the game and, in fact, all of football. Grange brought football out of the smoke-filled back room into the living room, legitimizing it for the American public. And so, when father or son or cousins sit awkwardly on the sofa to watch the game on Monday night or Thanksgiving Day and there is nothing else to talk about, they can at least talk about football. Grange's career provided this de facto symbolic language, according to his biographer. Perhaps this explanation is the key to the unique athleticism of Wheaton: the chosen sport provides an entry point for interpreting the human experience. For Greg Aagaard, running creates a spiritual zone for meditation, preparing him for the responsibilities of business and leadership. Kevin Jones, playing soccer in foreign lands, saw firsthand the wreckage of Third World poverty, deciding to relay something of his happy childhood to deprived people through social assistance. Similarly, the Chicago Eagles use soccer as a passage into spheres of ministry. Wayne Wray, critically injured on the gridiron, shifted his vocation from oceanography to therapy, seeking to assist others with spinal trauma. Mike Lee, boxer, raises funds for needy villages in Bangladesh. Jordan Kemper, former football and basketball player, offers through seminars his passion for health and spiritual well-being. Keaton Halley, artist and lecturer, dancing from foot to foot with extraordinary dexterity as he kicks the Hacky Sack, inspires youth to focus their energies. For the thoughtful athlete, sport is simply a gateway through which he engages the pressing issues of life.

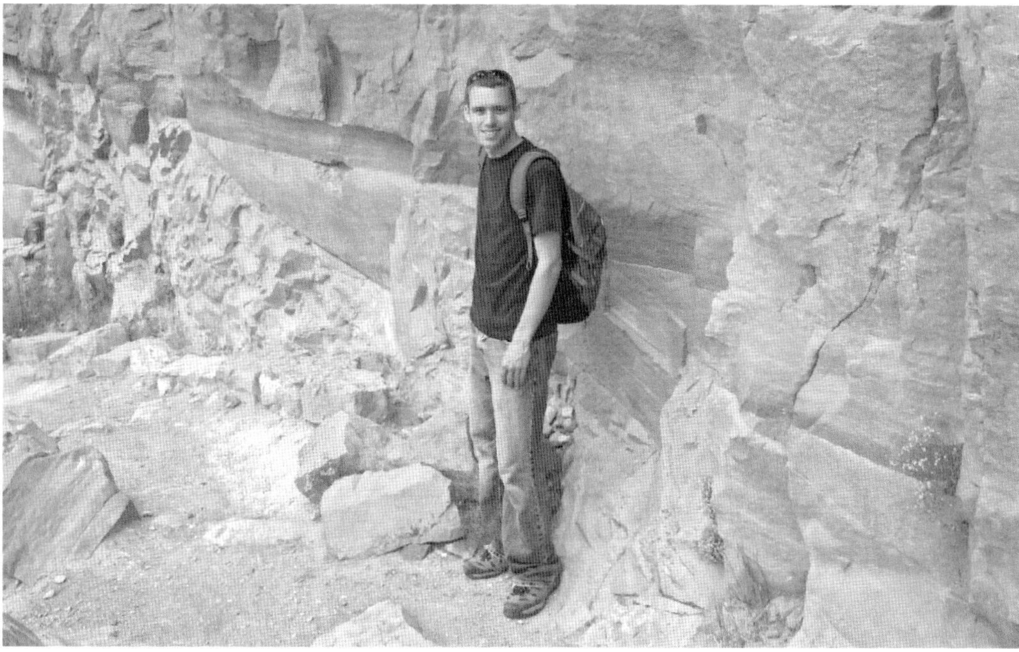

Keaton Halley
Halley hikes the Grand Canyon, "the house of stone and light." Together with Scott Davidson he took second place in Open Doubles Freestyle at the World Footbag Championships in 2007. Halley has a keen interest in the origins controversy, and promotes Young Earth Creationism in various forums including churches and schools. He also volunteers with the Midwest Creation Fellowship. Halley is self-employed as a web designer. (Courtesy of Keaton Halley.)

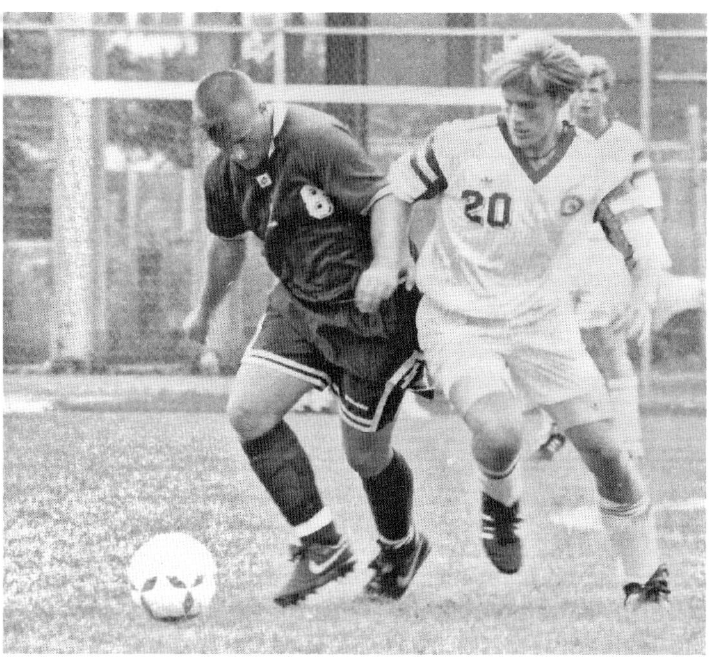

Kevin Jones
After spending his early childhood as the son of missionaries in Colombia and Venezuela, Jones (right, No. 20) moved to Wheaton in the third grade, acquiring a vision for community as a value to be shared, not isolated. A brilliant soccer player at Moody Bible Institute, Jones organized matches on the South Side of Chicago. Ending his athletic career, he now assists families with locating housing in nurturing neighborhoods, like the one he knew in Wheaton. (Courtesy of Heidi Stauff.)

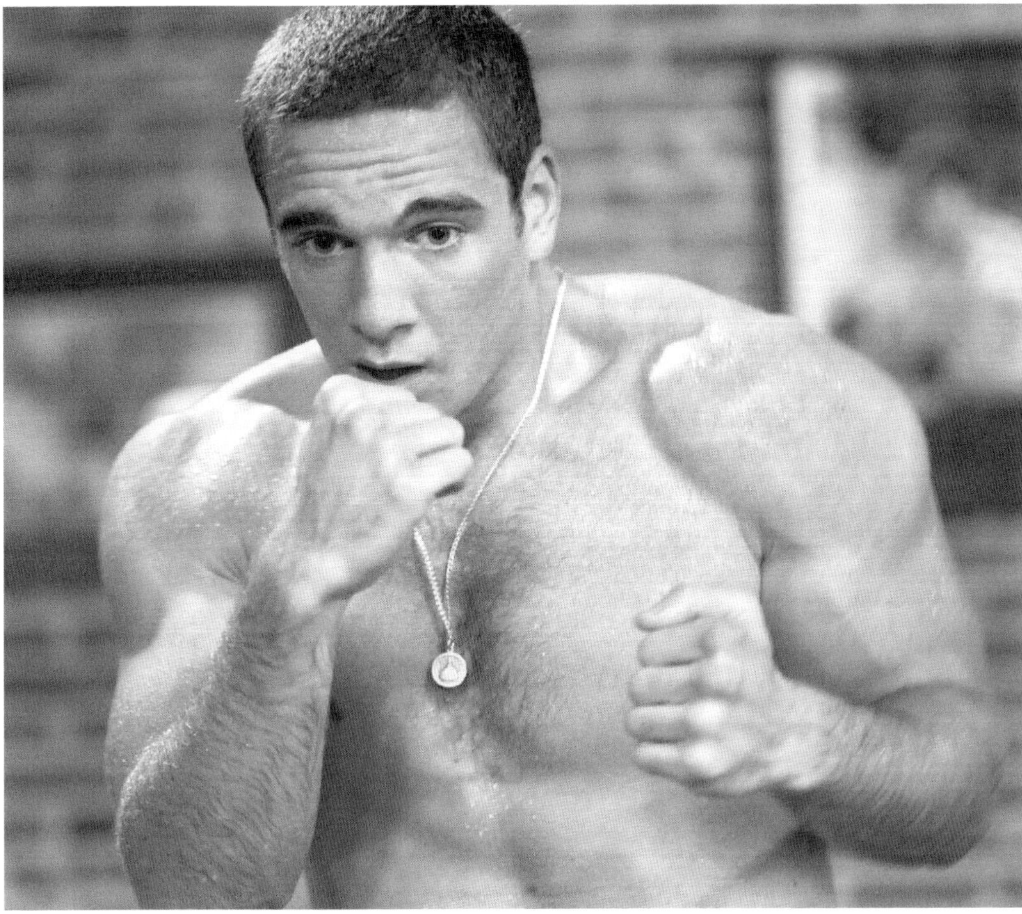

Mike Lee
Considering the fact that he possesses a degree in finance from the Mendoza College of Business at Notre Dame University, Lee does not fit the stereotypical profile of a professional lightweight boxer, defying the assumption that the toughest fighters emerge from the harshest origins. Growing up in the protected affluence of Wheaton and graduating in 2005 from the Benet Academy in Lisle, Lee frequented boxing gyms on the grittier South Side of Chicago, learning the art of pugilism. Attending Notre Dame in South Bend, Indiana, he was three-time winner of the "Bengal Bouts," an intramural boxing tournament begun in 1920 by the legendary Knute Rockne. It was at Notre Dame that Lee first stepped into the ring. After graduating, he completed the 2009 Chicago's Golden Gloves competition, defeating five opponents, winning his class. He also volunteered at a Bangladeshi school, eventually establishing his own foundation to assist funding for the Holy Cross Missions. In 2008, he personally visited Bangladesh to see how funds raised for the mission were being positively implemented. In addition to boxing, Lee desires to give back. Profits from the Mike Lee Foundation also go to the Robinson Community Learning Center, the Ara Parseghian Medical Research Foundation, and the Kelly Cares Foundation. He is renowned for throwing himself with gusto into all aspects of life, as well as his arduous training and boxing. Well-spoken and admittedly shy outside of the ring, he efficiently pounds his opponents senseless inside the ring. Lee is an undefeated professional boxer in the light heavyweight class. His popularity increases with each fight as he attracts fans who are not necessarily boxing enthusiasts. He resides in Houston, Texas, where he trains with Ronnie Shields, who mentored Evander Holyfield among other world champions. (Courtesy of Chris Farina, Top Rank Inc.)

A WRAY OF HOPE

by Gary Taylor
Ass't. Football Coach

Three emergency major surgeries in three days. Three occasions for neurosurgeons to say "no hope." "The worst type of neck injury ever confronted. We don't expect him to live out the night." A day passes, another, and another for Wayne Wray and his hope in an intensive care room.

A crucial week passes. Wayne's still alive. Barely. Conscious, praying for the Lord's will in his life, he is aware of the magnitude of his injury while playing football for the Wheaton College Crusaders.

His athletic goal was to be the starting defensive end for the Crusaders. He earned the position only to break his neck on October 7, 1972, while tackling the ball carrier on a kick-off late in the game. Wayne's play on the field that day had certainly been a ray of hope for the team.

Today, confined to a wheel chair after two years of total paralysis, he has become a WRAY OF HOPE, not just for himself, but for the hundreds of lives his injury has affected. Coaches, players, and fans followed his slow progress in five hospitals and rehabilitation centers. "He cheers and lifts you up when you go to see him. He's not bitter, he would play again if his body were healed," his visitors relate.

Wayne's faith in Jesus Christ has given him the courage to meet each operation, each therapy, each day, with the great expectation his life has purpose. Many of his classmates, friends of the college, friends in the sports world, the opposing team's student body, the colleges in the conference, have contributed tremendously financially to assist with his medical expenses. With hospital costs over $100 a day, the expense has been awesome. Insurance funds were exhausted long ago. Unpaid medical bills still total over $20,000.

A WRAY OF HOPE campaign has now been planned to erase the remaining medical bills and to provide funds for Wayne's education. He is taking courses and plans to receive a degree in counseling so he might instill a WRAY OF HOPE in others like himself who have suffered paralyzing injuries. Wayne desires to inspire others to fight on, to overcome circumstances and to live meaningful lives from a bed or wheelchair. Even now, he is learning to type, write, and print so he can communicate with others needing encouragement.

A foundation has committed itself to a $10,000 gift to the WRAY OF HOPE Fund if alumni, students and friends contribute $10,000 by December 31. Gifts to the Alumni Fund may be designated for this purpose. In the past two years over $30,000 has been given to defray the tremendous costs. The continued prayers and financial support of the "Wheaton Family" is greatly appreciated.

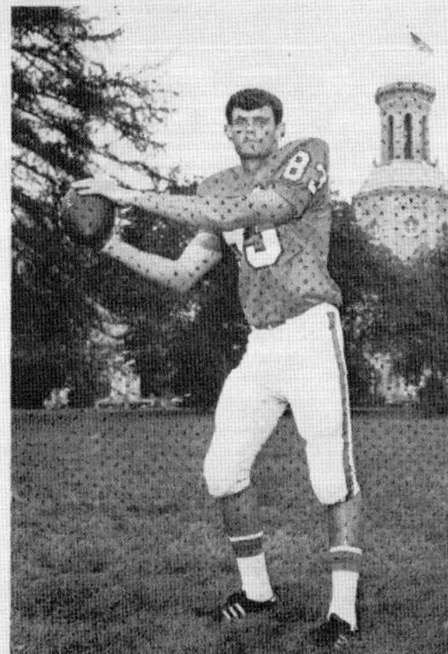

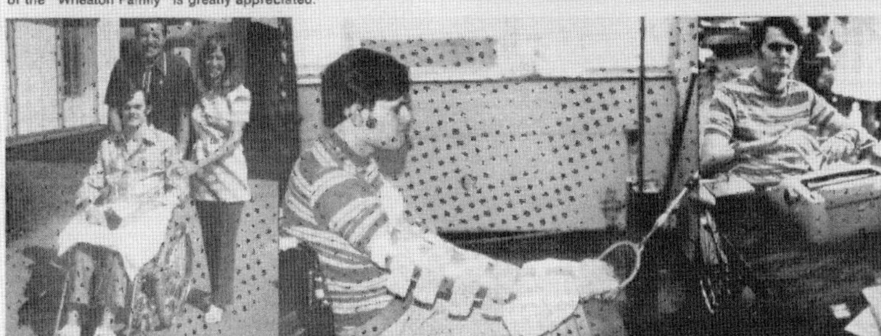

SEPTEMBER, 1974 3

Wayne Wray

When Wray enrolled at Wheaton College, his initial desire was to pursue veterinary medicine and oceanography, reflecting his passion for the outdoors. He wrote on his application: "I can offer Wheaton a life dedicated to Christ and believe your acceptance of me will give me advantages I will not find in all colleges. My hope is in Christ and I commit all things to His leadership." As a sophomore in the fall of 1972, his goal as an athlete was to be the defensive starting end for the Crusaders. Through grueling practice, he earned the position. During his first starting game as a varsity football player against Millikin University, while tackling the ball carrier on a kickoff late in the game, he received a critical injury, a fractured and dislocated fourth cervical vertebra. Suddenly, he was paralyzed from the neck down. Enduring three major surgeries in three days, each time the neurosurgeons declared, "No hope." As he lay motionless in the intensive care unit, Wray had much time to meditate on his faith and his life, now dramatically altered. Strengthened by the encouragement of friends and family, he did not surrender to despondency. Instead he set objectives, tackling his rehabilitation with the same single-mindedness with which he had played ball. Focusing, he learned to type, write, and print. "He cheers and lifts you up when you go to see him," visitors remarked. "He's not bitter, he would play again if his body were healed." Wray decided that he would encourage others as a profession. To assist with medical expenses, classmates raised $100,000 for the "Wray of Hope" campaign.

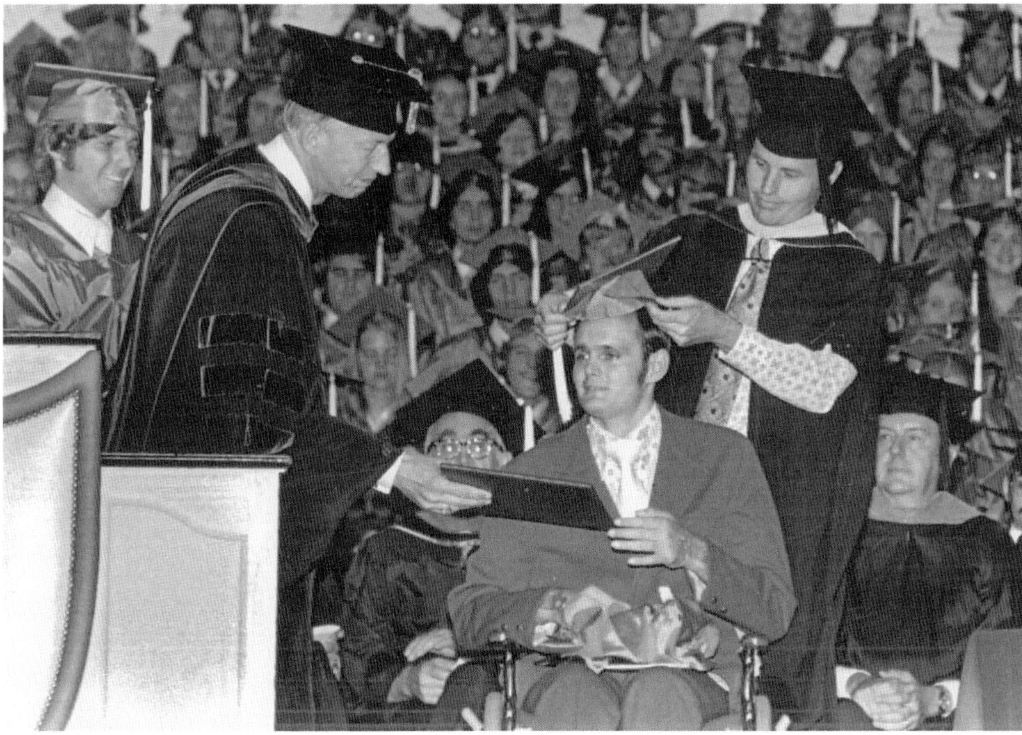

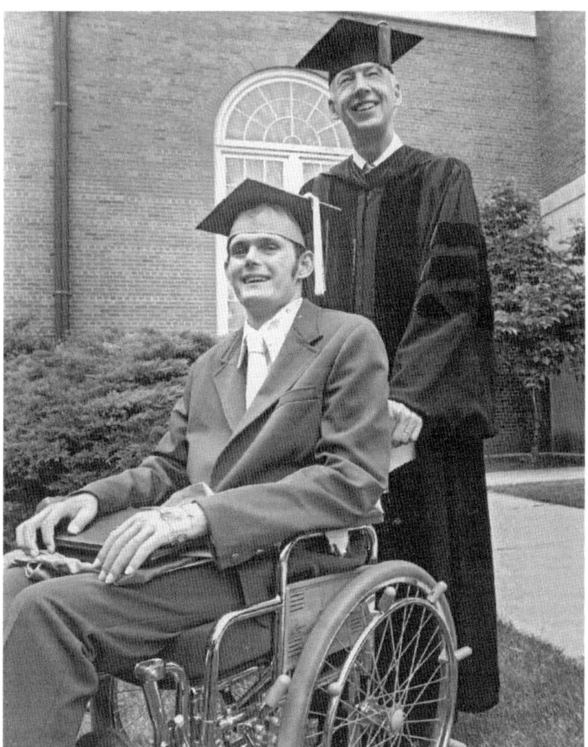

Wray Returns

In 1972, Wray returned to Wheaton College to receive an honorary degree from Dr. Hudson Armerding, president of Wheaton College. He later earned his associate's degree from Springfield Technical Community College and his bachelor's degree from Northern Colorado University. Fulfilling his desire to help others who had experienced similar injuries, he received his master's degree in rehabilitation counseling in 1982. That year he married Jeanette Gaffney, a physical therapist. Wray faced another challenge in 1986 when he was diagnosed with cancer. After battling illness for months, he died in 1987 at age 34 at his home in Florida. A scholarship in Wray's honor was established at Wheaton College to recognize, encourage, and financially assist any upperclass student who is facing personal adversity, and who shows continued growth in faith, academic performance, and contribution to campus life.

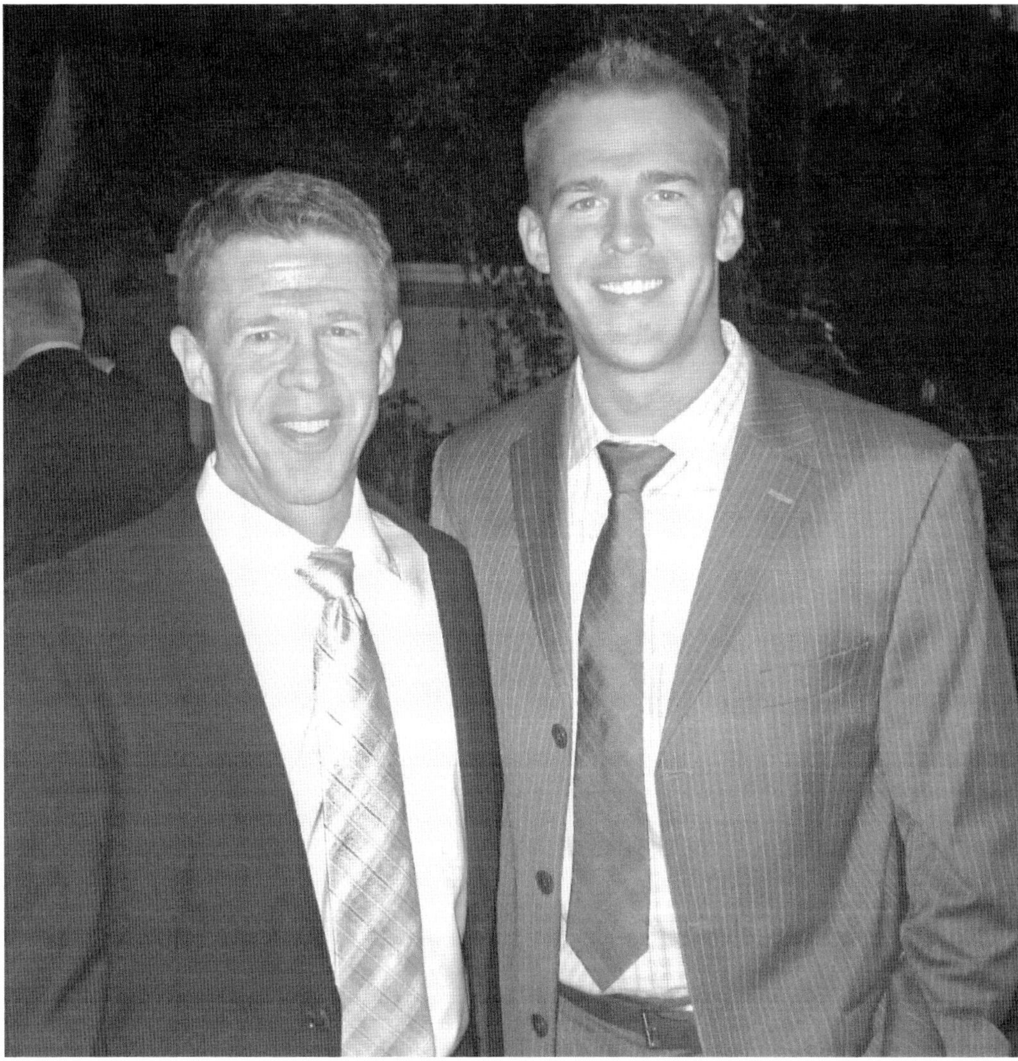

Greg Aagaard

With clockwork regularity, Aagaard (right) runs straight through the center of Wheaton, nodding crisply to his neighbors as he zooms past. As Olympian Eric Liddell remarked, "When I run, I feel God's pleasure." A similar reaction is observed in Aagaard's aspect as he strides his route. Born and raised in Wheaton, he is the second of five children. Attending Glen Ellyn Evangelical Covenant Church his entire life, he regularly participated in the student youth group; more recently he has led missions, both domestically and internationally. In this capacity, he is available to church youth as friend and counselor, offering advice if needed and a measure of stability. Aagaard studied business at Augustana College where he also played soccer, graduating in 2005. He is currently employed in the finance/investments business. He experiences life most fully in his interaction with students, fellow believers, and with the people God has so graciously placed in his life, particularly his family, who provide loving support. With him stands his father, Dr. Jon Aagaard, graduate of the University of Iowa Medical School. Dr. Aagaard treats patients of all ages and attempts to incorporate education to improve health. He has practiced medicine for 33 years and is a member of the American Academy of Family Physicians. Greg considers his father to be his greatest inspiration. (Courtesy of Greg Aagaard.)

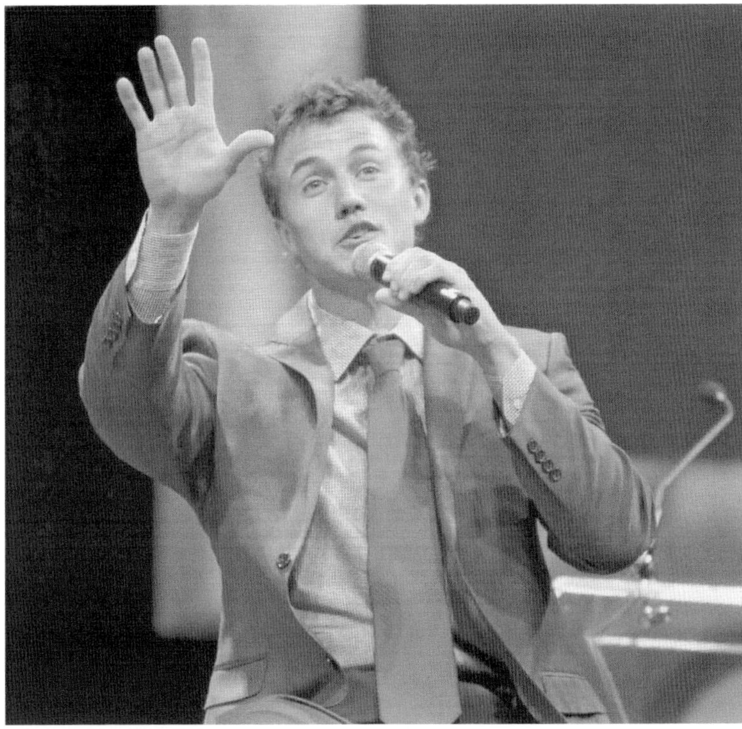

Jordan Kemper
As a motivational speaker, professional arena football player, entrepreneur, Universal Pictures stunt double, and fitness and nutrition expert, Kemper exemplifies the fully engaged man, both physically and mentally. In his frequent lectures to capacity crowds, Kemper's infectious enthusiasm inspires countless hearers to aspire ever higher, not only in health but in all aspects of life. He is a USANA Health Sciences Diamond Director and co-founder of OneBody International. "As I leaped out in faith with my USANA business, my network and influence started to grow," he says. "It didn't take long for me to see people are hurting physically, emotionally, financially, and spiritually. USANA became a vehicle for me to help people." (Courtesy of Jordan Kemper.)

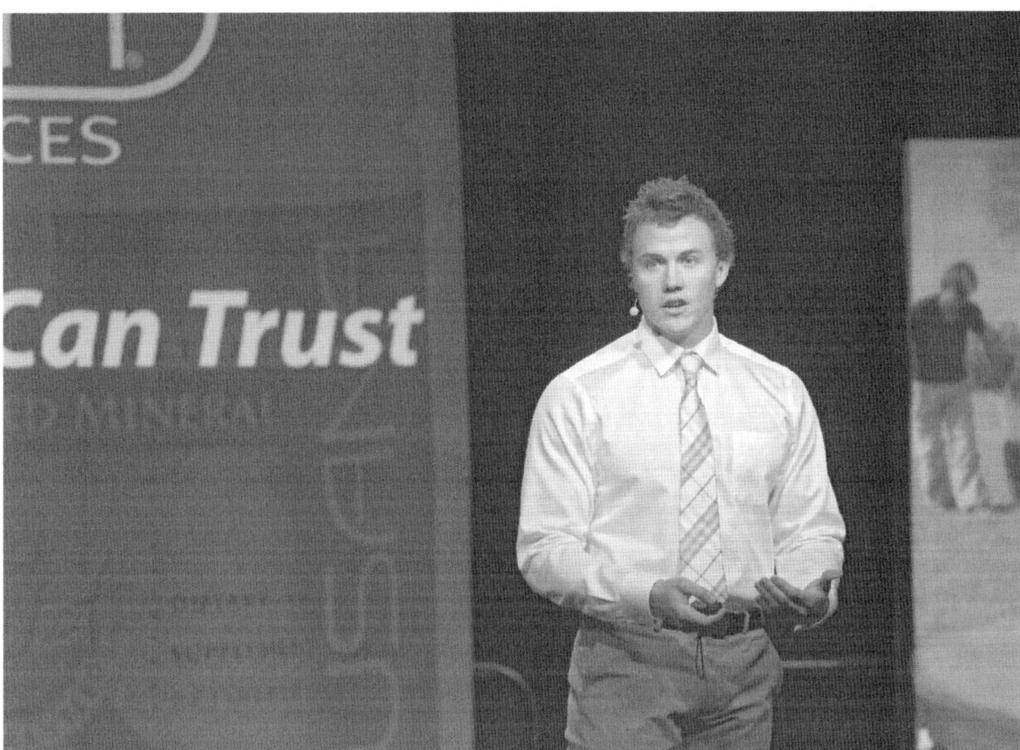

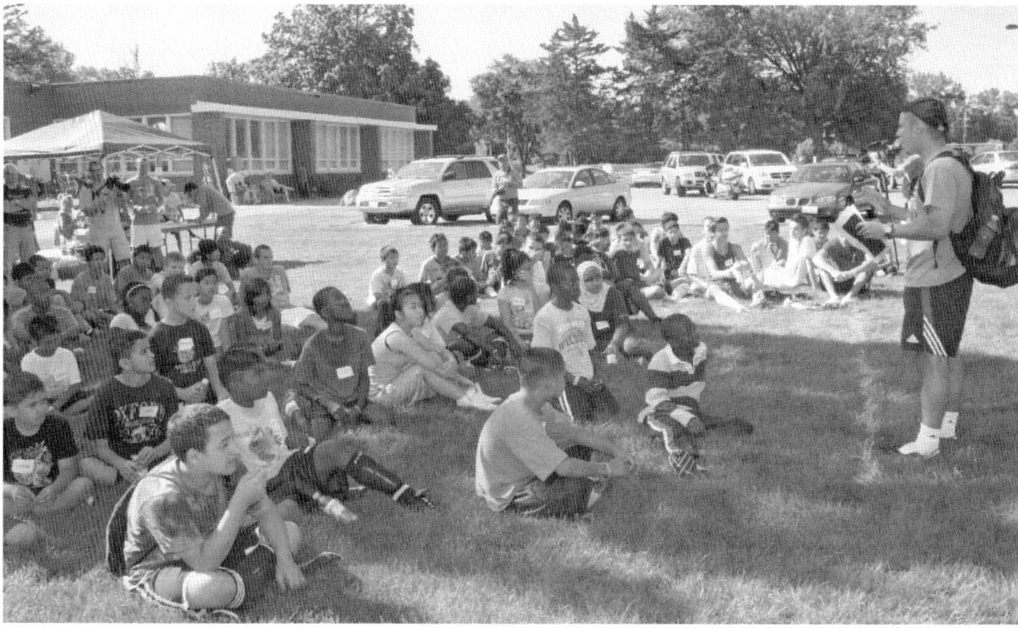

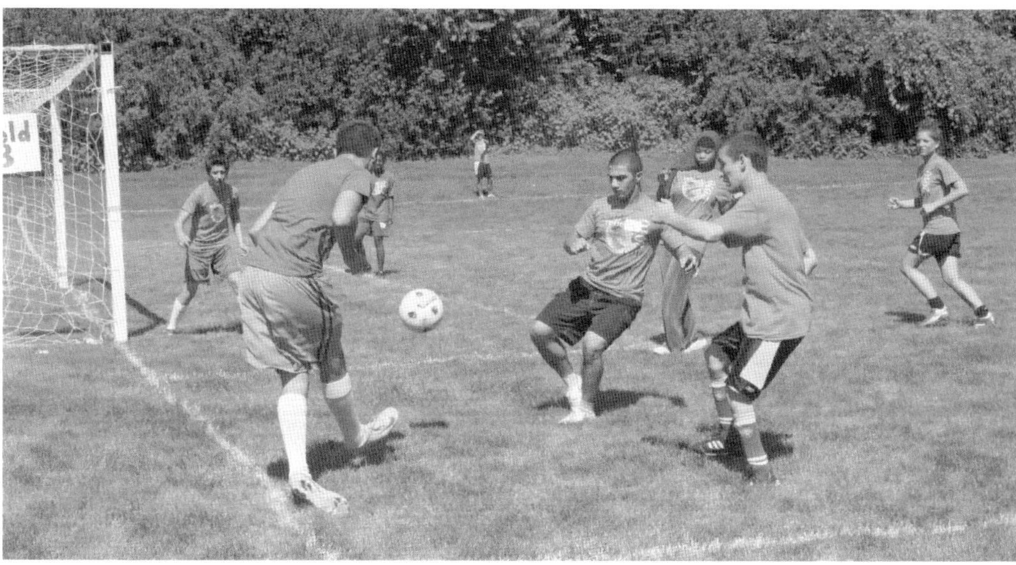

Chicago Eagles

Leandro Medeiros of Missionary Athletes International (MAI) instructs players at soccer camp. MAI was founded in 1983 to preach the Christian faith to the thousands the world over who enjoy soccer. At one of three MAI locations (the others are Charlotte and Los Angeles), the Chicago Eagles host a summer academy, refugee ministry, leadership training, urban ministry, and various internships. MAI is a nonprofit Christian soccer organization and support-based faith mission with each staff person raising his/her own funds to serve with the ministry through tax-deductible contributions. The Chicago office began in 1997, with the vision of working primarily with collegiate and high school athletes. Though a variety of programs, its goal is to train and equip young men and women as sports ministers. The Chicago directors are Rick and Janice McKinley. (Courtesy of the Chicago Eagles.)

CHAPTER TWO

The Artists

Since Wheaton is frequently compared to a Norman Rockwell painting, it is entirely appropriate that Rockwell's second wife, Mary Barstow, niece of Elbert Gary, founder of U.S. Steel, was born and raised here. The association with wholesome Americana is exactly right. With its straight streets and stately homes, landscaped parks and canopied trees, Wheaton not only inspires artists, but in some respects is a work of art. Its historic architecture, much of it constructed when Wheaton functioned as a haven for Chicago's wealthy merchants and farmers, is explored in *Life in a Small American City* by Marcia Gray Martin, Chip Krueger, and Barbara Hall. Architects such as Frank Lloyd Wright and Jarvis Hunt designed buildings for Wheaton. At least two novels, *The Silver Trumpet* by John Wesley Ingles and *The Tower, the Mask and the Grave* by Betty Smartt Carter, are set in the city, while Tim Peters is currently fusing fact with fiction in *The Exit Exam*, chronicling his perspective. Writers like Andrew Himes and Jon M. Sweeney, raised in Wheaton, discuss their attitudes toward conservative evangelicalism in deeply personal memoirs. Award-winning photographers Orlin Kohli and Ron Stewart established renowned studios. Television writer and producer Coleman Luck grew up in Wheaton, as did animator Don Toht. Multitalented Marjorie Gieser designed and displayed her spectacular banners and other art, while Barbara Fackler continues strumming her harp for friends and audiences. Sergio Villanueva composes songs vibrant with Latin rhythms and records his music. Actor Robert Maher pretends deliciously at Wheaton Drama and elsewhere. Janis Herbert writes readable, thoroughly researched histories for children. Stefan Bechtel, writer, and his brother, Lawrence Reid, sculptor, grew up in Wheaton before moving on to outstanding creative careers. Even poet Carl Sandburg, riding his bike from his home in Maywood, wheeled regularly through town, perhaps as he did composing poetry or ruminating on Lincoln. Just as a sport represents an opportunity for the athlete to engage the greater issues of life, art, whether dance, music, sculpture or literature, expresses the hidden epic of the soul.

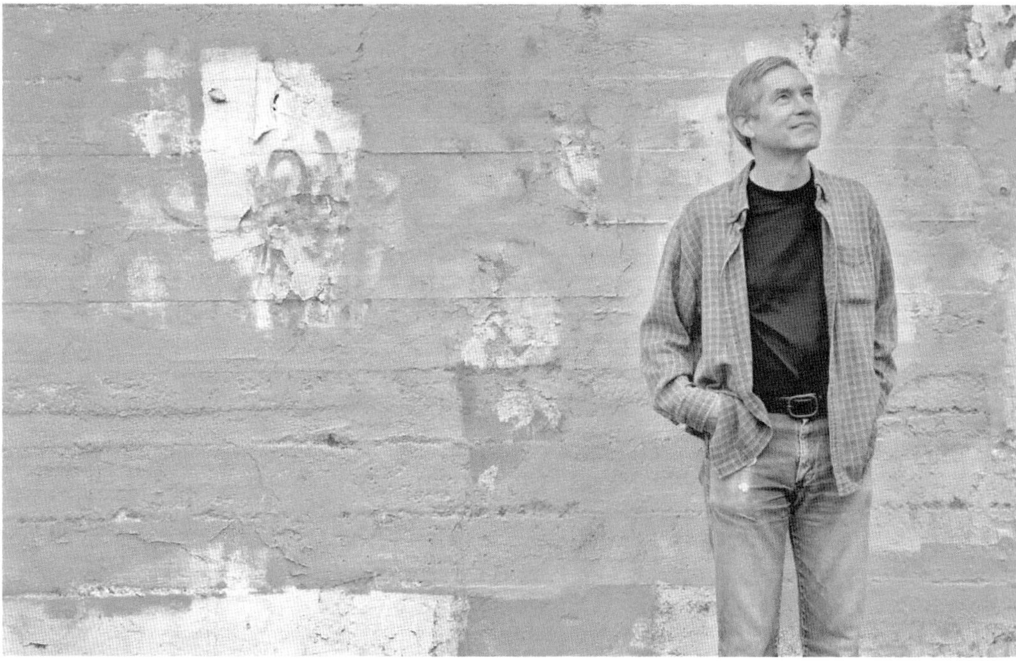

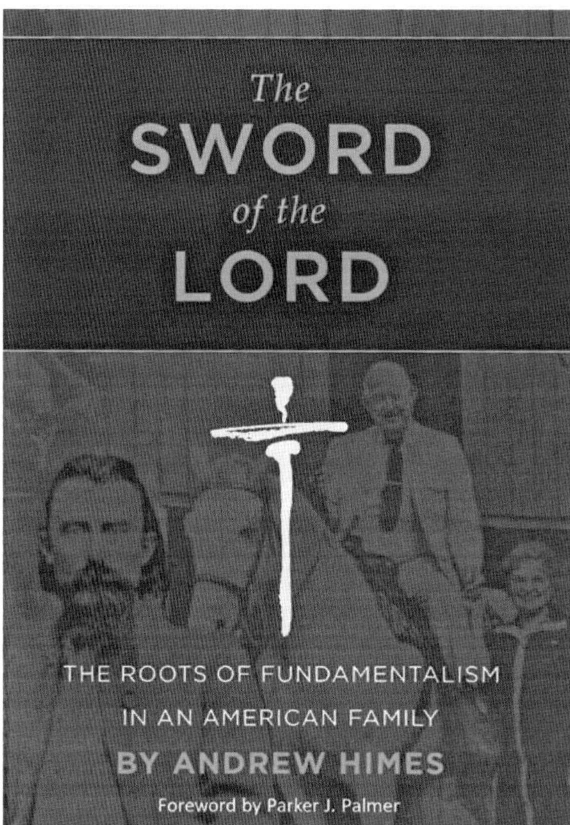

Andrew Himes

Raised in Wheaton, Himes, grandson of John R. Rice, pastor, editor, and evangelist, comes from a long fundamentalist lineage. "This book is not intended to be an exposé . . . or polemic against fundamentalists," Himes states in his memoir, *The Sword of the Lord*. "It is important to me to try my best to explore the truth about my family, our faith, and our history over the generations. So I have approached my task with humility and all the compassion I can muster. I am grateful for my fundamentalist family for instilling in me a profound love for others, high moral standards, and a deep commitment to justice." At the end he writes, "Here is what I have learned from my post-fundamentalist family: Honor truth. Love well. Live your faith." (Courtesy of Andrew Himes.)

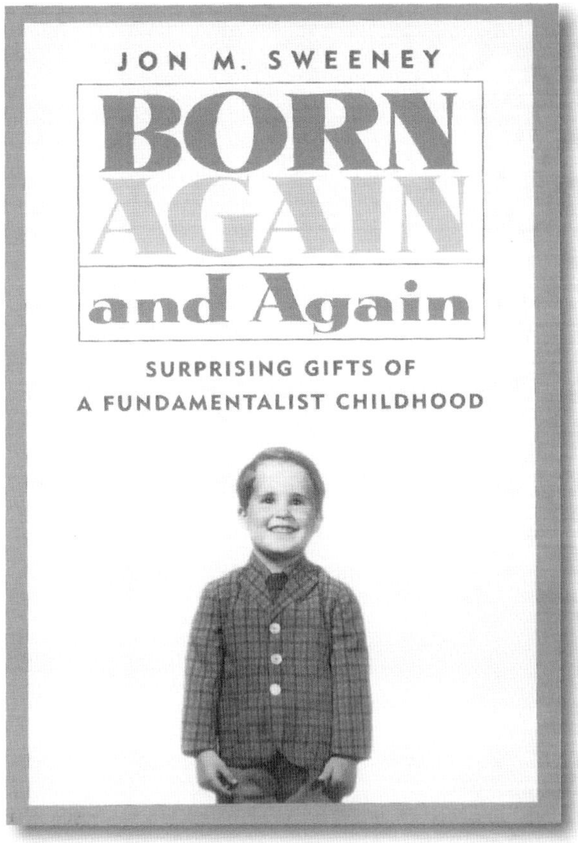

Jon M. Sweeney

"We lived in Wheaton, Illinois," Sweeney writes in his memoir, *Born Again and Again: Surprising Gifts of a Fundamentalist Childhood,* "where there were probably more churches per capita than in any other city in America." This title was named one of the Best Books of 2005 by *Spirituality & Health* magazine and recognized with an Award of Merit in the Spirituality category by *Christianity Today.* Beginning with his upbringing in a conservative Baptist church, Sweeney traces the circuitous path of his spiritual development, moving from Moody Bible Institute, where he began an undergraduate degree before transferring to Wheaton College, then on to graduate work at North Park Theological Seminary, noting his gradual attraction to liturgical and less dogmatic forms of worship. Along the way, he sojourned at the Monastery of Gethsemani in Kentucky, made famous by Thomas Merton in his autobiography, *The Seven Story Mountain.* Sweeney briefly considered joining, hoping to become a monk. "I love how miracles can happen in a monastery," he writes. "One serious obstacle to joining a monastic community for me, however, was that I have never found much comfort or satisfaction in religious groups." He is careful not to castigate his evangelical heritage as he examines his history, seeking rather to emphasize its positive qualities. In 2009, he became a Roman Catholic on the Feast Day of St. Francis. Sweeney cites Francis and Clare of Assisi among his heroes and has written several books about them, including a joint biography, *Light in the Dark Ages: The Friendship of Francis and Clare of Assisi*, which was a History Book Club and Book-of-the-Month Club selection, and *The St. Francis Prayer Book.* Other books include *Verily, Verily—The KJV, 400 Years of Influence and Beauty*, an appreciation of the Authorized Version, and *Cloister Talks: Learning from My Friends the Monks.* Sweeney was the co-founder and editor-in-chief of SkyLight Paths Publishing, a multifaith trade publisher in Vermont, until he joined Paraclete Press as their associate publisher. He speaks at conferences, retreat centers, and churches, and lives with his wife and three children in Vermont. (Courtesy of Jon M. Sweeney.)

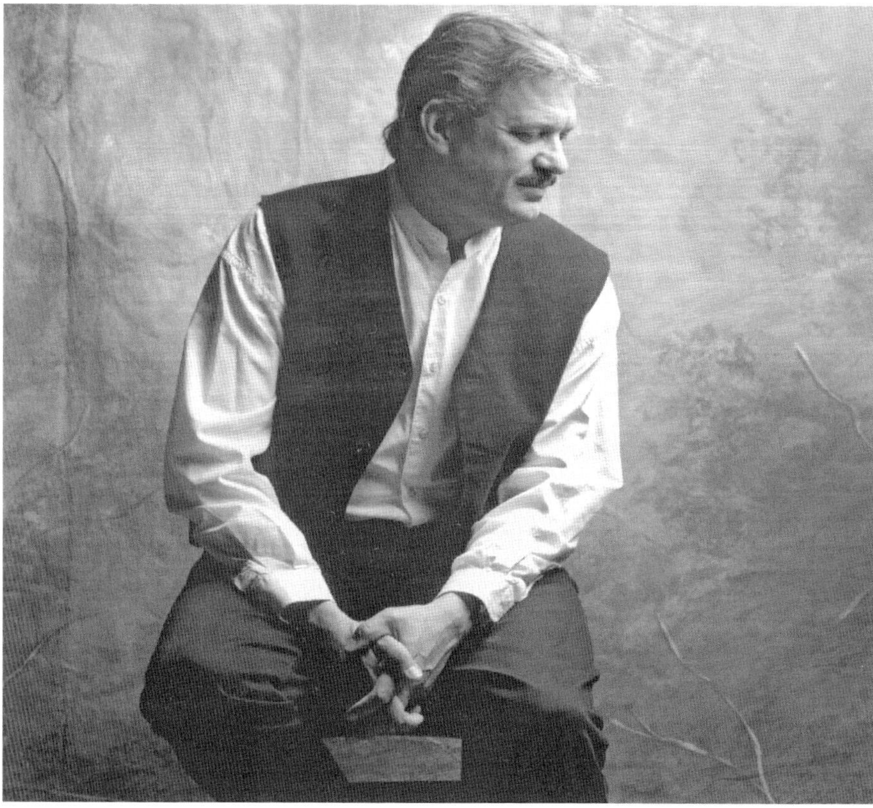

Timothy Botts

As a lad in sixth grade, Botts began noticing letterforms when he found a Speedball lettering book in the process of creating a circus poster. That small project opened the door to a magnificent career. Attempting to combine ancient letterforms with contemporary graphic design principles, Botts enjoys an international reputation. Interweaving background, text, and image in an effort to achieve unity, he is constantly attempting to strike a balance between the legibly visual and the lending of expression to the spiritual. He earned a BFA from Carnegie-Mellon, where he studied under renowned calligrapher Arnold Bank. He exhibited a childlike wonder about everything he encountered, remembers Botts. It was as if he were seeing our surroundings for the very first time each day. After studying with the master, Botts spent three years in Japan teaching conversational English. While there, he was influenced by the rich tradition and freedom of brush writing, and acquired a deeper understanding of space, asymmetry, and simplicity. As senior art director for Tyndale House Publishers, he has designed more than 600 books, and has published 10 of his own titles, including a Bible illustrated in his expressive style of calligraphy and *Horizons*, co-produced with poet Luci Shaw. Botts has received two Gold Medallion Awards. He is a part-time instructor at College of DuPage and has taught workshops internationally. His work is part of the permanent collection at the Newberry Library in Chicago. Botts also helped create and is artistic director for Masterpiece Ministries, which conducts an annual camp for high school students in the arts. It is a youth ministry with a mission to help young people identify and develop their gifts in the arts and to encourage them to become wholehearted followers of Jesus Christ. *Imaginative appropriateness* sums up what I have learned from my experience in publishing, he writes. I m always trying to come up with fresh ideas which get right to the heart of the message. He and his wife, Nancy, are parents of three grown children and 12 grandchildren. (Photograph by Gary Irving; courtesy of Timothy Botts.)

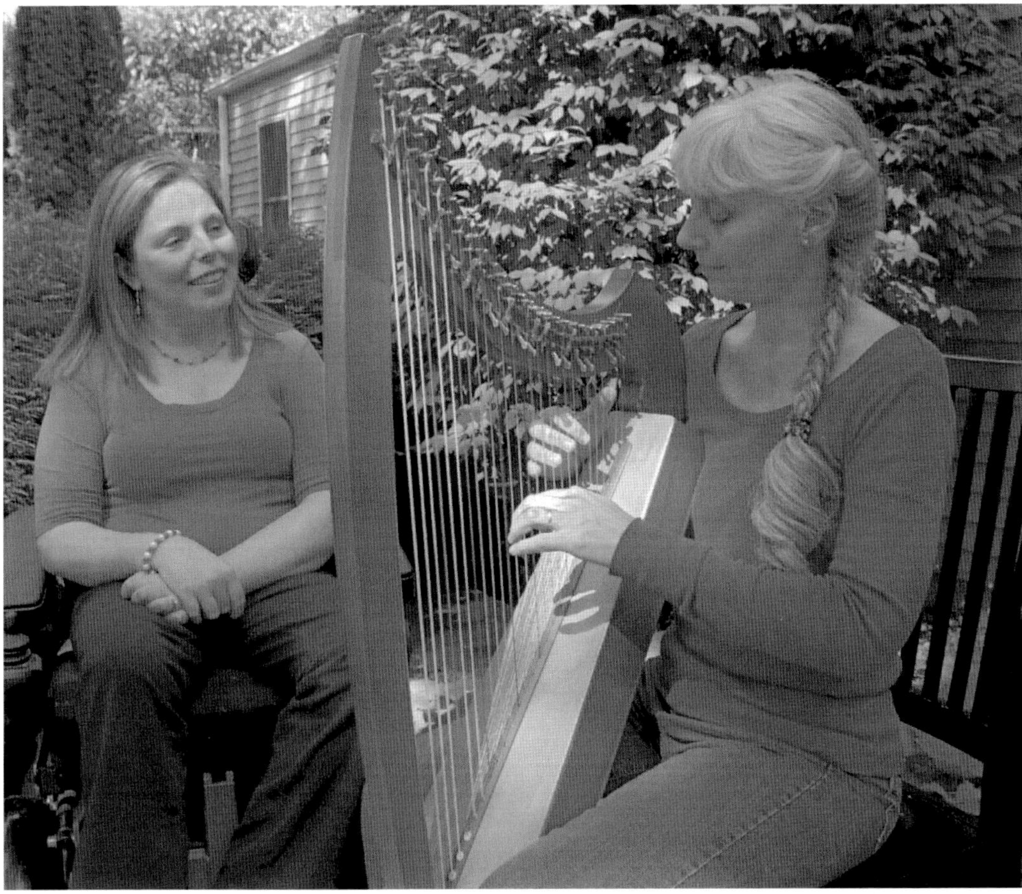

Barbara Fackler

Fackler plays harp for her friend, Ileana Blake, who suffers from multiple sclerosis. When Ileana experiences a bad day, Fackler plays for her. An inspiration to Fackler, she draws attention to her abilities rather than her failing body. Occasionally Ileana, whose expertise is in marketing, assists Fackler with publicity ideas or CD covers. As a friend, she emphasizes strengths, not weakness. "Therapeutic music gives a bit of control to those who are suffering," Fackler writes. "Think of what it is like to be very, very ill. The illness takes on a life of its own, dictating much of the daily routine: diet, medications, environment; it all becomes managed to a point that personal choice is nearly eliminated. When I take music to someone who is stuck in that kind of a routine and they choose what music they hear, they get a little bit of control back. It's a chance to make a decision that is not influenced by the needs of the illness and it is comforting and empowering. It is a positive moment in the midst of discomfort and struggle." She believes music achieves more than entertainment: "Primarily, music should be beautiful. There's no point at all if it isn't lovely beyond just the notes, but lovely in the deeper sense of reaching out to touch the need for beauty in our lives." As a four-year-old, she surrendered to the charm of the harp, its haunting strings lingering in her heart. "Very often my audience has not heard a harp up close before so the response is wonderful. I see their delight as they hear new and wonderful music for the first time. In concert settings, the response is only slightly different from therapeutic settings. Concerts focus on the beauty of the moment, art caught in motion and held in the memory. Therapeutic sessions focus more on the response to the music, relaxation, a slowing of responses and drifting away to absorb the loveliness of the music while abandoning the discomfort of the moment." (Courtesy of A. Woods.)

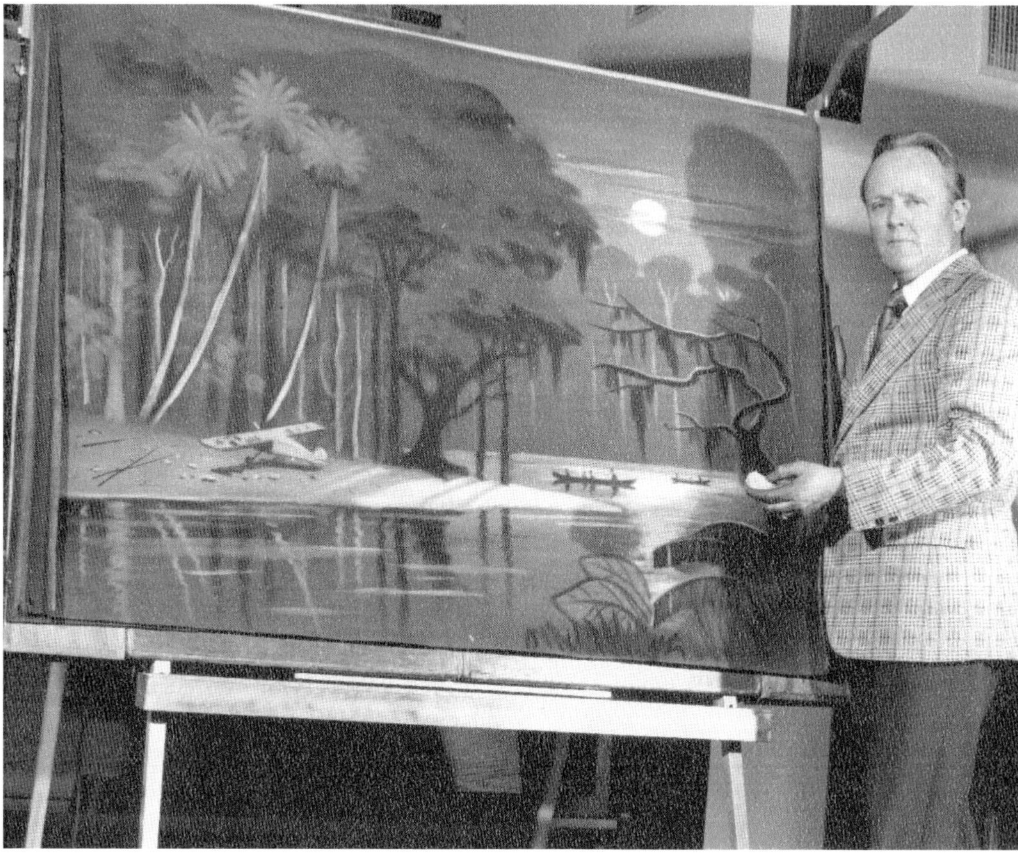

Phil Saint

"Dad taught me the fundamentals of art," writes Saint, whose father designed the stained-glass windows at the National Cathedral in Washington, DC, "with patience and devotion that I would not have met in any art school. He was a hard taskmaster." During high school, Saint assisted cartoonist Herbert Johnson at the *Saturday Evening Post*, learning valuable draftsmanship. As a "chalk talk" evangelist at Wheaton College, Saint drew pictures as he preached in churches and youth camps. Interestingly, Saint was partly color blind, asking attendees to his meetings the color of his chalk, dividing the pieces appropriately on his tray. He recalls fondly, "The Wheaton of 1937 caught me up in a new world of studies, friendships, and extracurricular studies." Amid these activities Saint met his future wife, Ruth Brooker. Graduating with honors, he entered World War II where he distributed New Testaments for the Pocket Testament League. After briefly serving as a missionary in Japan and Korea, he eventually settled in Argentina where he established a conference center and studio. Curious about his son's revitalized spiritual life, he investigated the claims of Pentecostalism and finally joined them in the late 1960s after receiving a "baptism in the spirit," which he called his "spiritual earthquake." Raised among the Plymouth Brethren, his decision caused considerable consternation and some supporters discontinued funding his mission. But Saint never looked back, simply applying his gifts as teacher and artist to Pentecostal denominations. His books include *85 Drawings About the Here and Hereafter* and his humorous memoir, *Saints Alive!*, both illustrated with cartoons interspersed with commentary reflecting his conservative positions on religion and politics. His brother, Nate, was one of five missionaries martyred in Ecuador in January 1956. The scene of their murder at the hands of the Waodoni Indians is depicted in the painting on the easel. Saint's sister, Rachel, remained with the mission to continue the work. Phil Saint died in 1993 as the result of a tractor accident at Lake Valley Bible Conference Center in Cordobo, Argentina.

Saint's Caricatures and Cartoons

As art director for the 1942 Wheaton College yearbook, Saint humorously depicted staff and faculty, including this spot-on caricature of Pres. V. Raymond Edman. Saint's cartoons are also found in the *Record*, the Wheaton College newspaper. His caricatures were never cruel, but often quite direct when addressing issues such as abortion or hypocrisy. Saint endeavored to gently exaggerate features, habits, or traits, more often than not expressing deep affection for his subject.

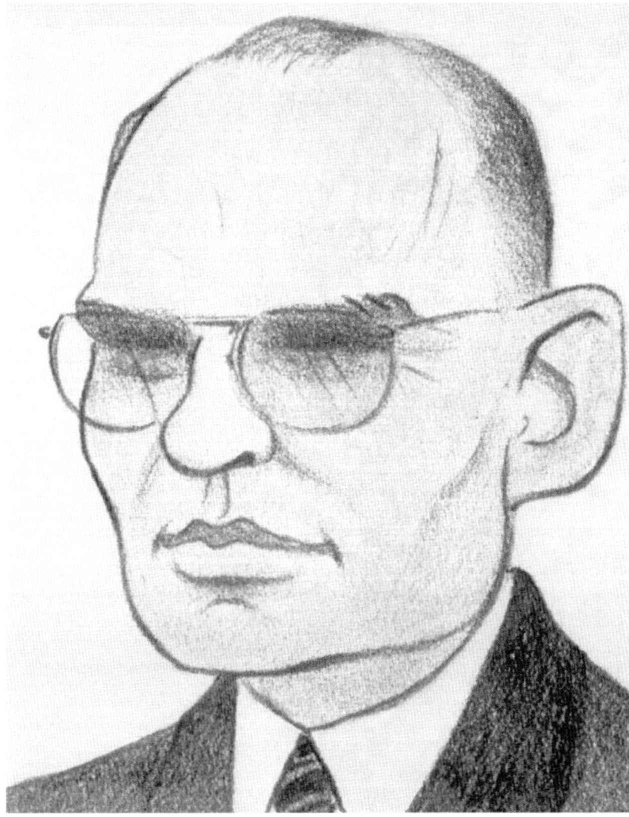

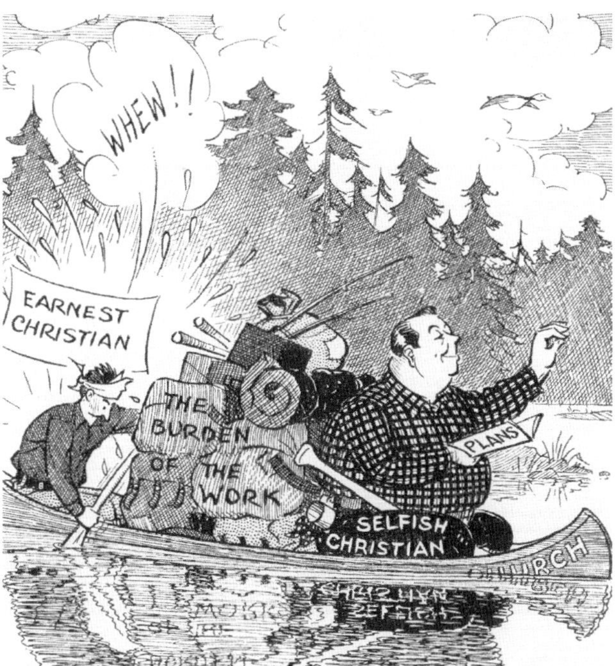

Saint's Christian Cartoons

This cartoon, also from the 1942 Wheaton College yearbook, portrays the fat, happy Christian selfishly enjoying the sacrificial labors of harder-working, leaner believers. Saint's work often poked fun at fellow Christians and politicians. His fluid style, dynamic figures, and dramatic expression were often compared to that of acclaimed graphic artist Will Eisner, creator of *The Spirit*. Saint during his early career also drew comic books and designed tracts.

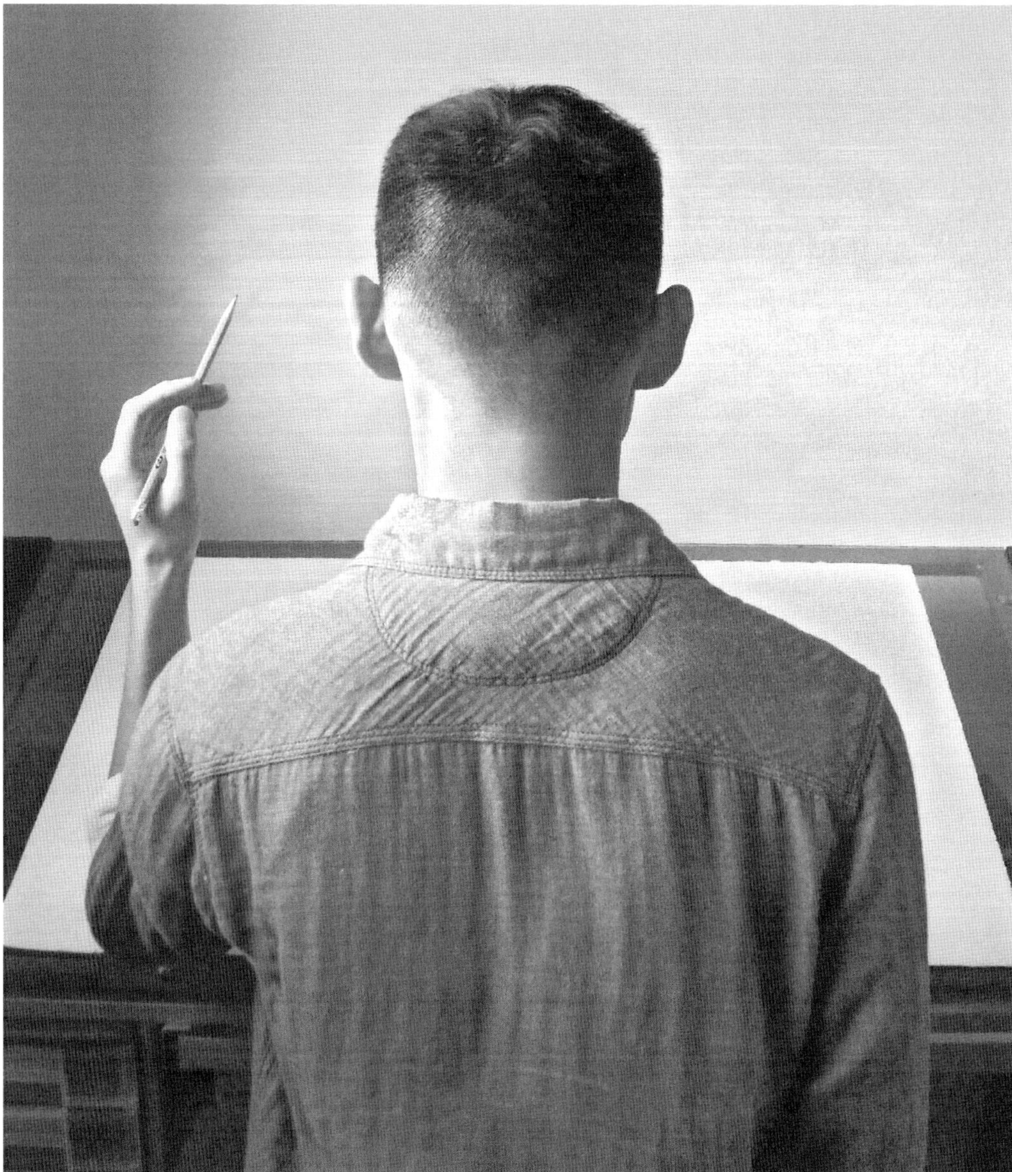

Ray Wu
A native of New York City, Wu received a BFA from Wheaton College where he studied figurative and representational painting, exploring the connection between faith and creativity. He has since freelanced as an artist and graphic designer, working on commissioned portraits, medical illustration, and theater set design. He also enjoys instructing high school students in drawing. Wu believes that his figurative style reflects people's intrinsic beauty and worth. He hopes that his art communicates this as well as other honest realities, such as faith, tragedy, loss, and redemption. He has been greatly inspired by music, dance, nature, and myth. Wu currently resides in the western suburbs of Chicago, where he continues to develop his artistic voice and pursue his creative calling while serving his local church and community through art. (Courtesy of Ray Wu.)

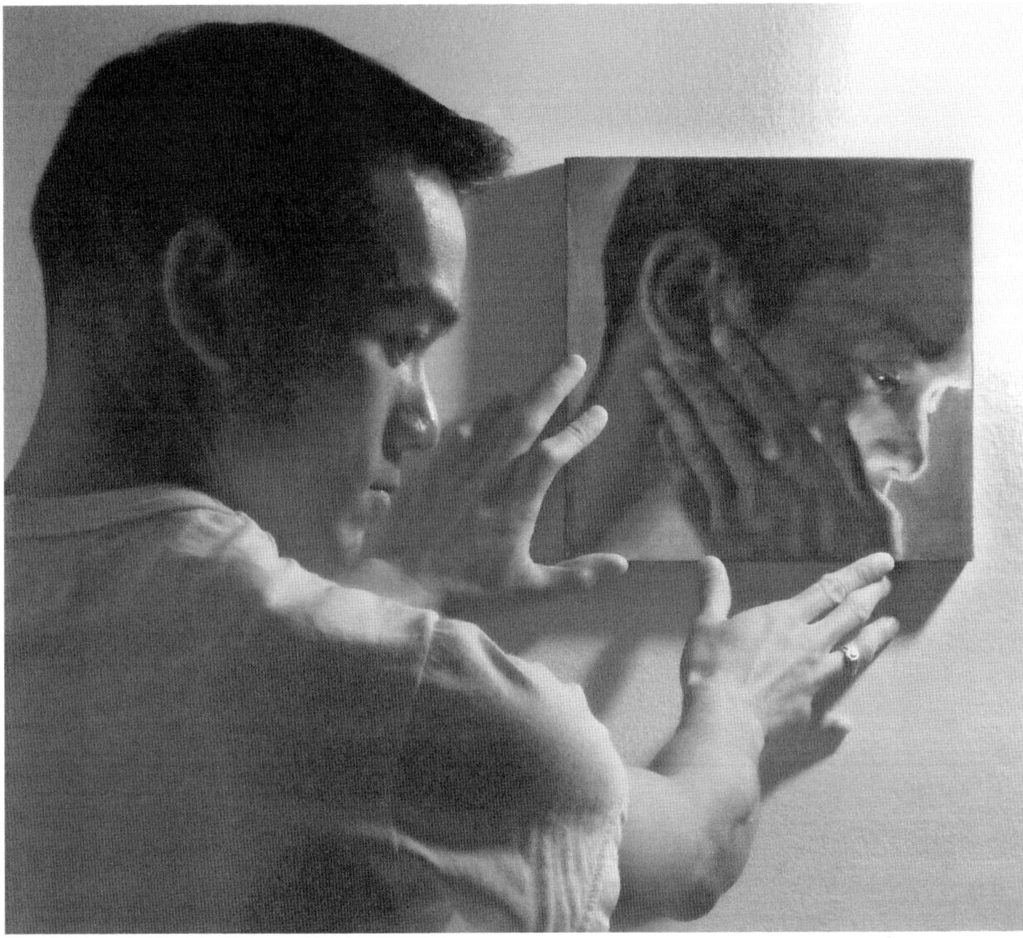

A Double Self-Portrait of Ray Wu
"I'm compelled to create works of art for two reasons," he says. "The first is that I deeply enjoy it. There is nothing so wonderful as losing myself in the process of capturing the subtle detail and overall form of someone's figure, onto paper or canvas. The second reason being, I love that I can potentially inspire people's lives by expressing some powerful or poignant truth or reality through art . . . My art tends to be realistic. That's how I am most satisfied and excited making art, being one so enamored with natural light, along with exploring unique and interesting compositions. I'm hoping to develop a stronger artistic voice as my art gravitates towards themes such as faith, tragedy, loss and redemption . . ." Right: Wu's "Noel" is seemingly alive with extraordinary delicacy of line. (Courtesy of Ray Wu.)

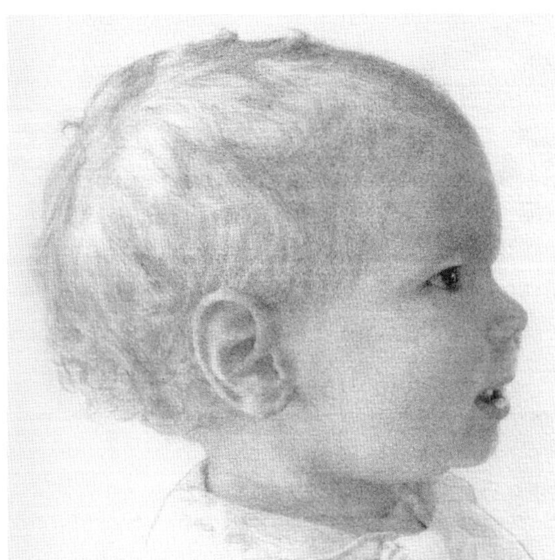

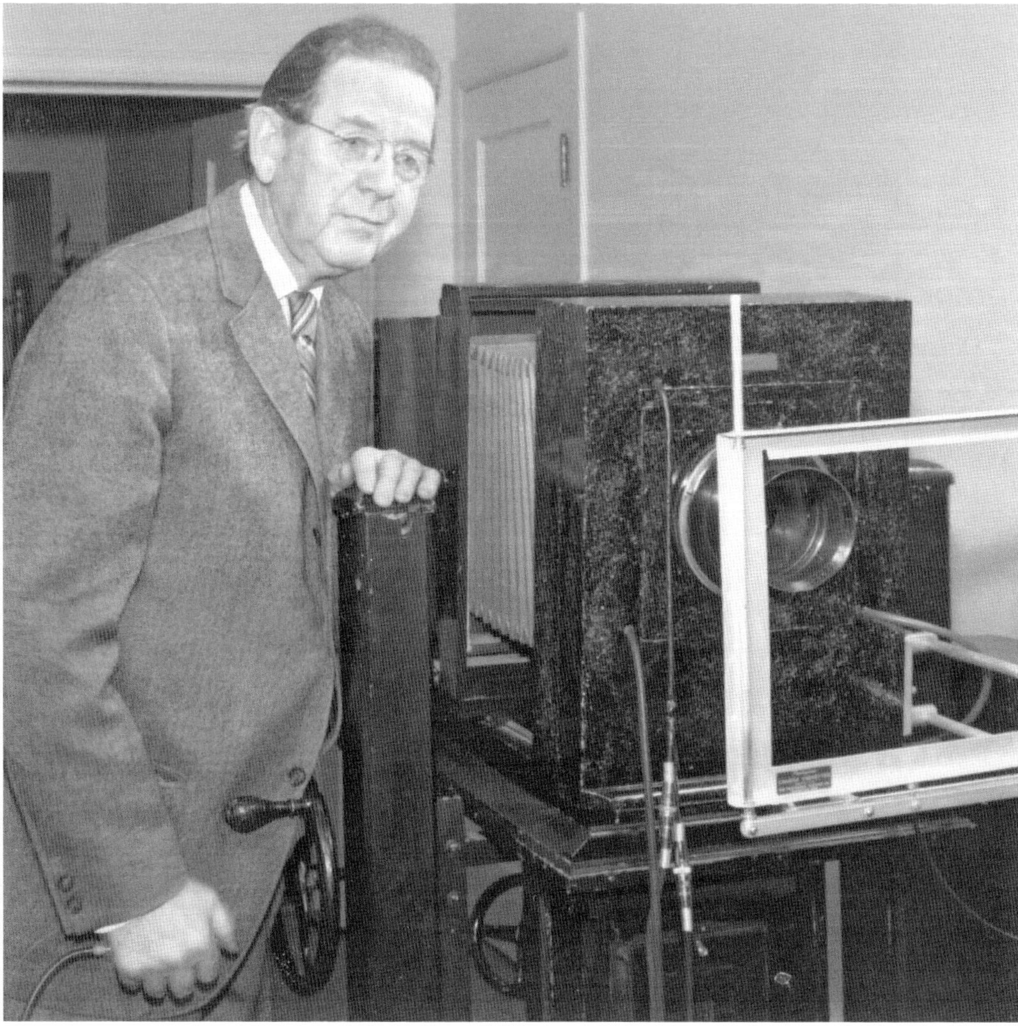

Orlin Kohli

After graduating from the University of Colorado in 1924, Kohli briefly taught school in Ft. Lewis, Colorado, and Hammond, Indiana, before discovering his passion for photography. Opening his first studio in 1926 in the Smith Building, he stayed until 1936 when he relocated to 212 North Hale. Through the years, his portraiture won national as well as community recognition. In 1953, the Professional Photographers of America honored him with the Master of Photography degree, recognizing excellence in photographic technique. In 1966, they again honored him with an award banquet for distinguished service to the profession, inviting him to exhibit 20 prints made throughout the years. In 1968, Kohli was honored as the official photographer by the city council and Mayor Karl F. Heimke, who stated, "Only once before has the city honored a specialist in his field in this manner and that was when another honored citizen was named poet laureate (Frank Herrick) for the city." Kohli was also a member of the Illinois Association of Photographers, serving as president from 1948 to 1949. When not creating portraiture in his studio, he served for 12 years on the Wheaton Public Library board, including a term as president. Kohli served two terms on the school board for District 95 and was active in YMCA work. In addition, he was a charter member of the Geneva Road Baptist Church. He died in 1972 at age 74, leaving a widow and three children.

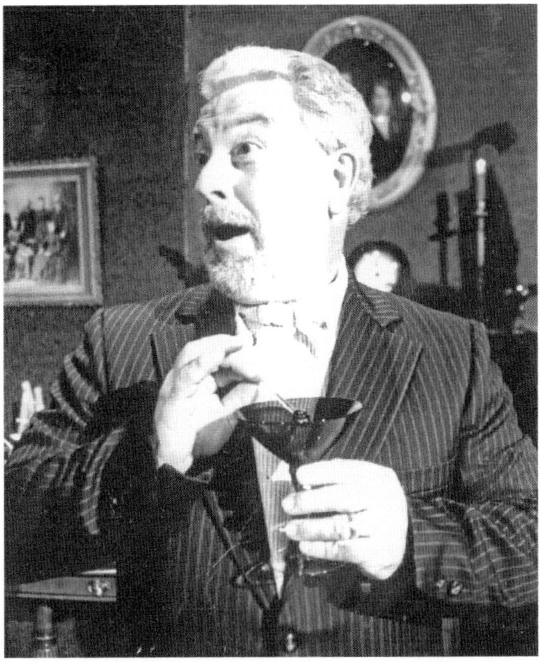

Robert Maher

Maher performs in *Musical Comedy Murders of 1940*. Growing up in California with a character actor (Harry "Pappy" Chesire) as his grandfather, Maher acquired the show business bug early, employed first as a Dapper Dan at Disneyland. In the past 50 years, he has appeared in more than 100 theatrical productions, three movies, and over 200 commercials, performing on-camera or voice-over. Adept in comedy or drama, his energies are now largely devoted to old-time radio re-creations, but Maher hopes to appear in a stage production every two years or so. For WMBI in Chicago, he portrayed D.L. Moody, careful to accurately inflect the evangelist's speech with Bostonian cadences. Below: Maher acts with Shon Little in Neil Simon's *God's Favorite*. He has performed duologues with actress Michael Learned, raising funds for the Einstein Academy in Elgin. (Courtesy of Robert Maher.)

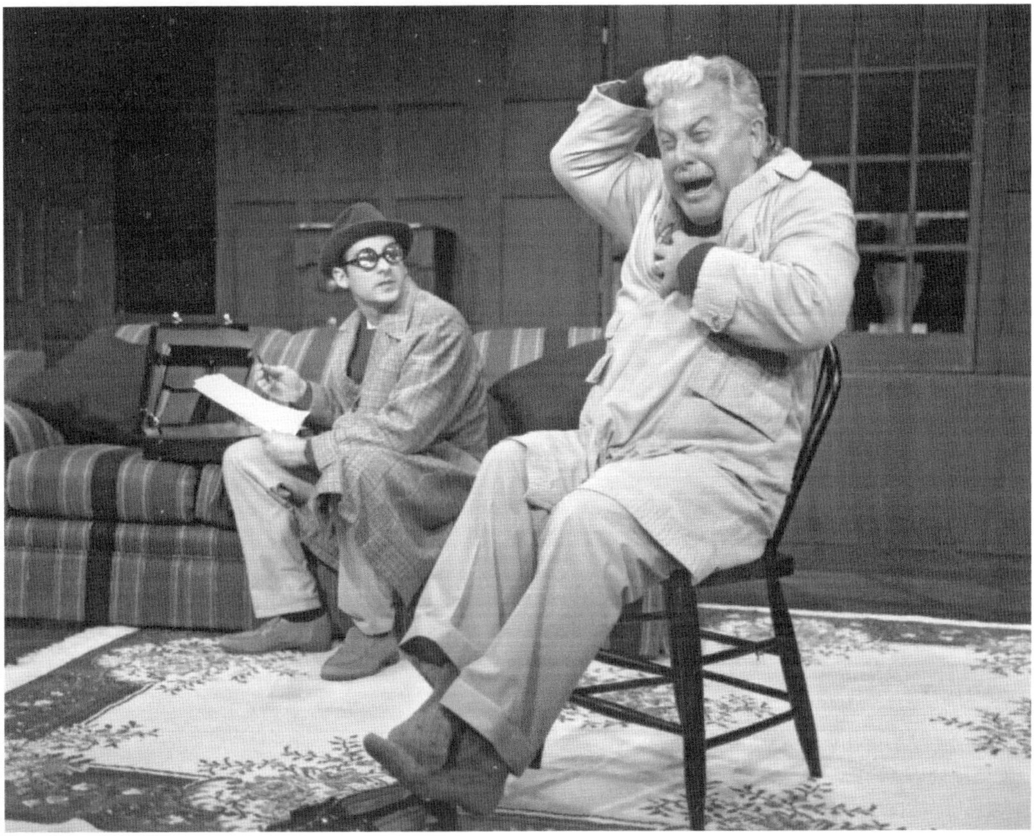

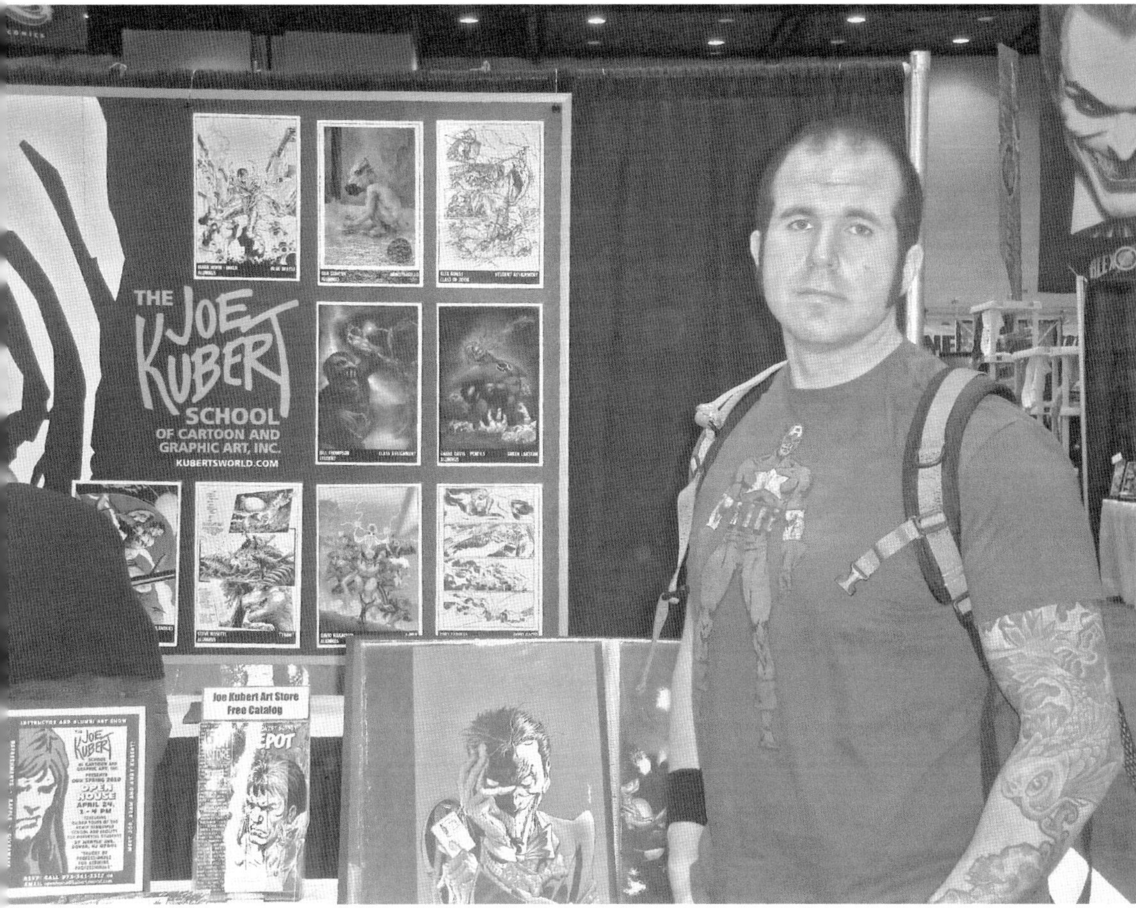

Michael Pellegrini

Wearing his favorite shirt as he wanders the aisles of Chicago ComiCon, Pellegrini pauses beside an exhibit featuring the work of graphic artist Joe Kubert, whom he esteems as a pioneer and teacher. Like the eponymous character from Ray Bradbury's fantasy, *The Illustrated Man*, Pellegrini has tales to tell, a few coloring his tattooed arm but most etched deeply in his soul. He is a martial artist, insatiable reader, and veteran traveler, counting among his residences Panama, Germany, and Japan. "To this day," he says, "Japan still holds as my favorite place in the world and by far having the single largest impact on me as a person. It's where I learned to love art and respect culture." As such, he was the ideal final manager of Wheaton's Borders Books & Music, providing placid, knowledgeable leadership amid its corporate unraveling. He describes himself as "a geek, former athlete, and of course, lover of comic books. And while that description fits me, it's so much more than that. One thing alone has remained an undying love and source of comfort in my life since my earliest memories and that is art and words and story and magic. To this day I write, draw, and dream of publication not because I'm talented, but just because I love it. There was a time when money was so scarce that comic books were a luxury I couldn't afford. So for over 12 years all I had was my childhood collection keeping me attached to my passion. In the last five years or so I found an amazing woman who not only made me happy, but agreed to marry me. Next to the rest of her life, the second best thing she gave me was her support in returning me to my youthful love of comics and art. She encouraged me to stop dreaming and do it. Nothing is quite as freeing as someone else allowing you to be whole." In addition to illustrating, Pellegrini writes reviews and articles for *The Geek Files*, published by the *Coventry Telegraph*. (Courtesy of Michael Pellegrini.)

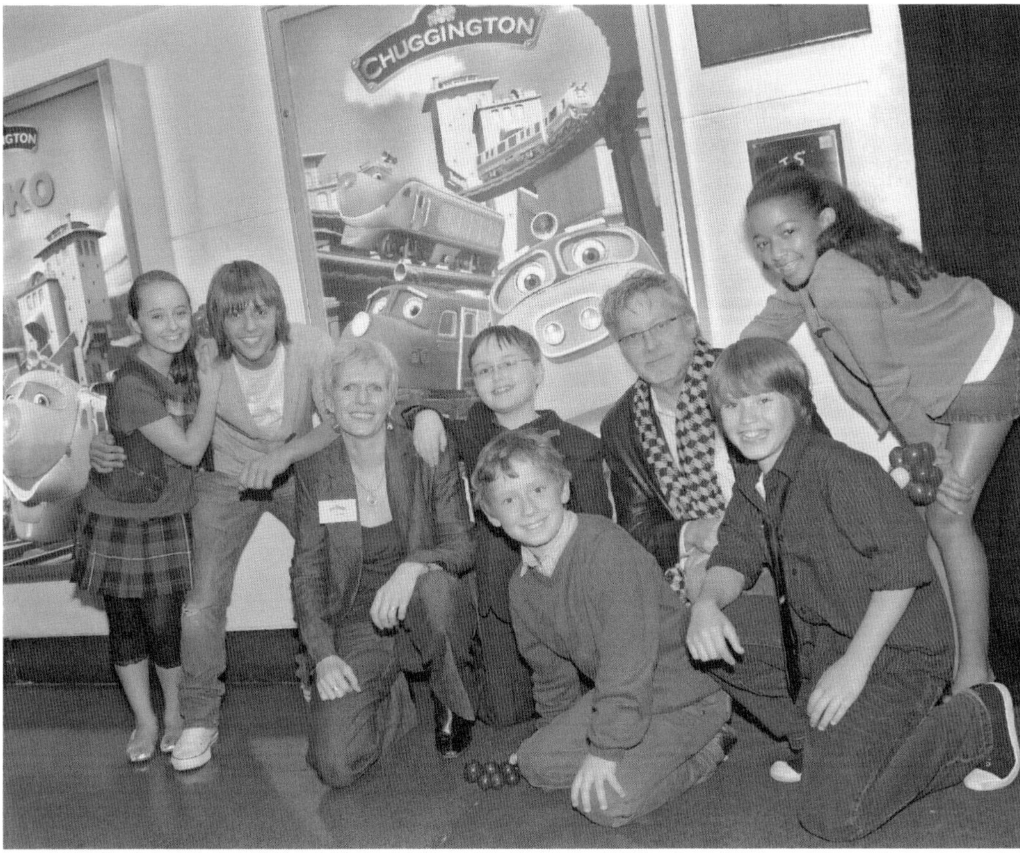

Don Toht

Toht poses with Sarah Ball, director and co-creator, and the show's voice artist cast at the premiere of *Chuggington*. Growing up in Wheaton near the tracks where the Chicago Metra and freight cars hourly rumble past, perhaps it was inevitable that trains should careen mightily through his imagination. As part of a collaborative team, Toht helped create *Chuggington*, a community of aged trains and their young "trainees," Wilson, Brewster, and Koko, learning how to be full-fledged engines riding the rails. Presented with a fresh look and state-of-the-art computer graphics, *Chuggington* seeks to promote such values as friendship, teamwork, and responsibility. Toht is executive vice president of concept and development at Ludorum, owners of *Chuggington*. Previously he served as creative director for an agency partner of McDonald's Corporation, developing Happy Meal toy programs. He joined Learning Curve International in 1995 as vice president of product development, managing research, design, and engineering, until it was acquired by RC2 Corporation, where he held the position of vice president of new products. "I have many important influences, Edward Hopper being just one," he writes. "One of my earliest was Disney, not Walt but the animation studio. On my first 'professional' visit to Disney Studios I stood on the corner of Mickey Mouse and Goofy Drives. I thought, 'I have finally arrived' because there was a photograph of that corner in a book belonging to my father, *The Art of Disney,* that I drew off, copied and traced since third grade. I have had so many influences and so much support it's hard to single out just one. In an odd, if not amazing way, my dyslexia was one of them. Being challenged by reading and writing, really schooling in general, I relied on my drawing to fill in those gaps. I would draw on my homework and reports and many of my teachers graded those doodles as part of the work. More often than not those doodles pulled the work from a failing mark to a passing one." Toht divides his time between London and Wheaton. (Courtesy of Don Toht.)

Muriel Fuller

Witty, wise, and sensitive to fine literature, editor Muriel Fuller was responsible for rescuing from slush piles more than a few blossoming authors, including Margaret Landon, her former Wheaton College roommate and author of *Anna and the King of Siam*, and Frank Yerby, author of *The Hounds of Yarrow*. She was born to the task, possessing a rare gift for not only placing her finger on exactly what was wrong with a manuscript, but also offering pointed suggestions toward correcting the problem. As a result of her perceptive editorial guidance, 15 published books are dedicated to her. As a student she wrote, "Someone once remarked that any graduate of Wheaton who did not become a missionary, minister or a school teacher was entitled to a refund of his tuition . . . but our college is turning out a surprising number of men and women who are finding their way in other professions . . .Why not have archaeologists, artists, musicians, inventors, architects, engineers, critics, and people in other equally absorbing lines of work on the roster of Wheaton's alumni?" She may have been thinking of herself. In fact, as a child she wanted to be a drama critic or a book reviewer. After graduating, Fuller secured employment at Rand McNally in Chicago; but soon she returned to Brooklyn, New York, working for publishers, among them Thomas Nelson, Abelard Press, and Greystone Press. She read manuscripts for *Redbook* and was the book reviewer for *Child Life* magazine. For more than 12 years, she served as assistant compiler for the O. Henry annual short story collections. Utilizing her expertise, she taught a course at Columbia University called "Editing and Publishing." She occasionally badgered the Wheaton College Alumni Association for their seemingly stingy recognition of female alumnae. In a 1968 memo to a friend, she bemoans the paucity of the fairer sex among its administration. "No woman trustee after a century!" Fuller complains. "Honestly. What is the matter with that place?" Since then, Wheaton College has not only produced graduates populating multitudinous disciplines, but it gladly recognizes many females among its faculty, staff, and trustees.

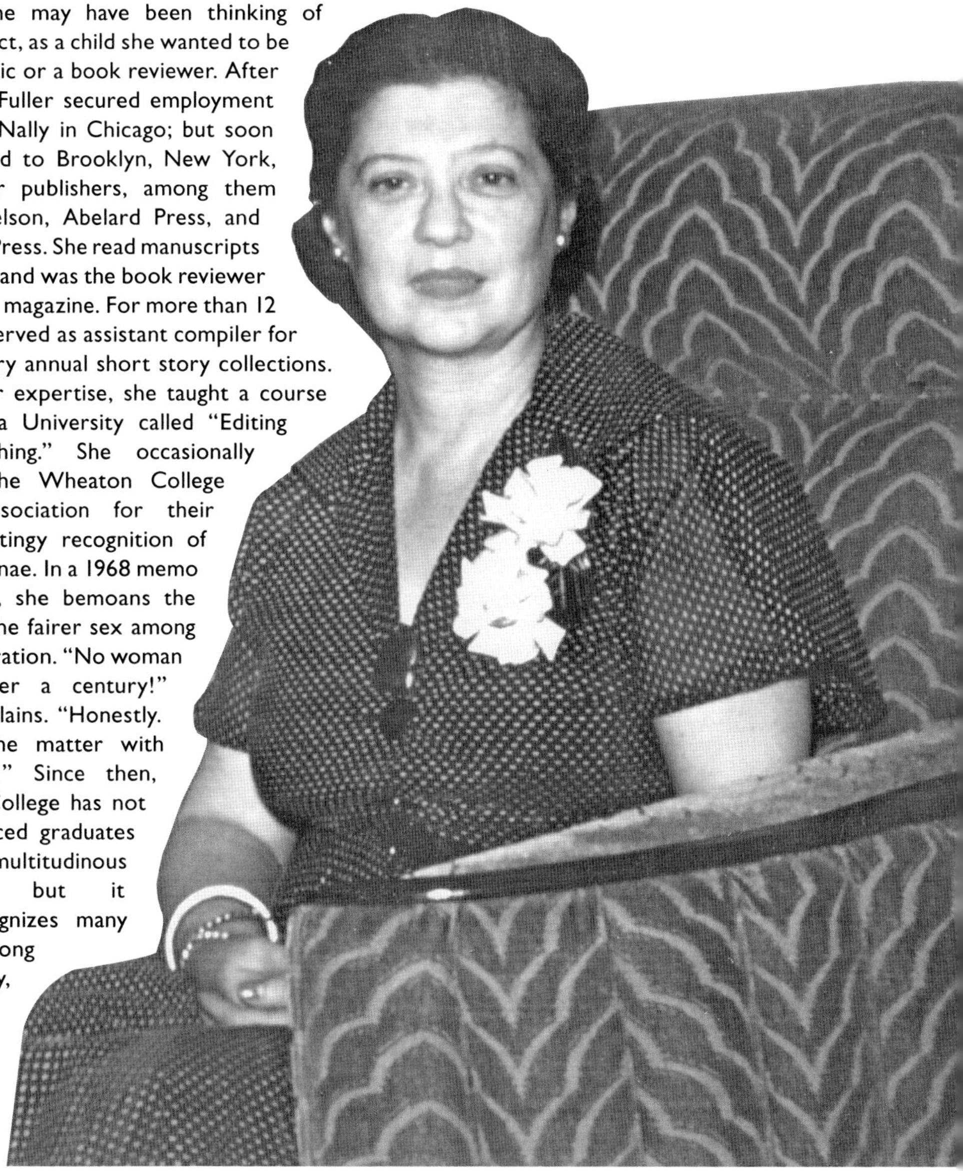

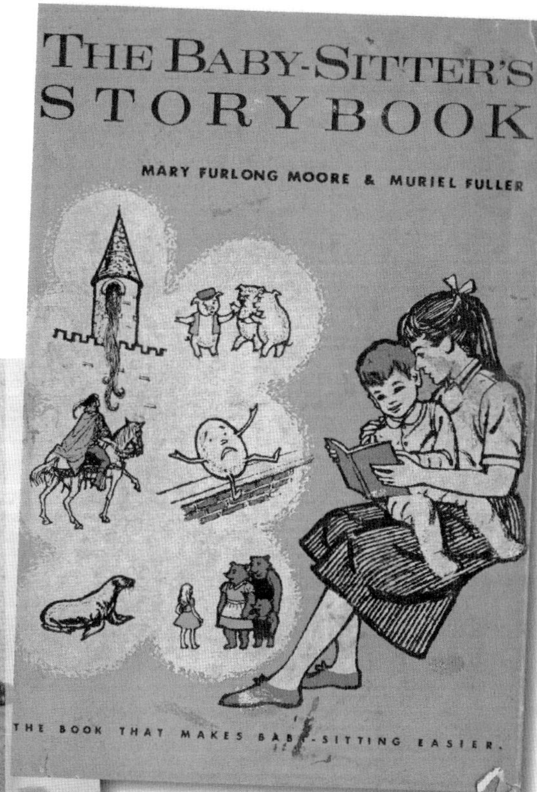

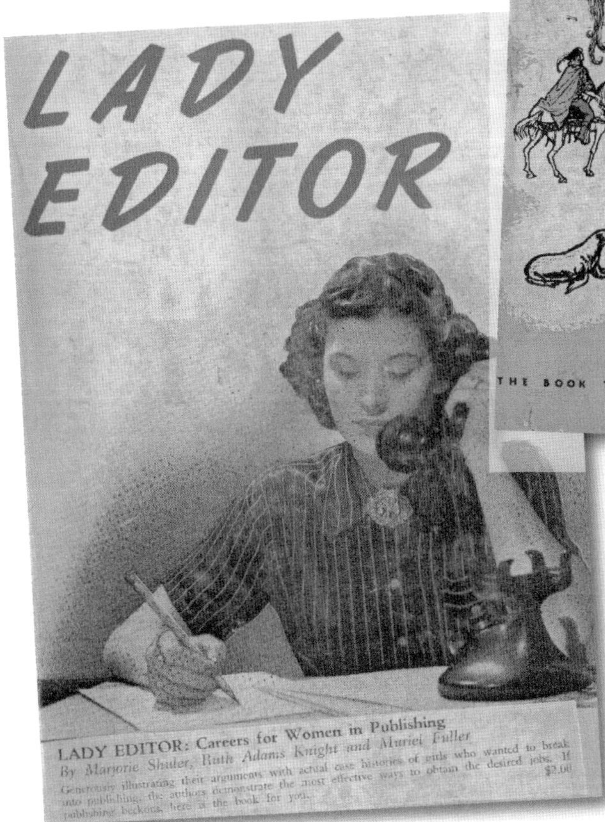

Fuller Children's Books

When not editing other people's manuscripts, Muriel Fuller wrote books for children, *The Runaway Shuttle Train, The Book of Dragons,* and *The Babysitter's Storybook*. One of the most relevant books she co-authored was *Lady Editor: Careers for Women in Publishing* (1941). She presciently observes: "A revolution in reading, thinking, publishing is ahead of us . . . Outmoded forms of publishing will disappear in every branch of the field, not only in books, but in magazines and newspapers . . . The publishing of tomorrow will combine the things we now know and blend the whole into something we cannot even dream of at present . . .The woman to be envied is the one who is now knocking on a publisher's door . . ." Reader, since the book you are holding was red-penciled by a lady editor, perhaps you should tip your hat in gratitude to Muriel Fuller the pioneer.

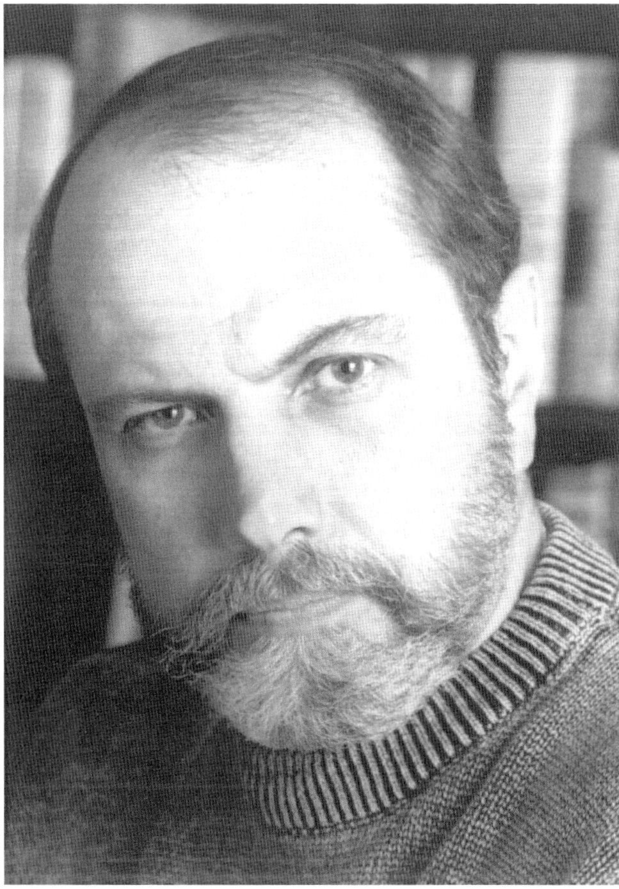

Coleman Luck

It has been observed that there is no agony like bearing an untold story inside of you. Through diligence and sheer talent, Coleman Luck Jr. is privileged to release from within tales of struggle, redemption, and grace, and his hearers are privileged to receive them. Born in Texas but raised in Wheaton, close to Chicago where his father, theologian Coleman Luck Sr. taught at Moody Bible Institute, Luck moved from grade to grade showing little interest in the classroom, but his innate ability to tell tales sustained him. A highlight of high school was the meeting with his future wife, Carel Super. After enrolling at a Dallas school, Luck soon transferred to Moody Bible Institute. Not surprisingly, his penchant for storytelling was not aligned with the prescribed courses of formal education. In 1966, he not only married Carel, but also enlisted in the Army where he was commissioned as a second lieutenant, fighting in Viet Nam. Returning to the United States and still desiring to spin yarns, Luck enrolled at Northern Illinois University where he wrote *Wintergreen*, his first screenplay. Receiving praise and a much-needed boost from film critic Pauline Kael of *The New Yorker*, he forged ahead with his hopes, moving to Los Angeles in 1977. Luck sold his first screenplay in 1980 to United Artists, and further scripts were purchased by Twentieth Century Fox, MGM, and Disney. After working on the manuscript for 25 years, he published his first novel, *Angel Fall*, in 2009. He has also functioned as a consultant and writer/producer on various television series, such as "Matrix" (1991–92), starring Nick Mancuso, and "The Burning Zone" (1996), starring Jeffrey Dean Morgan. Aside from widespread recognition for his writing, he has received the Combat Infantryman's Badge; the Bronze Star, Valor; the Bronze Star, Service; three Army Commendation Medals, Valor; and an Air Medal. He and Carel are the parents of three children and reside in the Sierra Nevada Mountains of central California.

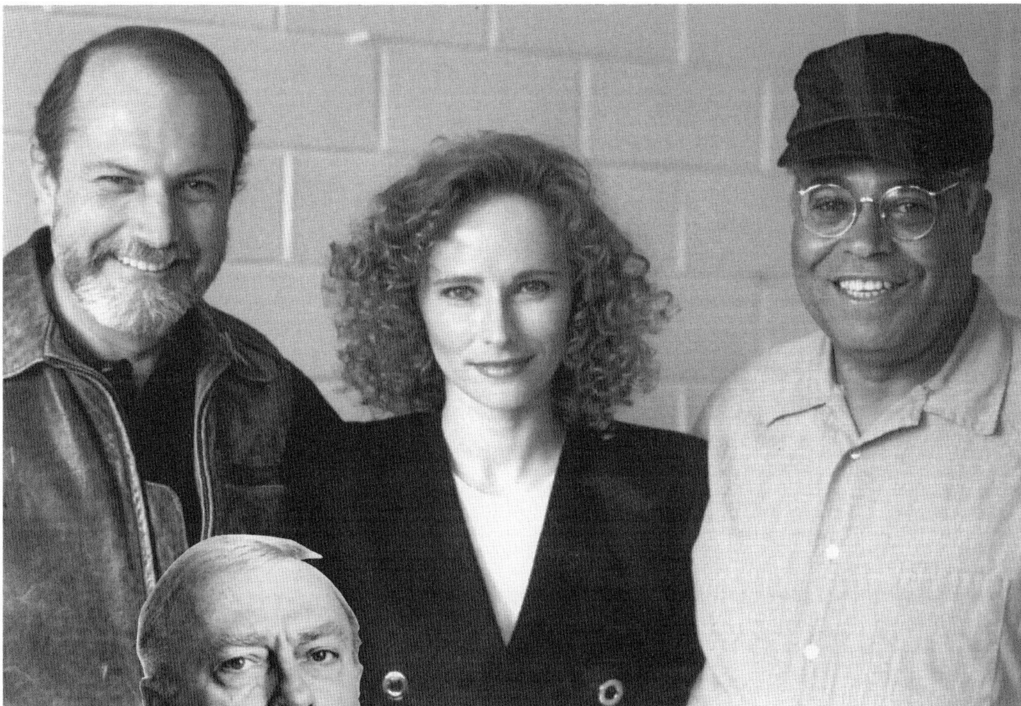

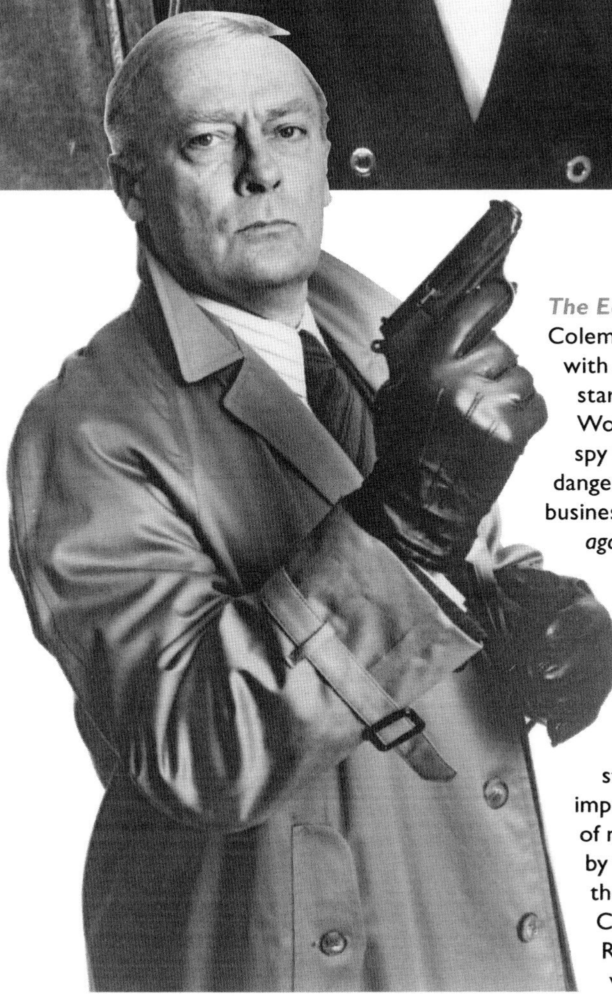

The Equalizer and *Gabriel's Fire*

Coleman Luck was hired in 1985 to assist with a new series called *The Equalizer,* starring the late British actor Edward Woodward as Robert McCall, former spy turned protector of people facing danger and injustice. McCall's memorable business card read *Got a problem? Odds against you? Need help? Call The Equalizer.* Luck advanced from co-producer to co-executive producer and showrunner. The series was nominated for a People's Choice Award. After *The Equalizer* was cancelled, Luck created and executive produced *Gabriel's Fire,* starring James Earl Jones, about an imprisoned Chicago cop wrongly accused of murder. *Gabriel's Fire* was nominated by the Mystery Writers of America in the Best Episode in a Television Series Category. Luck poses with actress Leila Robins and James Earl Jones (above), who won an Emmy Award for the role.

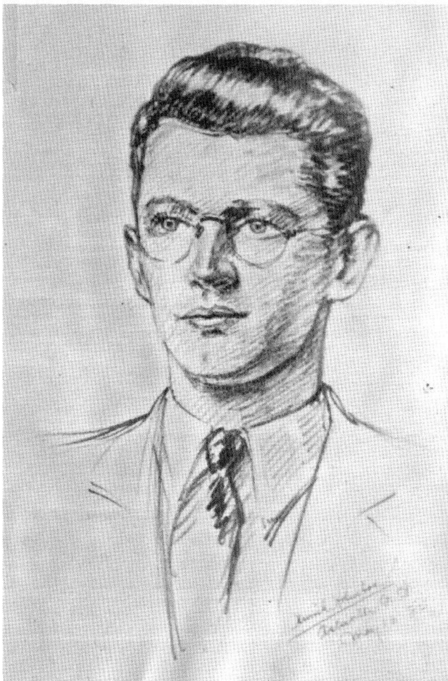

Elliot Coleman

This portrait is the frontispiece to *The Poems of Elliot Coleman*. Graduating from Wheaton College in 1928, Coleman attended Oxford to study for the Episcopalian priesthood. In 1945, he established the creative writing program at Johns Hopkins University while serving as resident poet. Coleman was privileged to teach several of America's finest writers, including John Barth and Russell Baker. Coleman counted T.S. Eliot and Dylan Thomas among his friends.

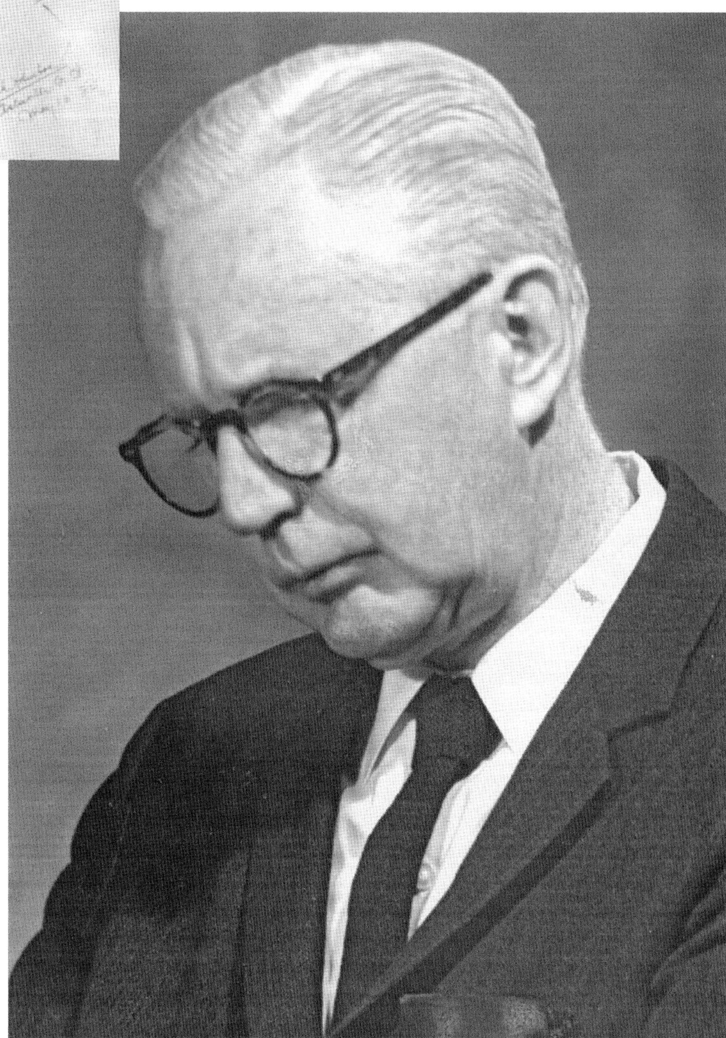

Coleman's Work

An interviewer observed: "There is, in fact, something of one's concept of the saint about Mr. Coleman . . . His high, humble presence is striking; to be with him is to feel that one is being presented with a rare gift, along with the giver's apology for having intruded." Coleman's books include a sonnet collection, *A Glass Darkly*, and *The Golden Angel*. He died in 1980 at 73 after a series of strokes.

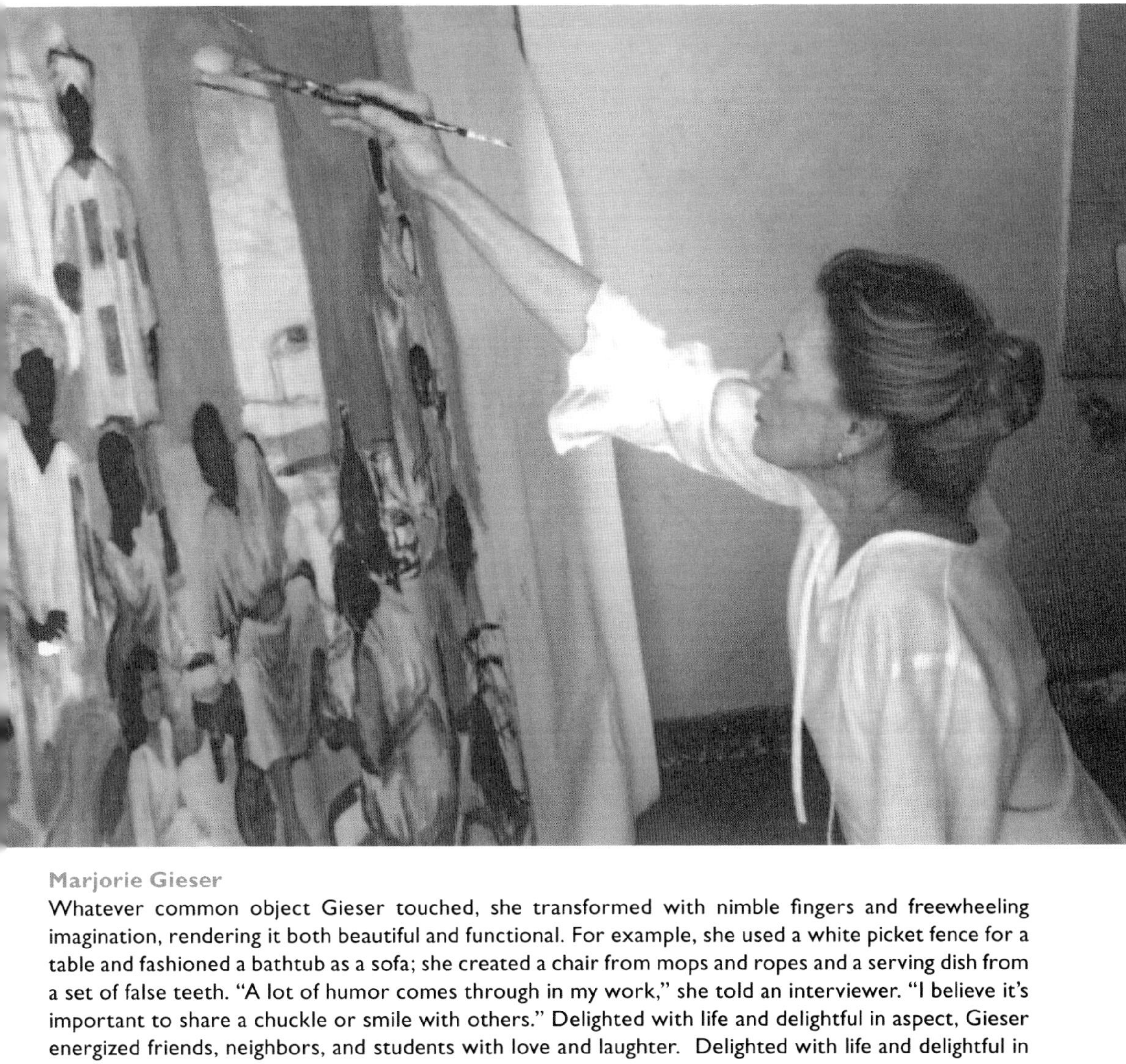

Marjorie Gieser
Whatever common object Gieser touched, she transformed with nimble fingers and freewheeling imagination, rendering it both beautiful and functional. For example, she used a white picket fence for a table and fashioned a bathtub as a sofa; she created a chair from mops and ropes and a serving dish from a set of false teeth. "A lot of humor comes through in my work," she told an interviewer. "I believe it's important to share a chuckle or smile with others." Delighted with life and delightful in aspect, Gieser energized friends, neighbors, and students with love and laughter. Delighted with life and delightful in aspect, Gieser energized...Raising three children in an English stone cottage with her husband, Richard, an ophthalmologist at Wheaton Eye Clinic, Gieser developed her varied craftsmanship during long hours at home, utilizing available materials. During the evenings, the Giesers frequently invited guests for a themed banquet or a mini-concert. She often traveled with her husband to Third World countries where he administered vision care. In 1980, Gieser was named Artist of the Month at Central DuPage Hospital, displaying her work on the second floor. She donated her paintings to Wheaton Academy and Wheaton Grammar School for fundraising. Her spectacular, luxurious three-dimensional banners, sporting figures so lifelike they might leap from the cloth, enliven the interiors of sanctuaries throughout Chicago, exhibited at College Church, Moody Church, Fourth Presbyterian Church, and elsewhere. At College Church, Gieser supervised holiday events, overseeing decorations, particularly the elaborate float for the Wheaton 4th of July parade. She shared her gifts through the instrumentality of teaching, instructing art classes in local schools and colleges. Whether painting, sculpting, cooking, photographing, or sewing, Gieser's prodigious talents burst into life as though from an unseen spring. She died in 2011. (Courtesy of Richard Gieser.)

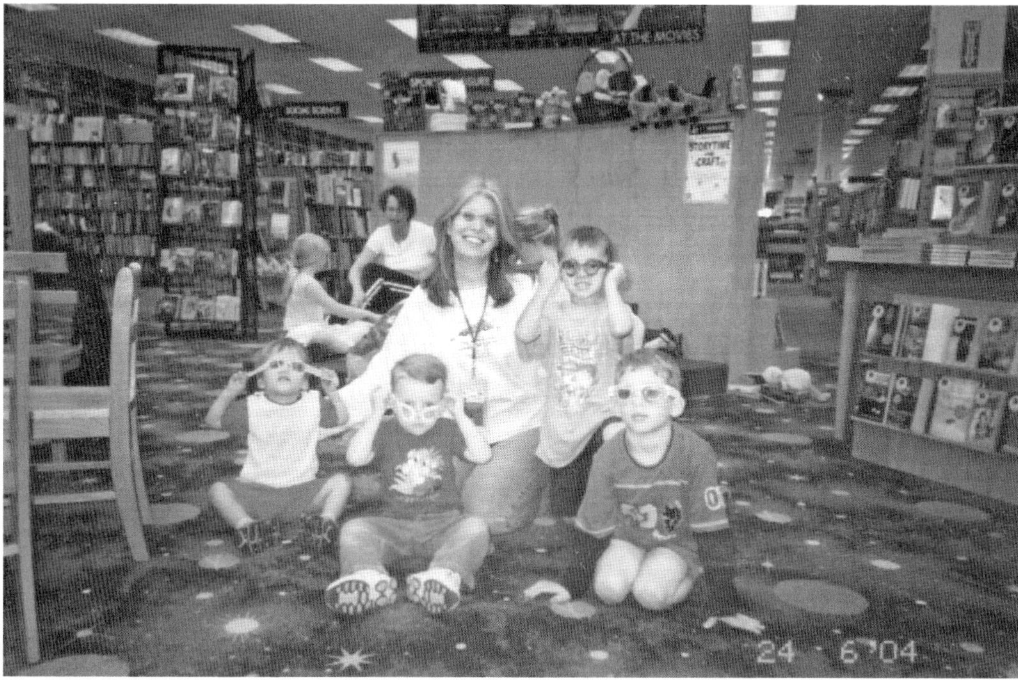

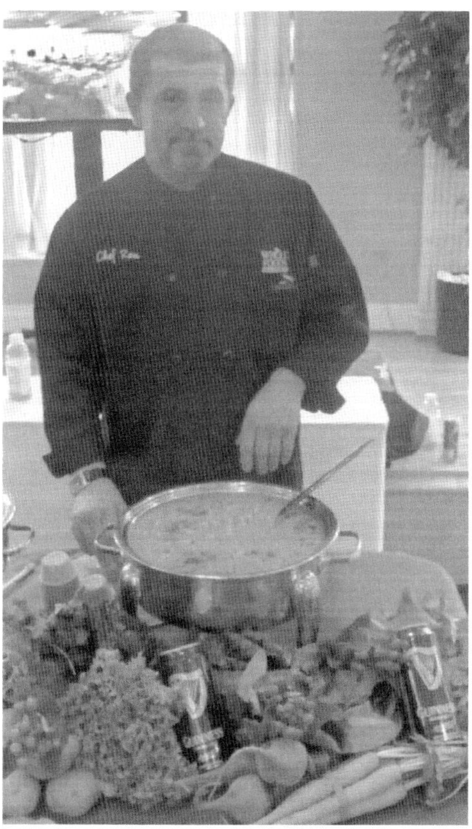

Janis Herbert

When asked to assume the storytelling responsibility in the kids' section at the Wheaton Borders, Herbert balked. Eventually, she developed a love for that task and the children who attended. Herbert has written six books, including *Marco Polo for Kids* and *Abraham Lincoln for Kids*. Researching the last title, Herbert traveled with her husband, Jeff, following Lincoln's route from Kentucky to Illinois to Washington, DC. (Courtesy of Janis Herbert.)

Ron Moore

Chef Moore, ever smiling, ever inventive, plies his trade at a DuPage PADS (Public Action to Deliver Shelter) auction. After 21 years of cooking at Dartmouth College, Moore relocated to the Midwest where he found employment with Whole Foods in Wheaton. Teaching children and adults, he uses a mobile kitchen that he designed. For his ancillary business, Just a Little Moore, he teaches the culinary arts in private homes. (Courtesy of Whole Foods.)

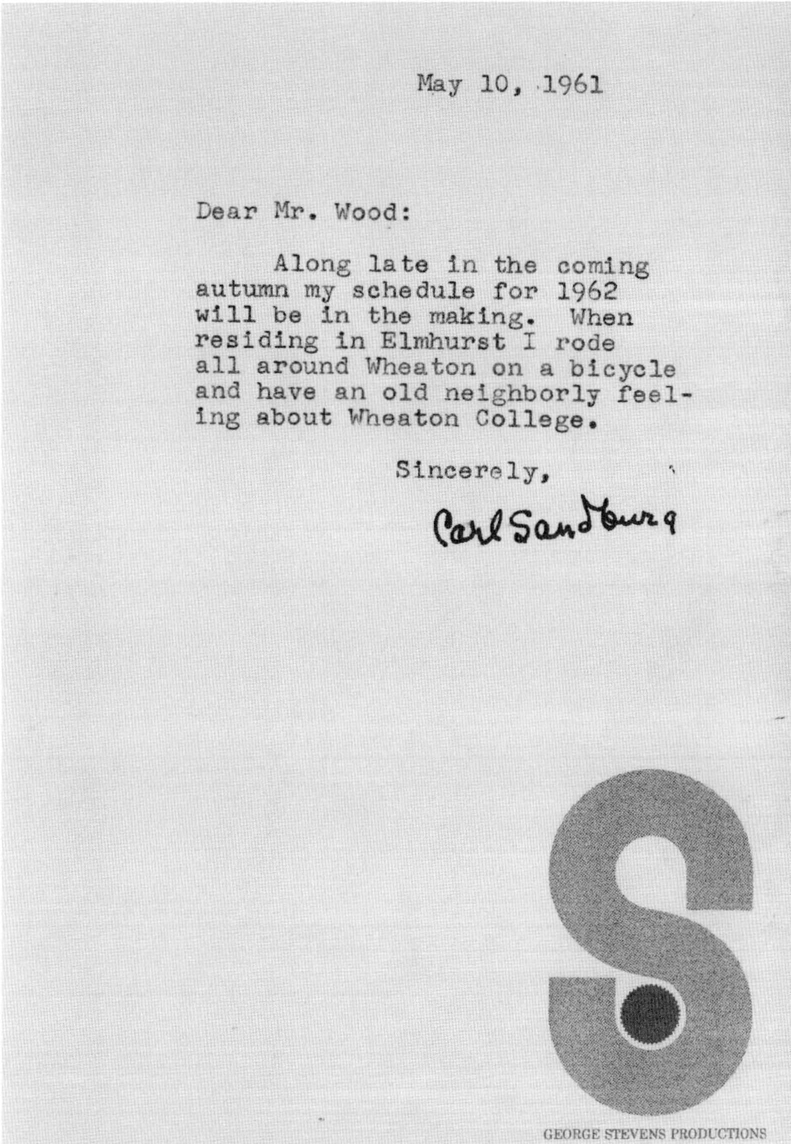

May 10, 1961

Dear Mr. Wood:

Along late in the coming autumn my schedule for 1962 will be in the making. When residing in Elmhurst I rode all around Wheaton on a bicycle and have an old neighborly feeling about Wheaton College.

Sincerely,

Carl Sandburg

GEORGE STEVENS PRODUCTIONS

Carl Sandburg

Carl Sandburg, poet, novelist, and Pulitzer Prize–winning biographer of Abraham Lincoln, wrote this response to "Mr. Wood" while living in Hollywood, crafting the screenplay to Fulton Oursler's *The Greatest Story Ever Told* (1961) for director George Stevens, whose name appears on the letterhead. When Sandburg lived in Maywood, Illinois, he often rode his bike to Wheaton, hence "the old neighborly feeling." Born in Galesburg, Illinois, where Knox College is located, Sandburg wrote of its second president, Jonathan Blanchard, who also served as the first president of Wheaton College: "The ghost of Jonathan Blanchard still goes stalking around Knox College. He was a lion, a bear, a buffalo, and in the realm of human behavior rated himself half horse and half alligator . . . He enjoyed controversy, seemed to create antagonisms for the secret fun he could have out of them."

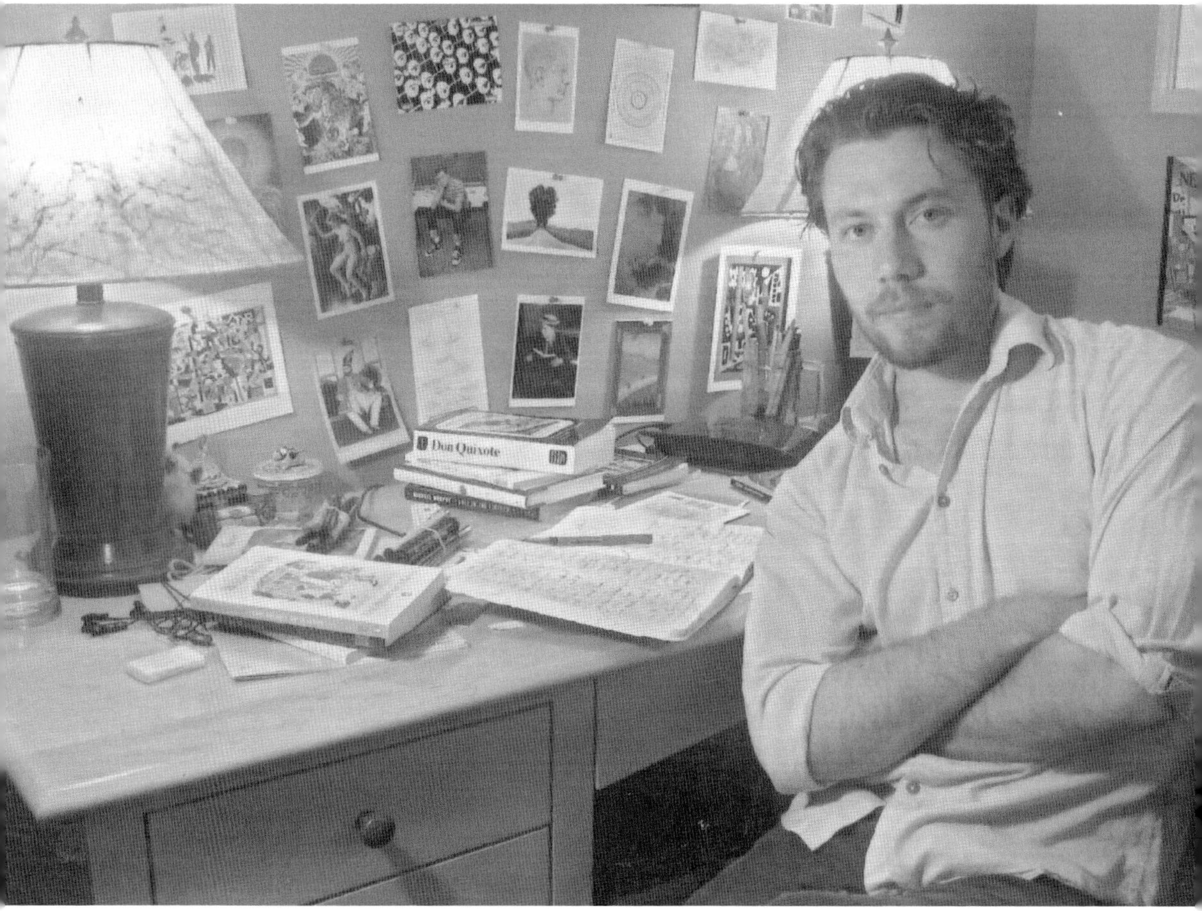

Tim Peters

In "Meditation on Wheels," one chapter from his digital novel, *The Exit Exam*, Peters explodes the universe, hardens it in the cool of space; then breaks the Earth into masses, developing its oceans, nations, and states; and finally amid the chaos, allows the emergence of his Illinois hometown and its 55,000 residents, over whom he lowers his magnifying lens. Like William Faulkner and Garrison Keillor, practitioners of regional fiction, Peters is engaged in the ambitious task of microcosmically chronicling a segment of the human experience. He writes, "I intend each chapter of *The Exit Exam* to be, in one form or another, the confessions of a young man very similar to myself about the variety of experiences, relationships, and thoughts he's had at some point in his life and that he wants to articulate and convey as simply and honestly as possible. I think of this novel as a sort of ultimate final exam—to have to say in a pithy but creative way what everything in your life so far has meant to you, and what it was all for, as you cross the threshold and head out into the real world." His hero, the ruminative cyclist, pedals through the peaceful, tree-lined streets of the city, stopping at Wheaton College, the Theosophical Society, and various shops and parks, familiar locales recruited as touchstones for his sharp and often amusing commentary on suburban wealth, religion, and politics. *The Exit Exam* falls somewhere between prose memoir and graphic novel. Peters's work has appeared at *McSweeney's Internet Tendency*, *Guernica*, the PBS NewsHour online, the *Point* magazine, and elsewhere. He studied philosophy at the University of Illinois at Urbana-Champaign and lived in Argentina, lecturing at a university and writing journalism courtesy of a Fulbright fellowship. Among his influences are David Foster Wallace, Hunter S. Thompson, Franz Kafka and Virginia Woolf. (Courtesy of Tim Peters.)

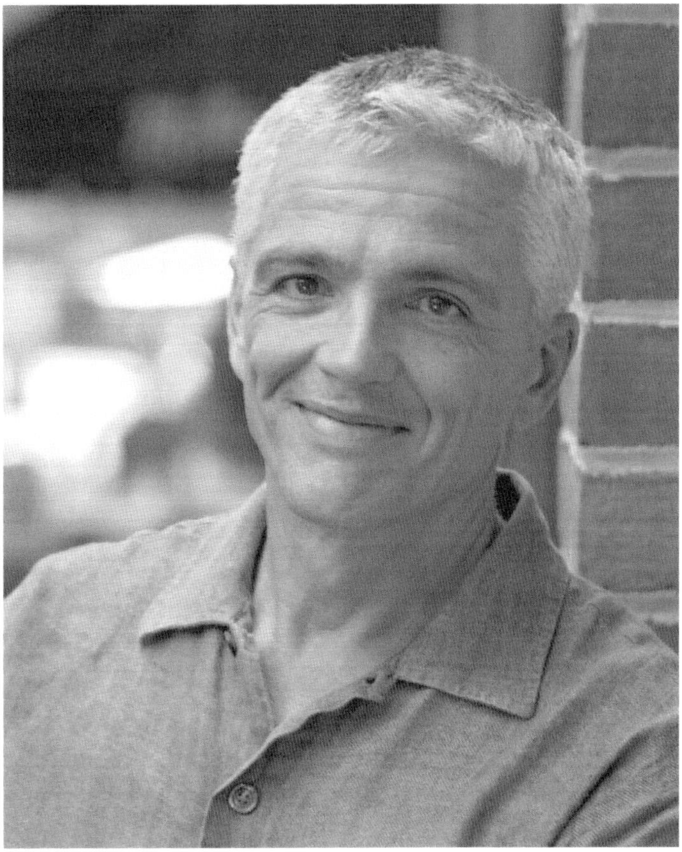

Stefan Bechtel

Writing his first story in the second grade, Bechtel knew he had the knack. His father, Paul, was an English professor and his mother, Mary, a librarian; consequently he grew up familiar with culture and books. But soon he realized that he required experience, a seasoning beyond academia. In the following years he traveled the world, including Africa, Alaska, Istanbul, and Patagonia, in addition to working as a reporter, house painter, gardener, street vendor, and entrepreneur. "Life itself, it seemed to me," he writes, "was the prize above all prizes." He secured a job as writer and editor at Rodale Press where he became involved in one of the more remarkable publishing stories of the 1990s. Working as a senior editor at *Prevention* (at the time the world's largest-circulation health magazine), he and his boss, Mark Bricklin, created a monthly newsletter called *Men's Health*, of which Bechtel was executive editor. The newsletter proved so successful that after two years of publication, they gathered existing material from back issues, generated new stories, repackaged it as a glossy magazine, and placed 200,000 copies on newsstands. Today *Men's Health* is the largest men's magazine in the world, outselling *GQ* and *Esquire* combined. Bechtel has published 10 books, including *Katherine, It's Time*, and *Mr. Hornaday's War*. His writing has appeared in newspapers and magazines including *Esquire*, the *Washington Post*, *Reader's Digest*, *Prevention*, *American Way*, and *Adventure Journal*. He is a longstanding member of the American Society of Journalists and Authors and a three-time Fellow at the Virginia Center for the Creative Arts. He serves on the board of the Center for Creative Voices in Media, a nonprofit organization dedicated to the preservation of independent voices in film, television, and printed media. Bechtel lives comfortably, he says, "writing books and articles and indulging a lifelong habit of staring vaguely into the middle distance with a kind of dreamy cheerfulness, wondering what's going to happen next." (Courtesy of Stefan Bechtel.)

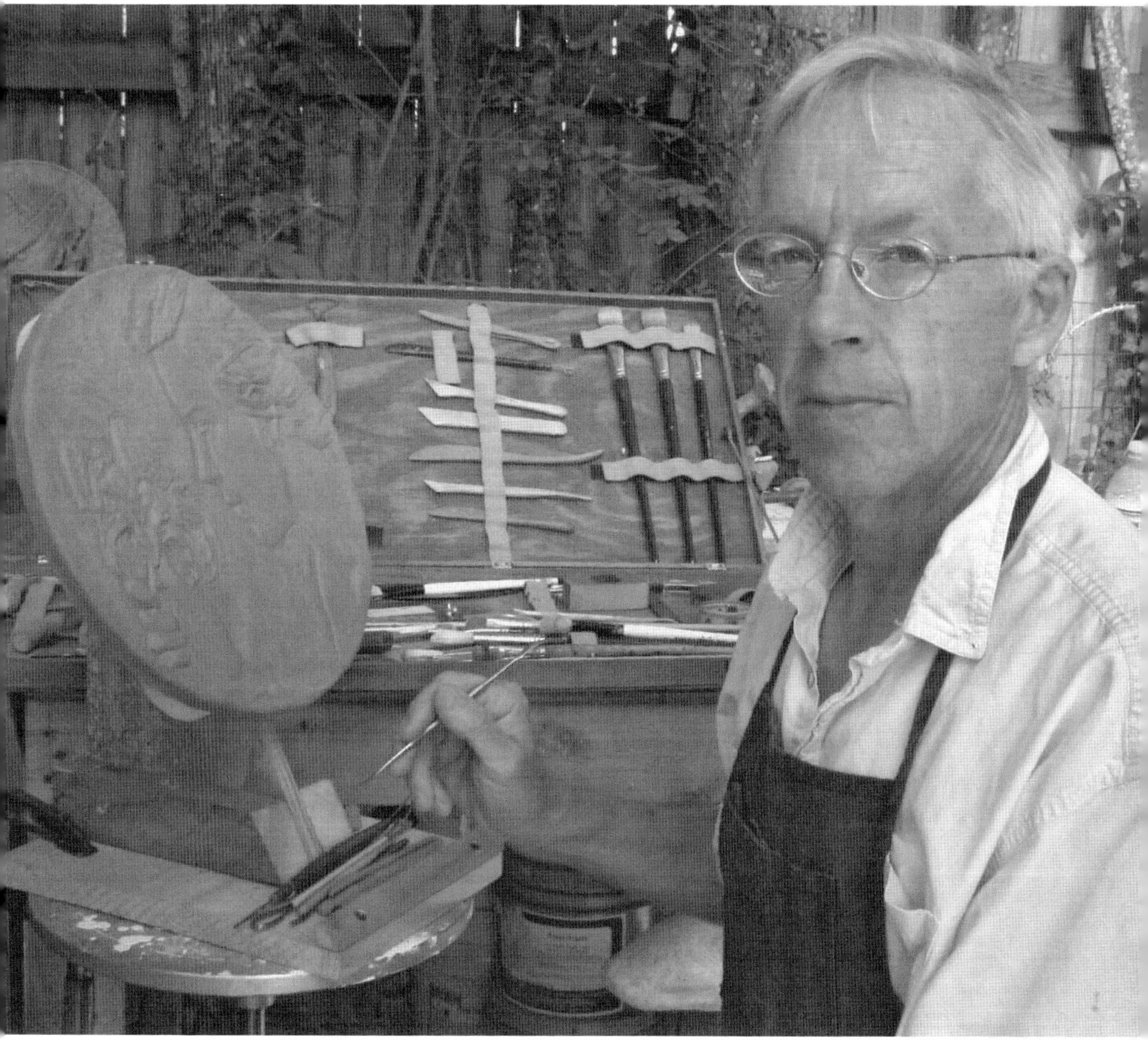

Lawrence Reid Bechtel

Like his brother, Stefan, sculptor Lawrence Reid Bechtel tells stories; but rather than using a keyboard, he employs clay and bronze. He writes, "Influenced by my mother's creativity and my father's love of great literature, I am as a sculptor drawn to projects which allow for personal expression and touch upon meaningful subject matter. In my public commissions, I love to immerse myself in sculpture as interpretation: giving tangible, symbolic form to community values. My artistic imagination was deeply shaped by my experience of growing up in Wheaton, in the shadow of Wheaton College, where my father taught English for many years. Innumerable boyhood adventures at Lincoln Marsh, which we knew simply as 'the swamp,' were also pivotal." Bechtel further reflects on his craft: "I see the work, in the context of my life, as a series of sculptural moments, which taken together, describe a long arc . . . Sculpture for me is an adventure. Portrait sculpture is about manifesting the mystery of personhood in a piece that's bronze. You're getting one moment of expression to somehow capture the soul and the lifetime of experiences of an individual. It's totally impossible, really. But art itself is an impossible enterprise. That's what makes it so challenging, so alluring." (Courtesy of Lawrence Reid Bechtel.)

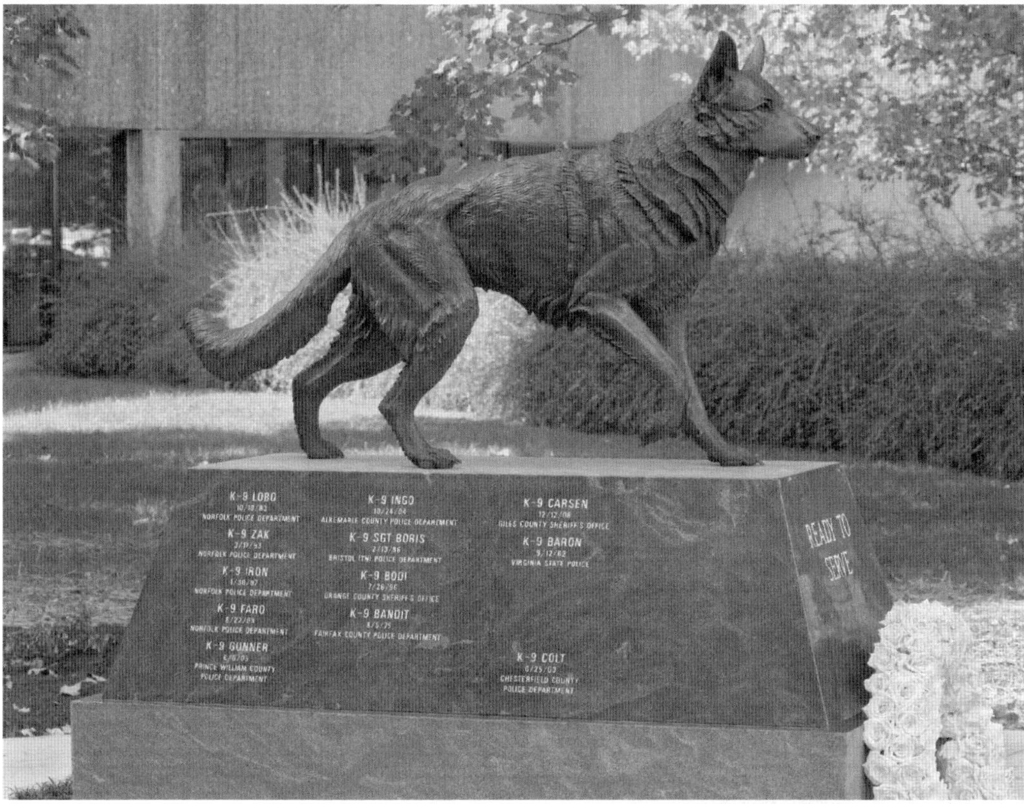

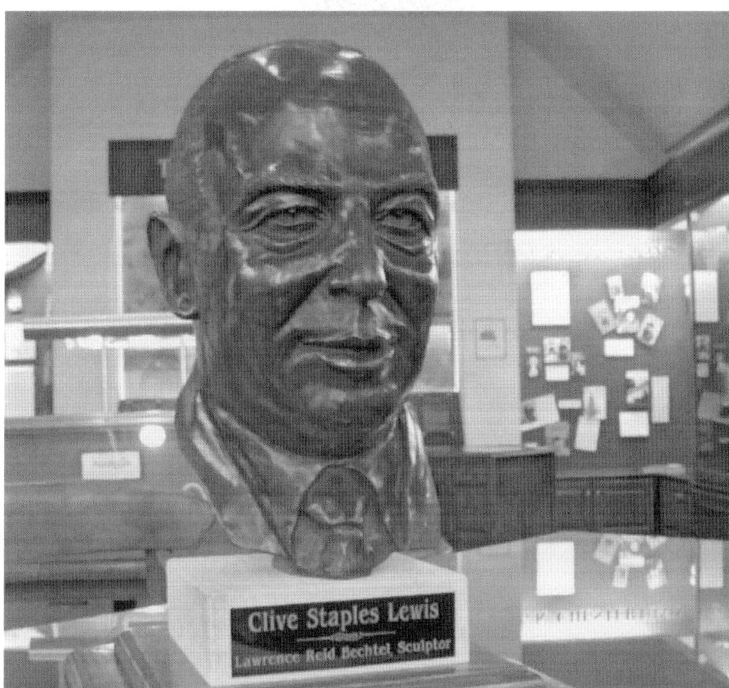

Bechtel's *Police Dog Memorial*
Police Dog Memorial is displayed at Virginia Tech. "Most people think in terms of [the sculpture's] narrative content," Bechtel says. "What does it look like? What is it about? What they don't appreciate, typically, is that the form can convey meaning and content, but it is registering to them at an emotional, subconscious level. Because I was raised in a home in which my father was an English teacher and my mother was a librarian, I do very much feel the literary background there. I am a storyteller . . . I very often think of a sculpture as a climactic moment in a narrative . . . So you have a sculpture that implies a past and implies a future. It's all contained in a moment . . . as all life itself." Right: *C.S. Lewis* is displayed at the Marion E. Wade Center. (Courtesy of Lawrence Reid Bechtel.)

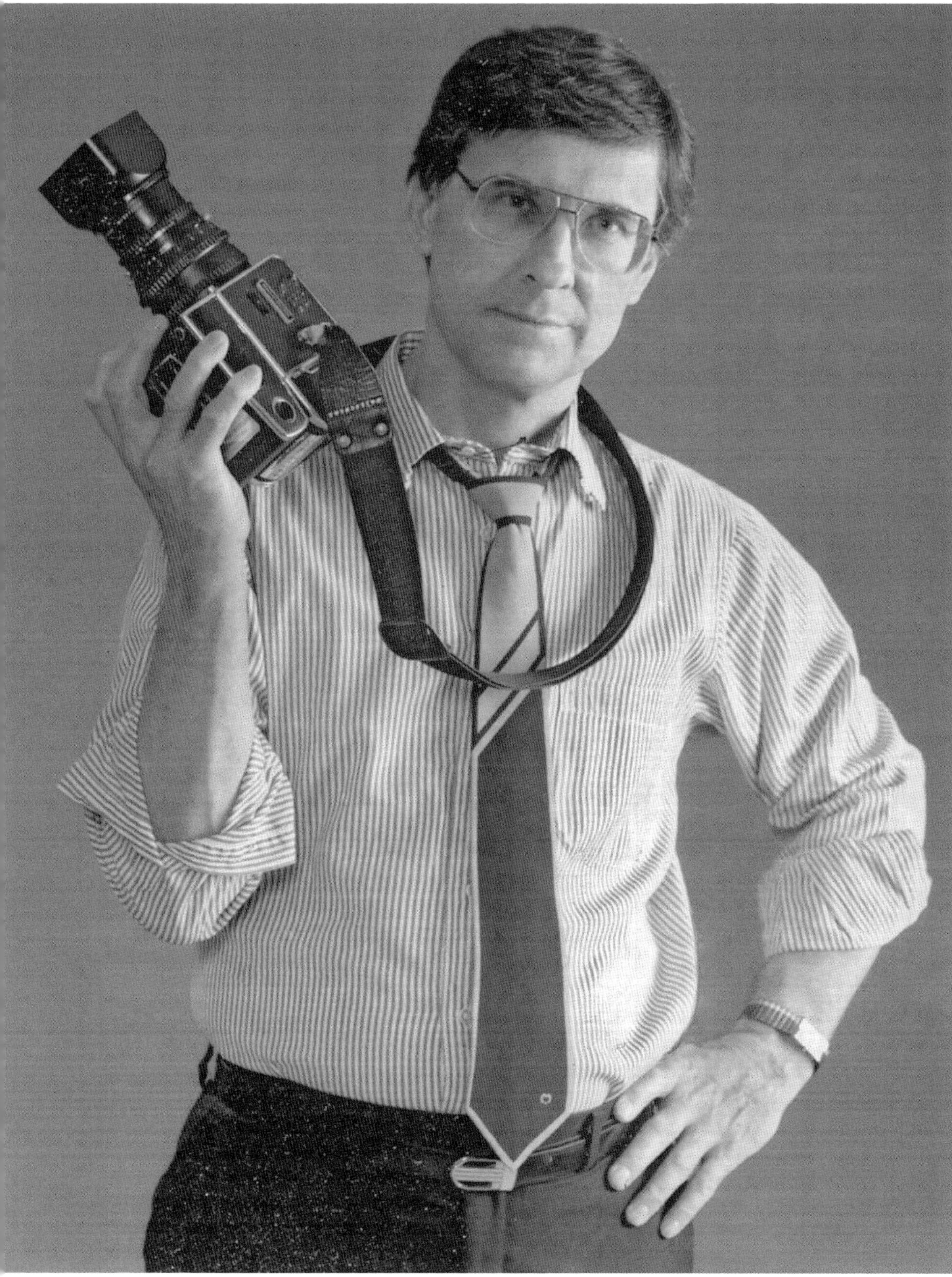

Ron Stewart (LEFT)
If photography is the art of seeing, Stewart sees with extraordinary clarity. Specializing in wedding and portrait photography, he opened his Wheaton studio in 1980 at 107 E. Front Street. A graduate of the Rochester Institute of Technology, he also attended Brooks Institute of Photography in Santa Barbara, California. He holds the professional photography degrees of Master of Photography and Photographic Craftsman, from the Professional Photographers of America, and he has been named Associate and Fellow by the American Society of Photographers. He is a Fellow of the British Institute of Professional Photography, the highest award given by the institute. Stewart is one of two photographers in the world to hold these five degrees. At the awards banquet held in the House of Parliament in London, Stewart received the Fellowship from BIPP president Eric Strange. The event was sponsored by Lord Jerry Wiggins, member of the Parliament. Stewart was among 16 photographers from around the world to receive this honor. The criteria necessary to attain Fellowship in the British Institute is: a portfolio of 20 prints representing the best work of the photographer; a thesis detailing the photographer's philosophy; and a personal interview. The portfolio and thesis were judged by a panel of BIPP Fellows, and the interview was conducted by a select committee in order to evaluate his contribution to the profession of photography. Stewart's portfolio was selected as the finest portrait entry of all who applied. The panel also selected an image from the portfolio to be displayed in the House of Commons. Stewart beat out 15,000 photographers in the Professional Photographers of America's print award competition. He is the founder and twice president of XXV, an organization of 25 top photographers worldwide that meets annually to advance the profession of photography. He serves as a member of their board of directors. (Courtesy of Ron Stewart.)

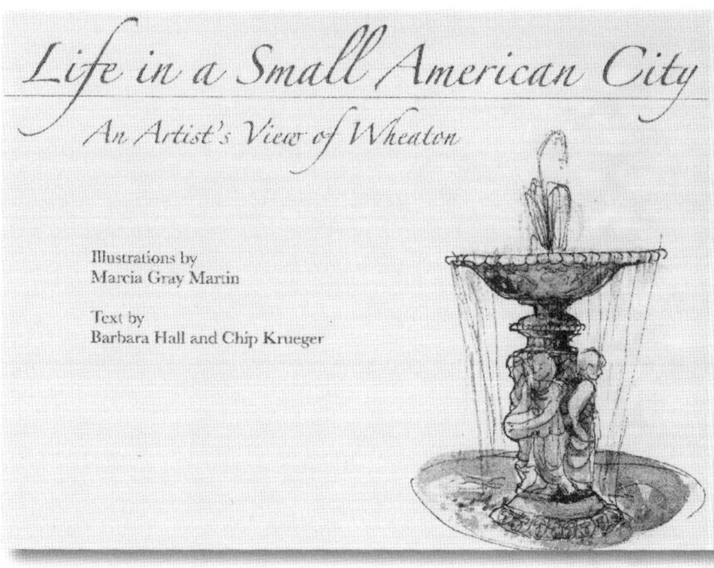

Life in a Small American City
This illustrated book offers a unique approach to the city's historical heart. Illustrated by Marcia Gray Martin and written by Barbara Hall and Chip Krueger, *Life in a Small American City* presents a series of sinuous watercolor line drawings depicting prominent homes, churches, and civic structures. Legendary architects graced Wheaton with their incomparable visions, including Frank Lloyd Wright, Edward Dart, and Jarvis Hunt. Martin, trained as an architectural and mechanical engineer, taught architecture at College of DuPage; Hall, graduate of the Illinois Institute of Design at Illinois Institute of Technology, taught graphic arts at College of DuPage; and Krueger, lifelong resident of Wheaton, was recognized in 2009 by Landmarks Illinois for his research on the influential Wheaton Colony. (Courtesy of Marcia Gray Martin, Chip Krueger, and Barbara Hall.)

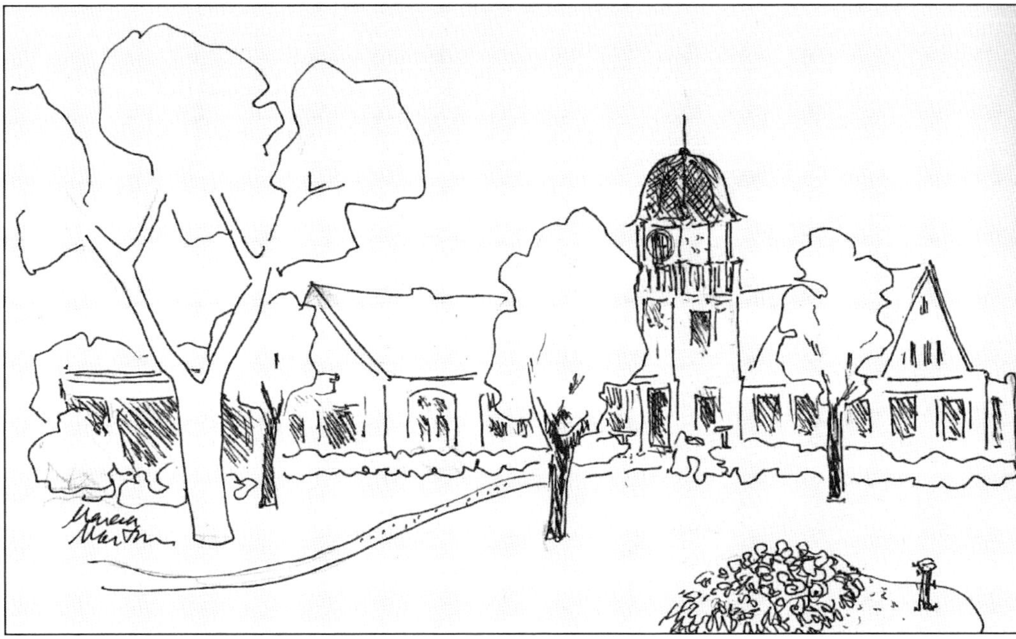

Marcia Gray Martin's Work

Located in Wheaton, Chicago Golf Club (drawn by Marcia Gray Martin) is the oldest 18-hole golf course in the country, and certainly one of the most prestigious. For decades, it attracted Windy City high society as a summertime playground. The clubhouse was designed by Jarvis Hunt. Below: This home by Frank Lloyd Wright (drawn by Martin) stood on Leask Lane. Exhibiting Wright's Usonian design, which he considered as singularly American and free of previous architectural conventions, the prefabricated structure was dismantled and moved in 2003 to Wright's estate, Fallingwater, in western Pennsylvania. It is now used as a portion of a luxury resort hotel. (Courtesy of Marcia Gray Martin, Chip Krueger, and Barbara Hall.)

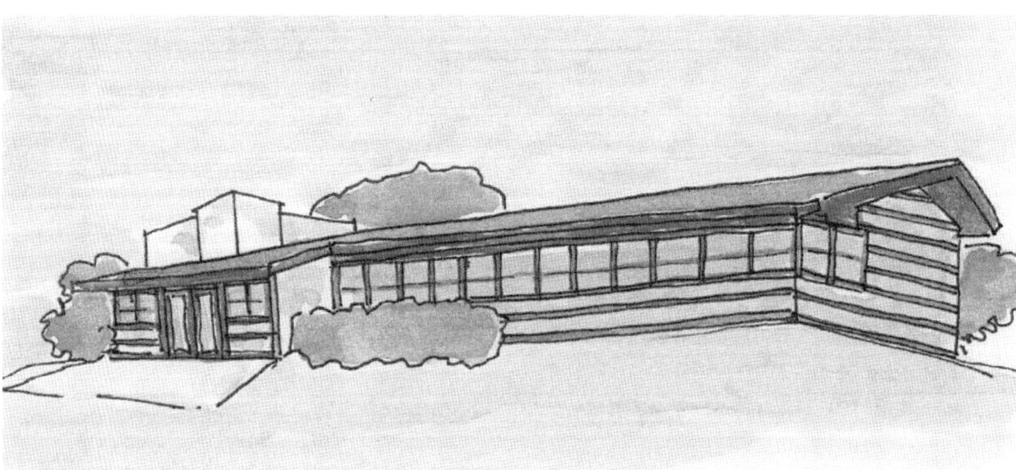

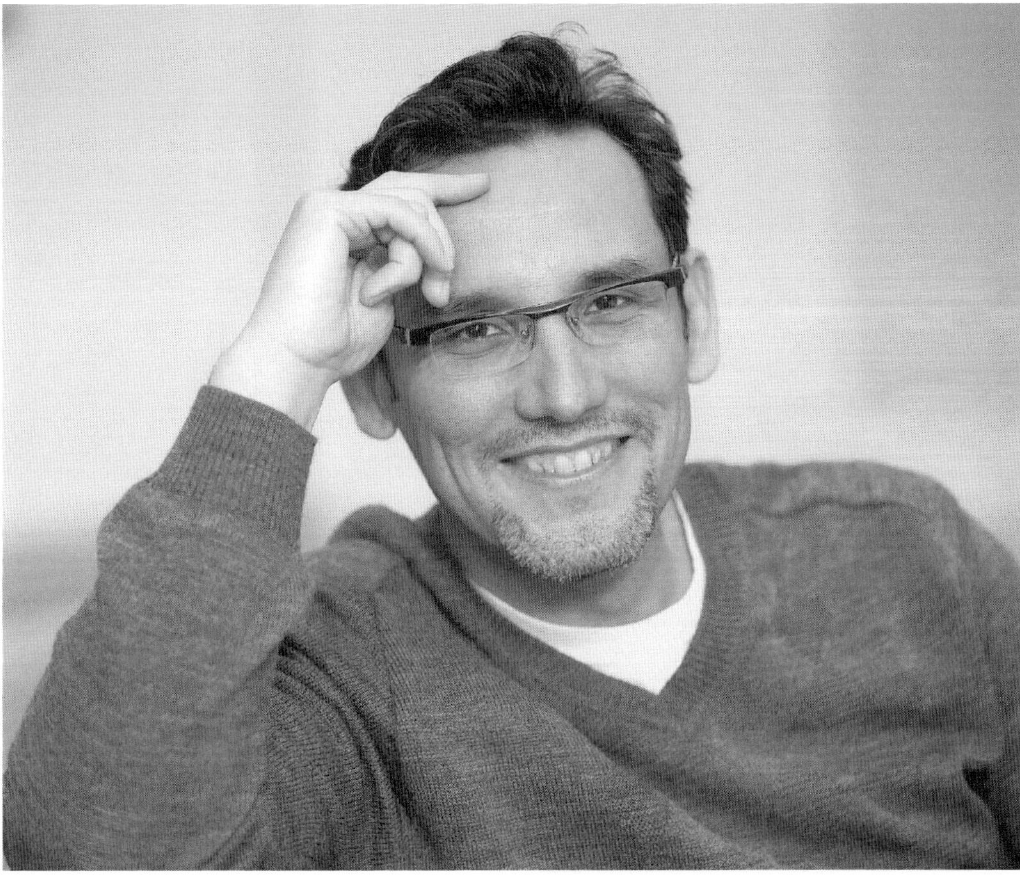

Sergio Villanueva

A native of Mexico, Villanueva has taught and led congregations in worship in Central, South, and North America. He is a singer/writer with a passion to create songs of celebration and confession. He is currently the pastor of worship and devotion at Iglesia del Pueblo, the Hispanic congregation of Wheaton Bible Church. His music is frequently broadcast on Latin radio. "La Casa de Dios" and "Hoy y Siempre te alabare" are performed by Costa Rican contemporary Christian musician Danilo Montero. Villanueva's other songs include "Un Millon de Arcoiris," "Eco de Tu Voz," "Bendecire," and "Dejate Amar." Villanueva is often surprised to attend worship services where his own music is performed. He lives in Lombard, Illinois, with his wife, Rosie, and his two sons, Gabriel and Daniel. (Courtesy of Sergio Villanueva.)

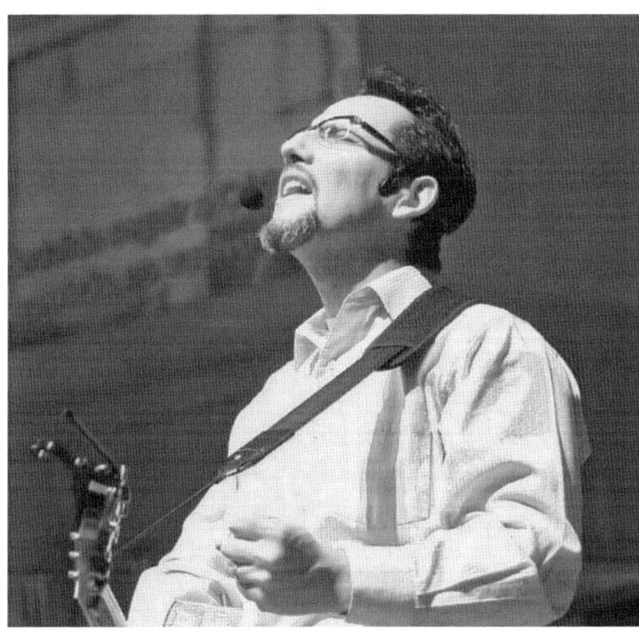

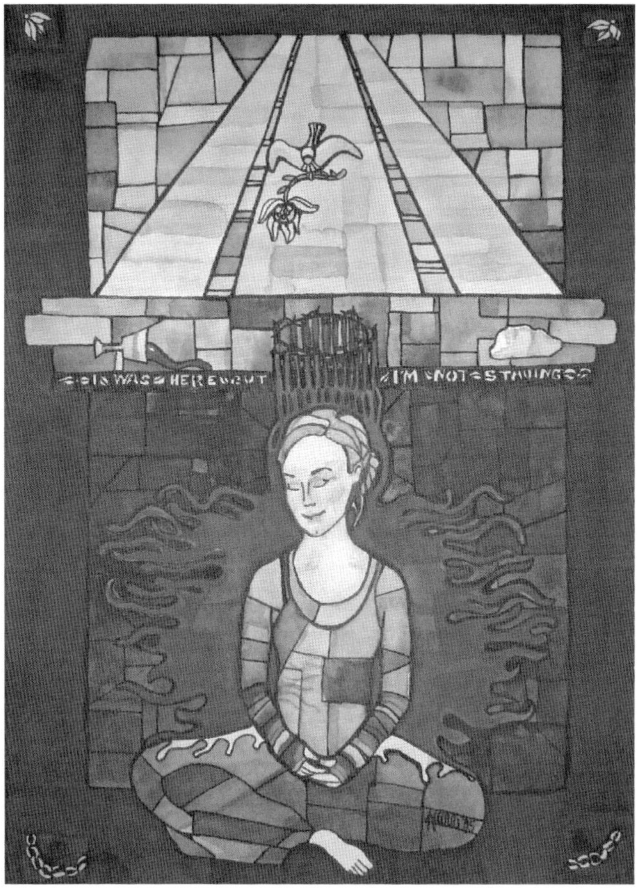

Hannah Maletich

The artist portrays herself meditating serenely in this painting, completed at Emmaus Bible College in Dubuque, Iowa. Calvin Seerveld, professor of philosophical aesthetics, might have had this work in mind when he wrote: "An art object is like an alluring, ambiguous wink hinting at matters worth experiencing, full of knowledge bottled for those who can open up its allusiveness and taste it aesthetically." Currently employed in commercial interior design, Hannah Maletich was raised on the mission field. She writes: "I imagine that there are many artists in this world that never live in the kind of peace and prosperity that allow for the development of something great and beautifully planned. But even in the villages of Eastern Turkey, where I spent several summers as a child, people find ways to dye the wool of their sheep and to hand-knot intricate rugs. These patterns and colors are not necessary to their survival. They have to work hard to put food on the table and deal with the elements of weather and political unrest. But still there is a need to create beauty. I see people as unique works of the artist God, created with a need to reflect their creator in whatever way they've been given talents and drive to do so. Whether painting, blowing glass, or refinishing wood furniture rescued from a Dumpster dive, I enjoy the process as much as the result. The innate qualities of the materials are themselves such an ingenious creation and I am humbled that I have the resources to enjoy beauty in this way. This summer my creative energies have been focused on doing well in my new career in commercial interior design. Once I am more settled at work I would like to take advantage of the open-hearted town of Wheaton. Because I grew up in Turkey, Iraq and Germany, I am excited that many people groups have found a safe place to live in Wheaton. I would like to create a place where refugees living in cramped apartments with limited resources could go to find joy in artistic and cultural expression." (Courtesy of Hannah Maletich.)

CHAPTER THREE

The Givers

"This city," said Judge Frank Herrick, poet laureate of Wheaton, with a vigorous sweep of his arms in a 1959 interview conducted on his 84th birthday, "has many things to be proud of. Wheaton is a citadel of Christian forces. Here Wheaton College has trained men and women for the greater part of this century to the work of God. The city is the headquarters of many great forces for good, both Protestant and Catholic. Her schools are of the finest, and her men turned soldiers when their country called." Surely the presence of innumerable churches, mission agencies, and other charitable organizations has contributed to its generosity, but not all the citizens of Wheaton claim to be Protestant or Catholic, or possess any faith at all. Nonetheless, the moral imperative for giving runs deep, possibly fed by a combination of wealth, graduate-level education, and pressing sense of obligation. Its expression assumes many forms. Giving might mean serving the physically or mentally challenged, or writing a life-changing book, or operating a welcoming restaurant or bookstore. Wherever one stands in relation to the motives for giving, Pres. Bill Clinton (of whom Herrick and most of his heavily conservative DuPage County constituency would strongly disapprove) presents a succinct, wide-ranging encouragement regarding the generous impulse in his book, *Giving: How Each of Us Can Change the World*: "There's so much to be done, down the street and around the world. It's never too late or too early to start . . . So much of modern culture is characterized by stories of self-indulgence and self-destruction. So much of modern politics is focused not on honest differences of policy but on personal attacks . . .Who's happier? The uniters or the dividers? The givers or the takers? I think you know the answer. There's a whole world out there that needs you, down the street or across the ocean. Give."

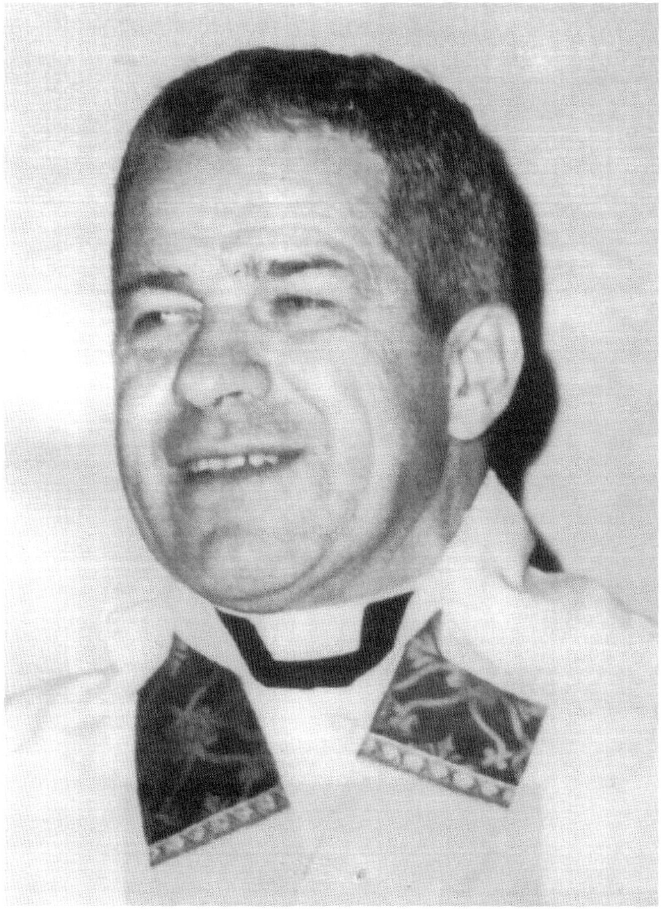

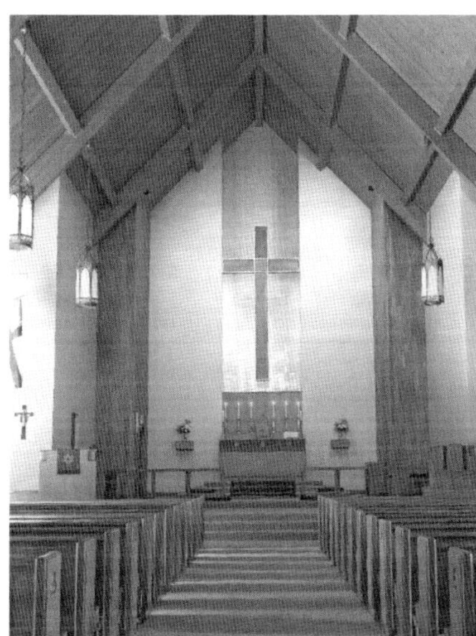

Richard Winkler

Former rector of Trinity Episcopal Church, Winkler is recognized as the "grandfather" of the Charismatic movement of the late 1950s. He was perhaps the first Episcopal priest to receive the "baptism in the spirit," introducing the Charismatic renewal into mainstream denominations. He oversaw a weekly prayer circle dedicated to spiritual revival and physical healing. Winkler preferred a humble "hidden" life. However, a 1964 *Saturday Evening Post* article featuring Trinity and similar ministries brought unwanted attention. (Courtesy of Trinity Episcopal.) Right: The chapel at Trinity as it appeared during Winkler's tenure. He moved to Hawaii in 1967. A fuller account of his extraordinary career is presented in Leanne Payne's memoir, *Heaven's Calling: A Memoir of One Soul's Steep Ascent.* "A very precious man of God he was," she writes, "and never one to vindicate himself in the face of public disapproval."

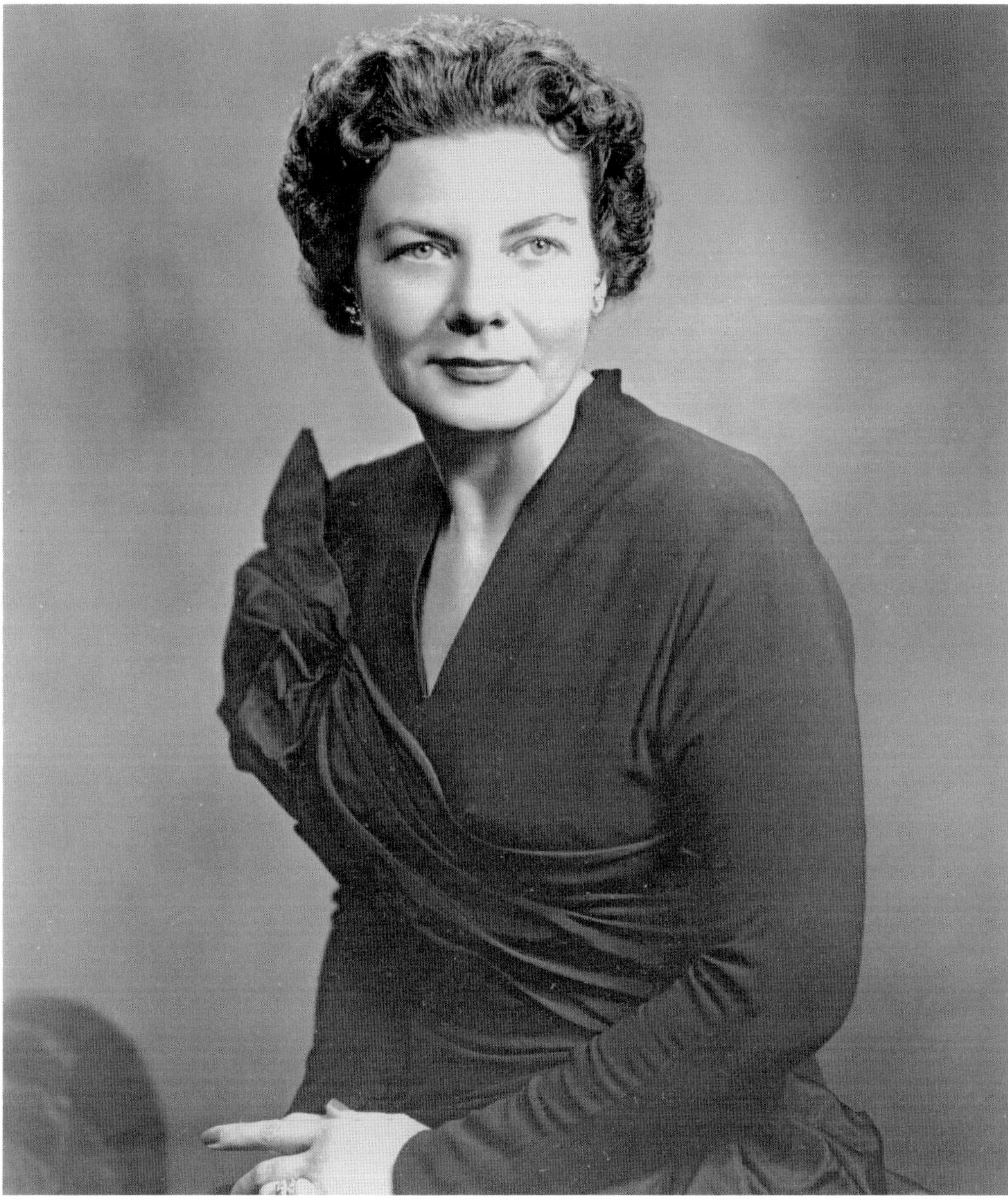

Catherine Marshall

Aside from the regular attendees of Richard Winkler's midweek prayer circle, several Christian celebrities joined him. For instance, Father Dennis Bennett, author of *Nine O'Clock in the Morning*, recounting his own pivotal experience with the Charismatic blessing, traveled from Anaheim, California, to pray with Winkler. Another prominent visitor was Catherine Marshall, author of *Beyond Ourselves* and *A Man Called Peter,* and widow of Peter Marshall, chaplain of the US Senate, joining the prayer circle at Trinity Episcopal Church whenever she was in the area. "Back in 1945," she writes in *The Helper*, "Peter and I could never have foreseen the amazing resurgence of the Spirit that began early in the sixties and by 1966–67 was in full swing." Marshall continued attending meetings and revivals centered on Charismatic renewal for the remainder of her life.

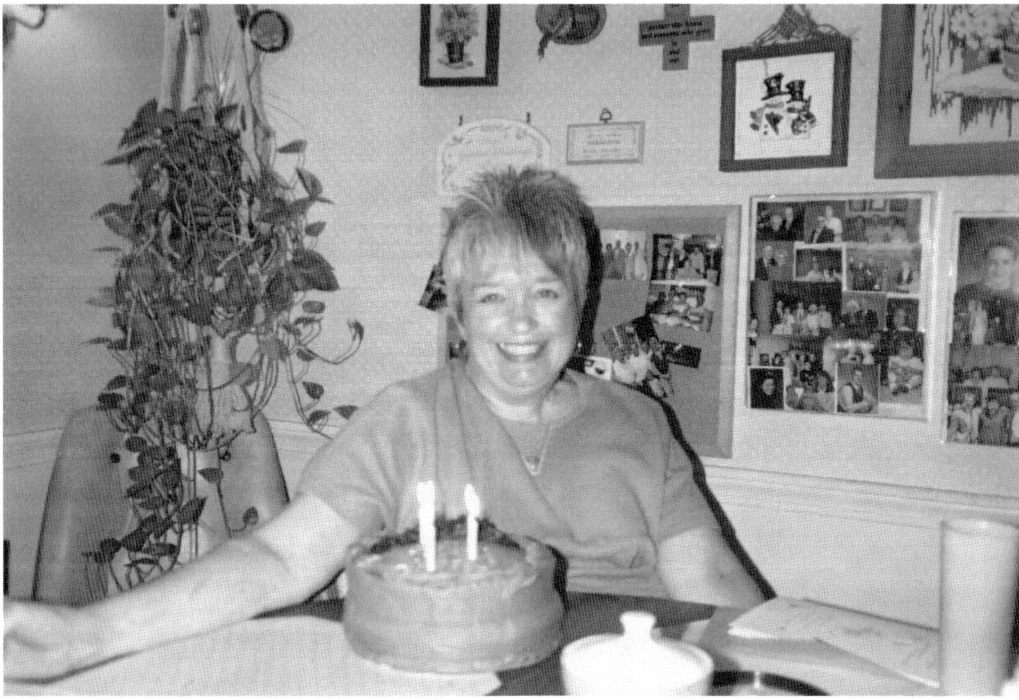

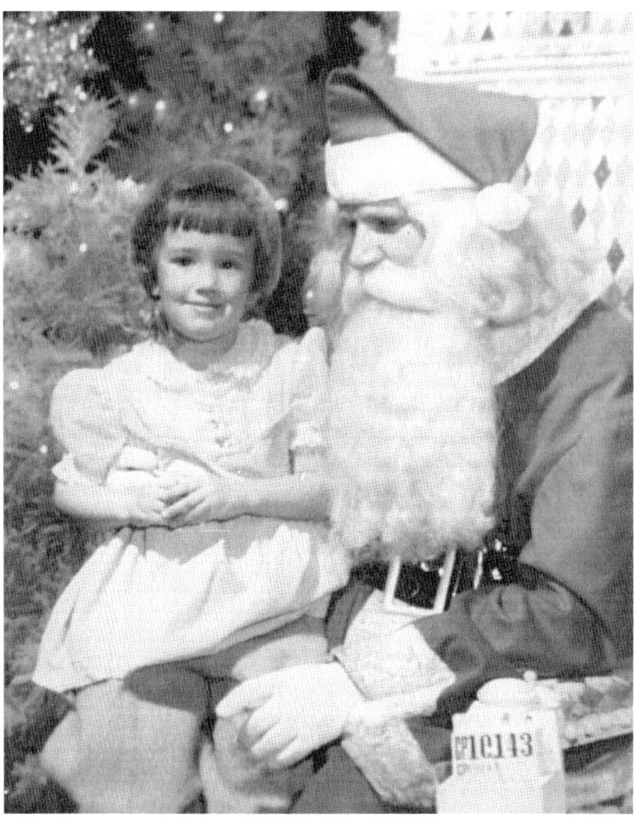

Vonny Albert

Perhaps little Vonny Albert is asking Santa Claus to gift her with a lifetime supply of joy. Albert, whose middle name is, in fact, "Joy," has throughout the decades generously dispensed abundant joy to her friends, family, and neighbors. Her abiding practice of generating "good clean fun," celebration, and neighborly concern daily bring light to whatever space she inhabits, whether it is the workplace, home, or church. She teaches Bible stories to two-and-a-half to three-year-olds at Wheaton Bible Church, sings songs, and supervises their rowdy play. Albert is the mother of two 20-something sons. (Courtesy of Vonny Albert.)

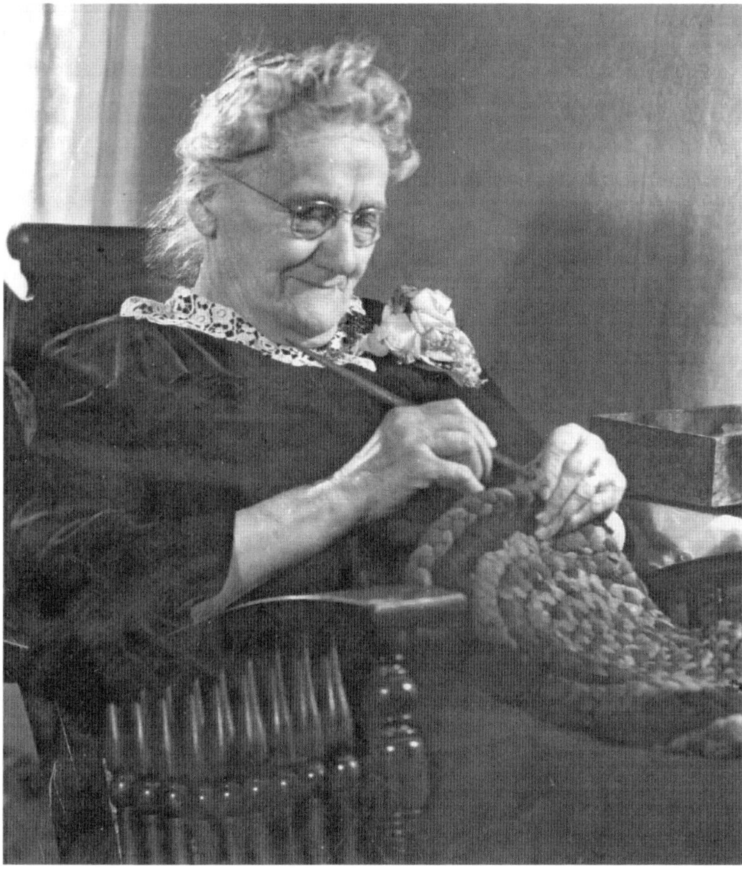

Louise Stoddard Wheaton

Louise Stoddard of Byron, Illinois, graduated from Wheaton College in 1889, one of 12 in her class. Two years later she married Warren Lyon Wheaton, the son of Warren Wheaton, one of the founders who donated land for the expansion of the college. Her mother, Catherine, a daughter of Jonathan Blanchard, founder of the college, was killed in a train accident, causing the family to be divided among relatives. For a short time after their marriage, Warren Lyon and Louise lived in Battle Creek, Michigan, but returned to Wheaton to care for the family estate. In 1944, Wheaton fell and broke his hip; despite her age and arthritis, Louise, trained as a nurse, tended him back to relative health. During the mid-1950s, she was the college's oldest alumna. An interviewer vividly notes her quaint, old-fashioned mannerisms in a 1955 article: "Having patted her pompadour neatly in place, she straightens the bustle of her ankle-length calico dress and flicks a speck of dust off the toe of her shiny black high button shoes." An oral interview was recorded in 1954 and broadcast on WMBI. "I still love Wheaton College," she wrote in 1949 to the alumni association, "and pray daily for all connected with her and trust the day will never come when the ideals and sacrifices of her founders will be only a memory." Warren Lyon died in 1945 at 95. She died at 91 in 1961 at a Naperville convalescent home. Louise faithfully attended College Church and, as her obit succinctly states, "was always interested in all good works." The Warren Wheaton home still stands on the corner of Roosevelt and Naperville Road, and is now used as a real estate agency. The Platonic ideal of the sweet, doughy old lady, Louise Stoddard Wheaton's reassuring image was occasionally used by Wheaton College during the 1950s for promotional purposes. Connected so directly to the history of the city and the college, she was often asked to speak to local history groups. At one point, she was asked to dress in the clothing she would have worn while in school for a "pioneer days" event.

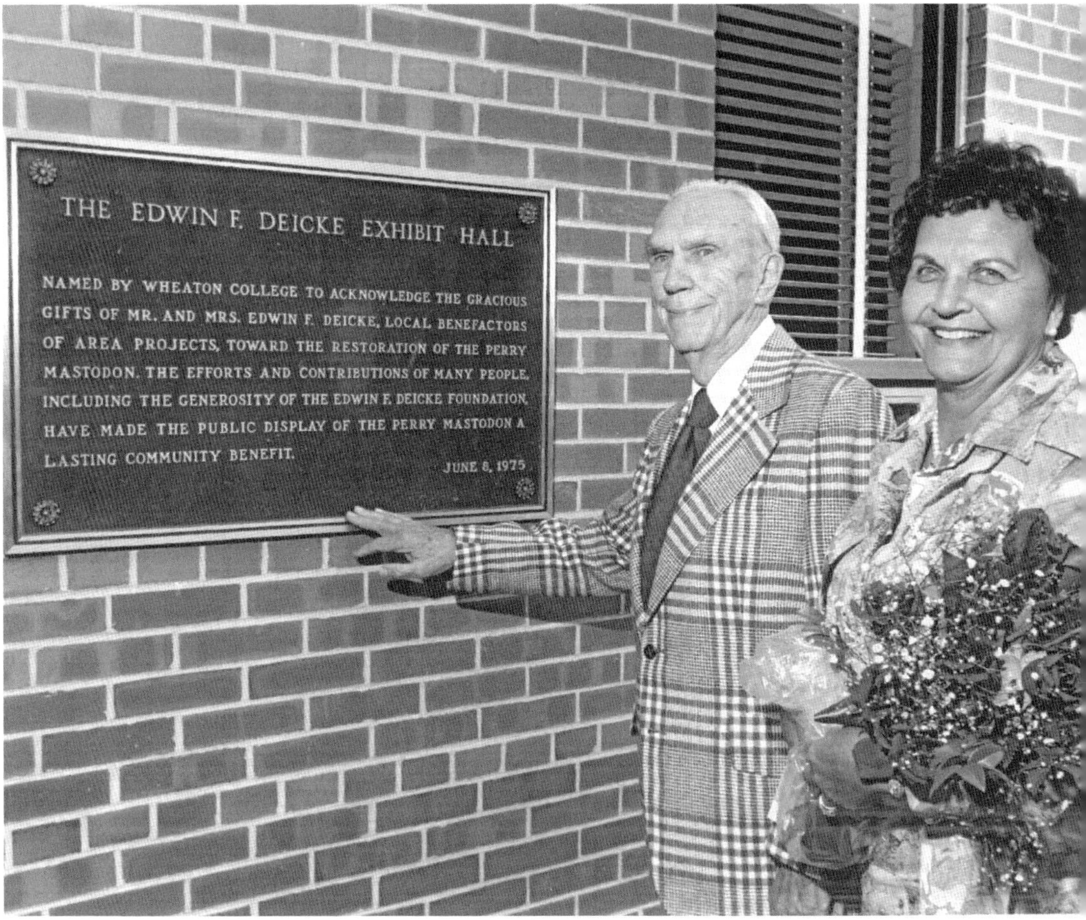

Edwin F. and Lois Deicke

Edwin F. Deicke, benefactor and businessman, contributed significantly to the social welfare of the citizens of Wheaton, the people of the western suburbs, and the overall well-being of cavies (guinea pigs) the world over. A veteran of World War I, he returned to the States to found a variety of organizations, including Suburban Casualty Insurance Company and the American Cavies Breeders Association. In fact, Deicke wrote *Cavies for Pleasure and Profit* (1944), the definitive collection of information pertaining to the gentle, easily startled rodent, addressing concerns such as feeding, odors, shipping, handling, and housing. Boundless in generosity, he helped found Elmhurst Memorial Hospital and the DuPage Area Council of Boy Scouts, in addition to founding the board of governors of Central DuPage Hospital in Winfield. After his first wife died in 1959, he married Lois Gerhardt of Houston. Together they simply continued his philanthropic mission through the Deicke Foundation, established in 1956, which granted scholarships to needy students, supported historic preservation, and funded facilities for the disabled. Contributions from the Foundation created the Deicke Visual Rehabilitation Center at the Wheaton Eye Clinic, one of the most renowned eye care facilities in the world. The Lions of Illinois Eye Research Institute at the University of Illinois houses patient care facilities for the Edwin F. and Lois Deicke Eye Center. The Deicke Foundation also enabled the City of Wheaton to purchase Deicke's red-brick office building, now used as city hall. A glass case featuring Deicke's honorary plaques, typewriter, and other significant objects from his life is displayed at the DuPage County Government Center. Edwin F. Deicke, whose munificence toward *homo sapiens* (human) and *Cavia porcellus* (guinea pig) alike is still appreciated in Wheaton and beyond, died in 1984.

Louis Evans Sr.

A notable American minister of the twentieth century, Evans was born in Goshen, Indiana, but raised in Wheaton. He attended Wheaton Academy, across the street from his home, for one year (1914–15), later entering Occidental College in Los Angeles. A remarkable athlete, he participated in football and basketball, winning multiple honors. After serving in the Navy during World War I, he acquired his theological education at McCormick Presbyterian Theological Seminary in Chicago. Evans led congregations in North Dakota, Pennsylvania, and finally Hollywood, California. As membership increased, swelling to the largest assembly in the denomination, so did Sunday School enrollment. Henrietta Mears, director of Christian education, was responsible for training these converts, implementing an engaging program that inspired hundreds of young people to enter full-time Christian activity. Among them was Bill Bright, founder of Campus Crusade for Christ. After serving for 12 years at Hollywood Presbyterian, Evans resigned in 1953, leaving a healthy congregation of 6,400 members. "It made a rancher out of me instead of a shepherd," he joked. For the next nine years he traveled as minister-at-large for the National Board of the United Presbyterian Church, U.S.A., speaking to universities and churches, appearing on radio and television. As he journeyed from one engagement to another, his wife, Marie, usually drove as he sat in the back, tapping out sermon notes on a specially built typewriter stand. He also served as President Eisenhower's summer pastor in Washington, DC, and was one of the co-founders and president of the Fellowship of Christian Athletes. *Life* magazine named Evans as one of America's Twelve Outstanding Religious Leaders, along with Norman Vincent Peale, Fulton Sheen, and George A. Buttrick. Writing eight books, he continued his public ministry until four months before his death in 1981. His memorial service was officiated by Dr. Lloyd John Ogilvie, who also served as a pastor at Hollywood Presbyterian and eventually as chaplain to the US Senate. "Rolled into one man," eulogized Ogilvie, "was the brilliance of an Apostle Paul, the impetuousness of a Peter, the love and tenderness of a Barnabas."

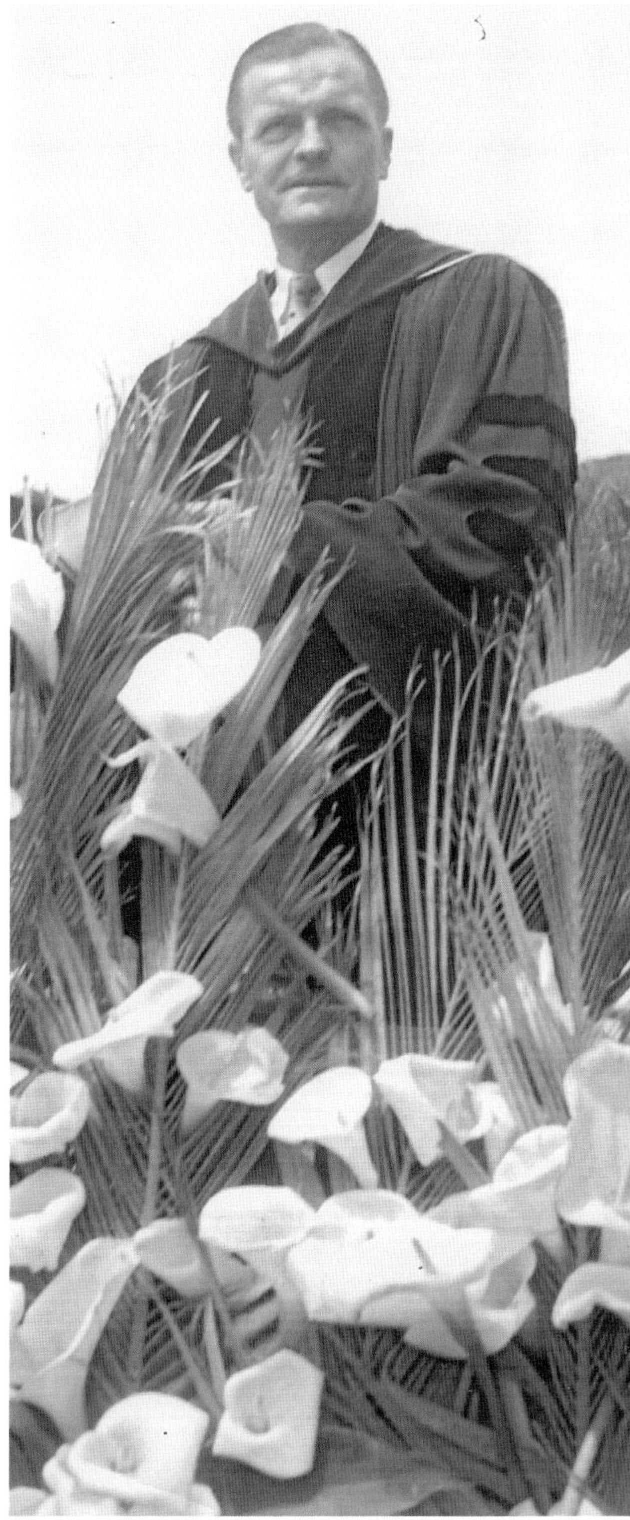

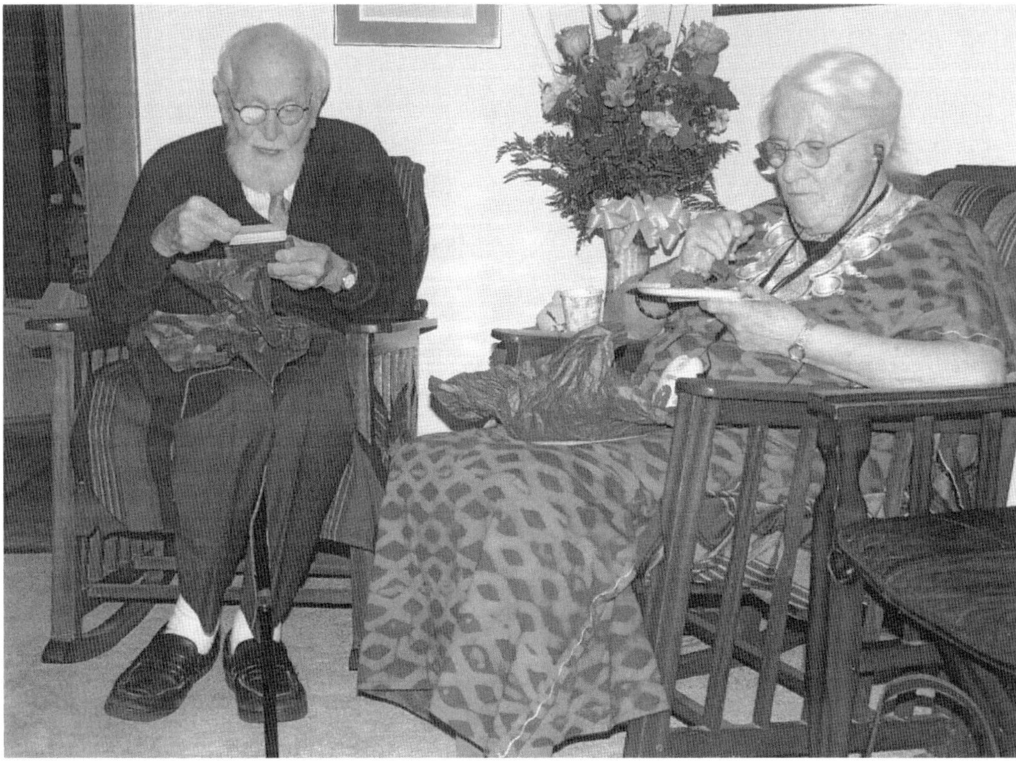

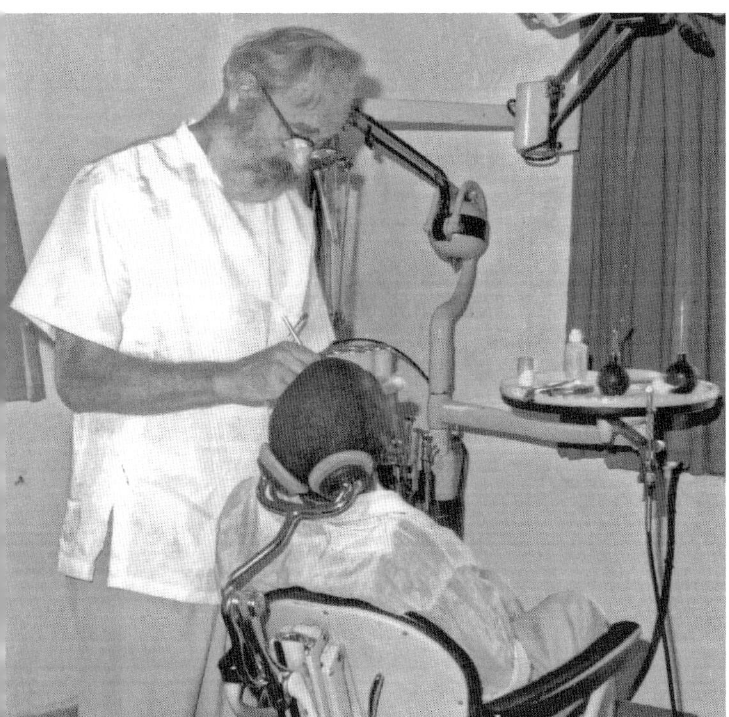

Lois and Behring MacDowell

For 53 years, the MacDowells labored as missionaries in Congo serving with Christian Missions in Many Lands. A revolution forced them to leave their beloved home and move to Wheaton to reside with family. Leading worship services for the people of their mission station, Behring also learned dentistry through courses to better serve their needs. Occasionally, the MacDowells hosted honored guests in their home, such as author and Holocaust survivor Corrie ten Boom. Lois at 91 is an indefatigable letter writer and encourager, while Behring at 95 daily attempts to comfort and cheer fellow residents at DuPage Convalescent Center. In 2011, the MacDowells celebrated their 65th wedding anniversary. Adored by friends and neighbors, they are exemplars of Christian charity, gentility, and generosity. (Courtesy of Lois and Behring MacDowell.)

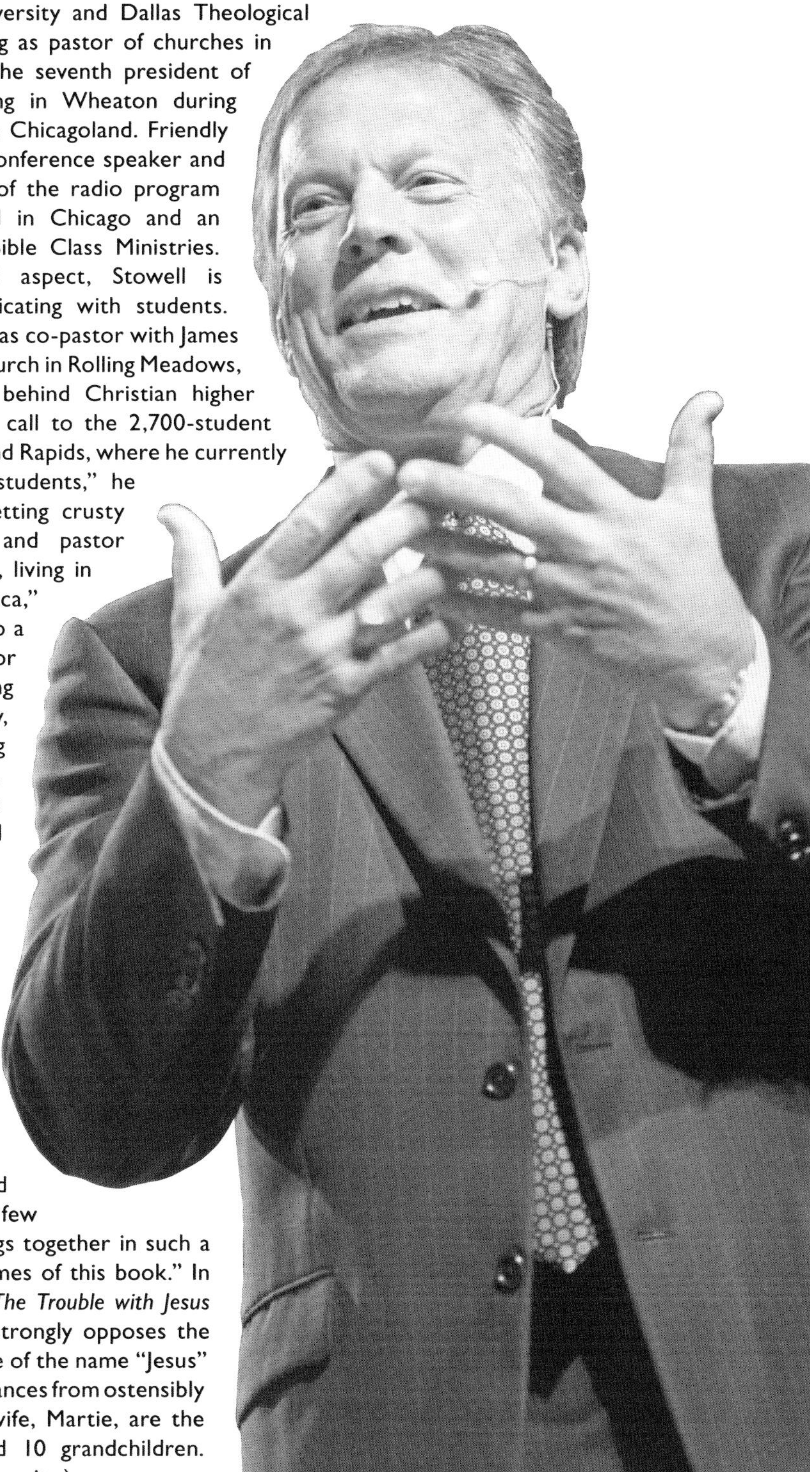

Joseph Stowell

A graduate of Cedarville University and Dallas Theological Seminary, Stowell, after serving as pastor of churches in Ohio and Indiana, served as the seventh president of Moody Bible Institute, residing in Wheaton during the early years of his career in Chicagoland. Friendly and engaging, he is a popular conference speaker and teacher. He is also the voice of the radio program *Proclaim!* broadcast by WMBI in Chicago and an associate teacher for Radio Bible Class Ministries. Exuding a positive, youthful aspect, Stowell is particularly effective communicating with students. After leaving Moody, he served as co-pastor with James MacDonald at Harvest Bible Church in Rolling Meadows, Illinois. Thinking he had left behind Christian higher education, Stowell accepted a call to the 2,700-student Cornerstone University in Grand Rapids, where he currently serves as president. "I love students," he says. "They keep me from getting crusty and calcified." The author and pastor occasionally jokes about when, living in Wheaton, the "evangelical Mecca," he found it difficult to step into a local shop to buy a newspaper or a cup of coffee without hearing from a clerk or stranger, "Hey, aren't you Joe Stowell?" Among his 20 books are *Far From Home*, *Strength for the Journey*, and *Jesus Nation*. Stowell was presented in 2007 with a Festschrift entitled *Proclaiming Jesus*. "I am sometimes asked who I think best models today the kind of preaching we're after," writes Duane Litfin, former president of Wheaton College and classmate from Stowell's Dallas years, in the last chapter. "I always say that one of the best models I know is the work of my friend Joe Stowell. Joe is one of the few preachers whose ministry brings together in such a genial package the various themes of this book." In the Moody Press publication, *The Trouble with Jesus* (dedicated to Litfin), Stowell strongly opposes the deliberate removal or avoidance of the name "Jesus" from public forums, in some instances from ostensibly Christian events. He and his wife, Martie, are the parents of three children and 10 grandchildren. (Courtesy of Cornerstone University.)

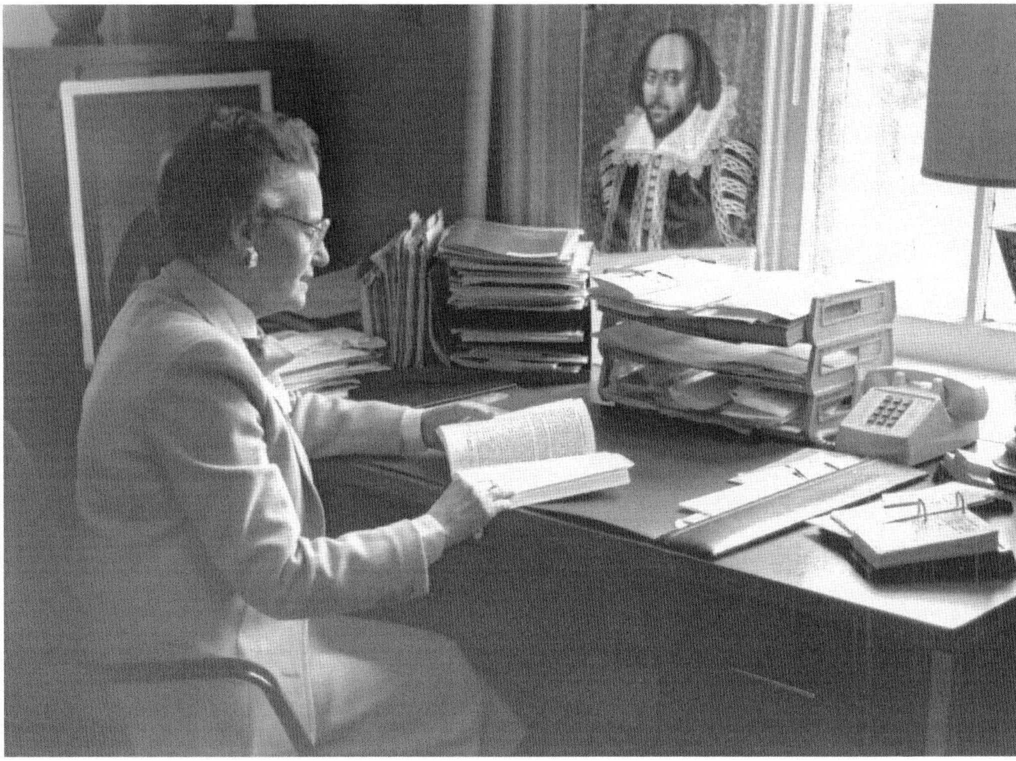

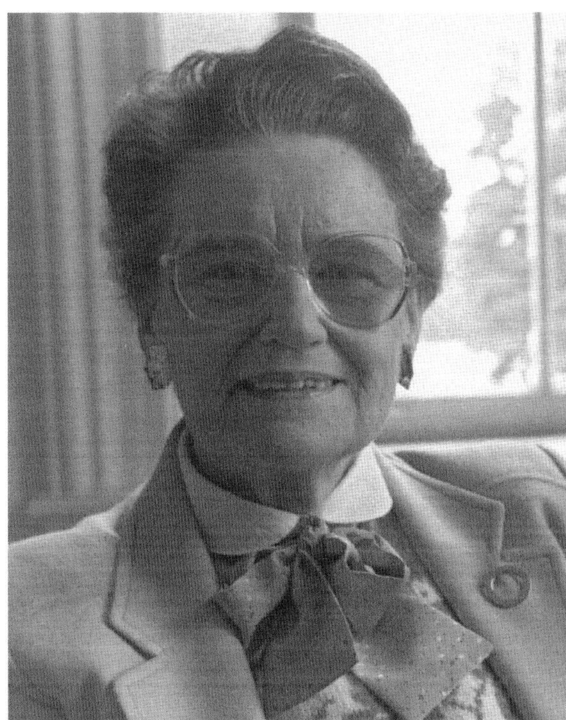

Beatrice Batson

Possessing a formidable knowledge of literature, irresistible Southern charm, and a genius for friendship, Batson has endeared herself to generations of students, influencing many toward careers in academia. Her extraordinary life exemplifies the integration of faith with high scholastic standards. Batson served as chair of the English Department at Wheaton College for 13 years and taught courses in Shakespeare for 33 years. She is the author or editor of 11 books, and has written for journals. "The best we can give is ourselves," Batson exhorts students in a public address. "Let's be sure that self is as strong and committed, as God-centered and human-hearted . . . as humanly possible." She is the coordinator of the Shakespeare Special Collection on Shakespeare and the Christian Tradition at Wheaton College. Batson is the recipient of the Wheaton College 2007 Alumna of the Year Award for Distinguished Service to Alma Mater.

Parkside Ministries

Smiling with his neighbor, Fisto, Aaron Fisher lives in the Parkside Apartments, a low-income housing complex comprised primarily of immigrants and refugees. Supported as a ministry of the Church of the Resurrection in Wheaton, Fisher and his neighbors intentionally relocated to the property, seeking to serve and learn from their neighbors. They have shared meals, led Bible studies, and offered everything from vocational assistance to a community garden. Below: The Parkside Community raised funds for purchasing prosthetic limbs for Andres, who lost his legs in an accident while working in the United States to provide for his family in Mexico. The mission of the Parkside Ministry is to seek the transformation of its multiethnic community through "incarnational" ministry and discipleship, striving to bridge a diverse community and the local church, blessing and transforming each other. (Courtesy of Aaron Fisher.)

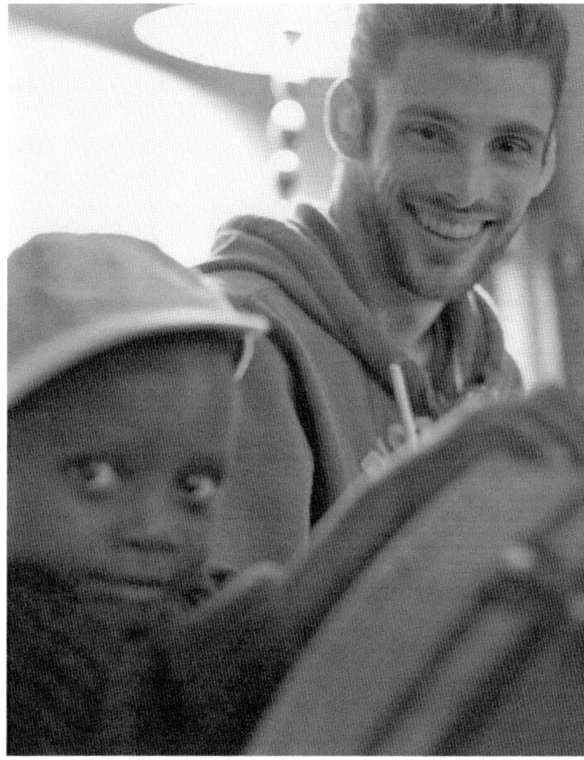

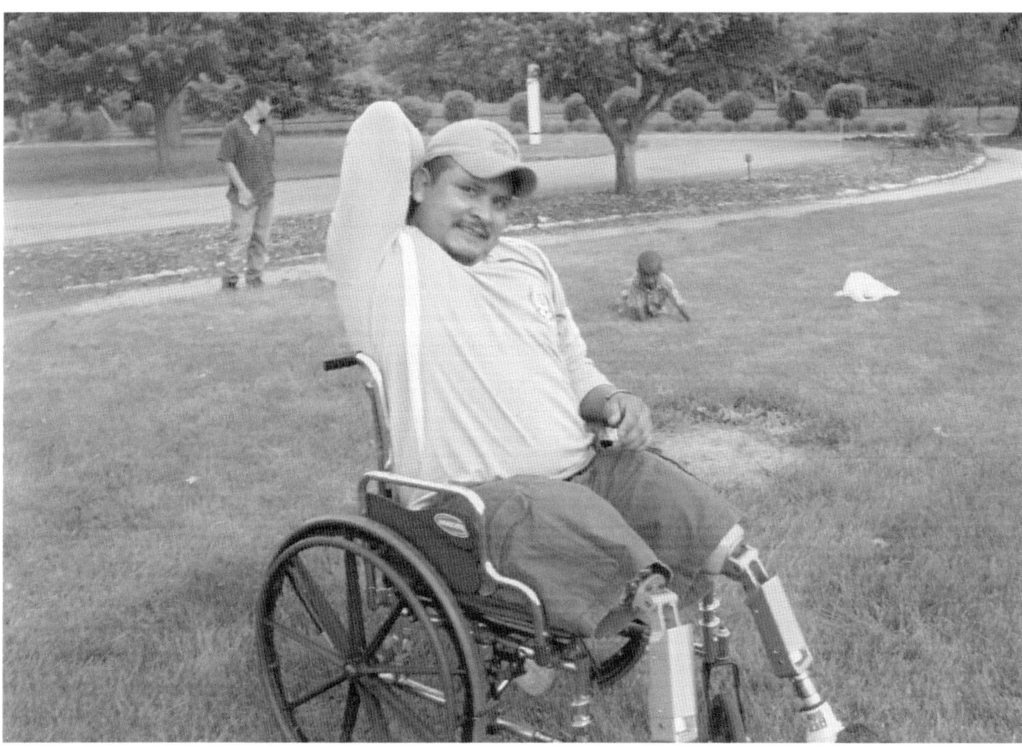

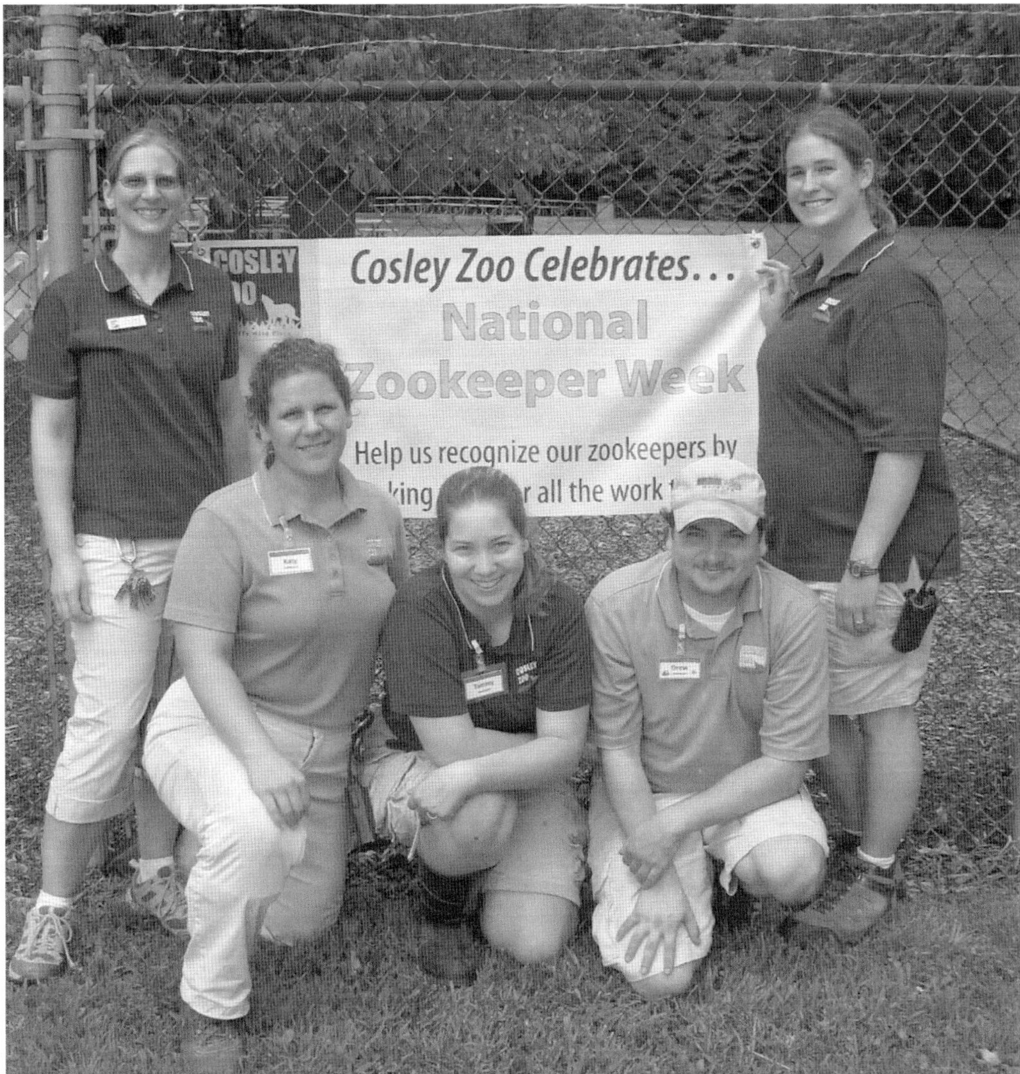

Cosley Zoo

During National Zookeepers Week, Cosley Zoo displays humans instead of animals: (left to right) Angie Dosch, senior animal acquisitions supervisor, Katy Briggs, Tammy Janik, Drew Kotche (kneeling), and Kristi Sampillar. Paula Jones in 1973 donated 2.65 acres of land to the Wheaton Park District in memory of Harvey Cosley, the previous landowner and a close relative, desiring to preserve the land from development. In the years following, its acreage expanded as well as the wildlife exhibits. In 1997, the Vern Kiebler Learning Center was completed, a $356,000 facility built to provide feed storage areas, hospital and isolation rooms, and office space. Cosley is presently partnering with other conservationist organizations to preserve various endangered animals. In 2008, Cosley Zoo worked with an Eagle Scout candidate to transform the caboose from an empty shell to an interactive educational experience. Cosley now boasts enlarged exhibits, a gift shop, and refurbished washrooms. Robustly alive and earthily aromatic with braying donkeys, hooting owls, slithering snakes, bobbing ducks, sly foxes, ponderous turtles, and laughing children, Cosley Zoo is an exhilarating reminder for DuPage County suburbanites that it is a privilege to share the Earth with creatures such as this. (Courtesy of Wheaton Park District.)

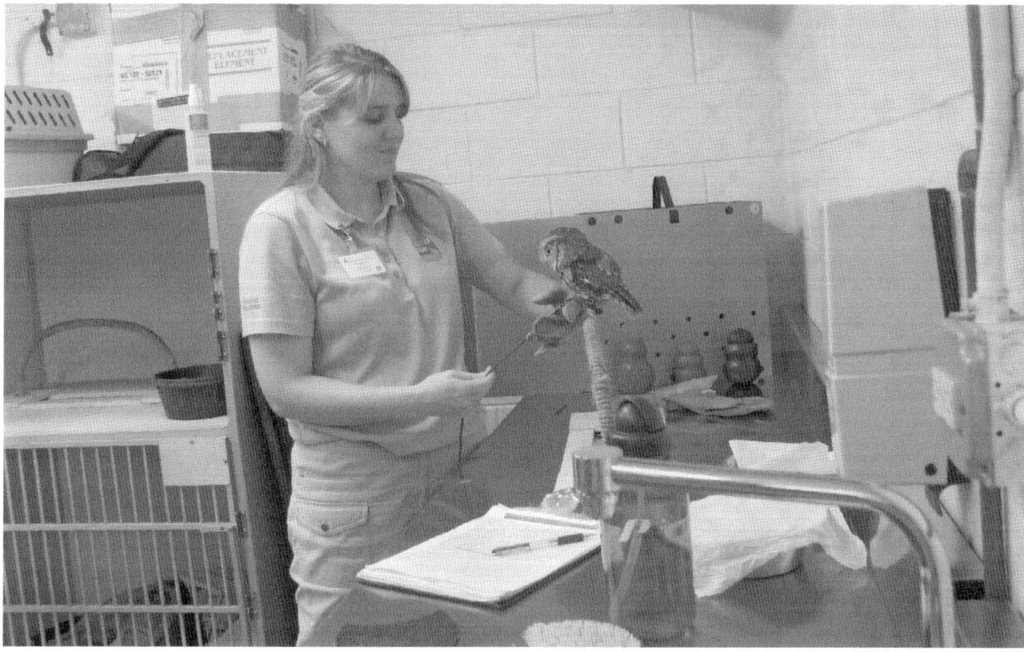

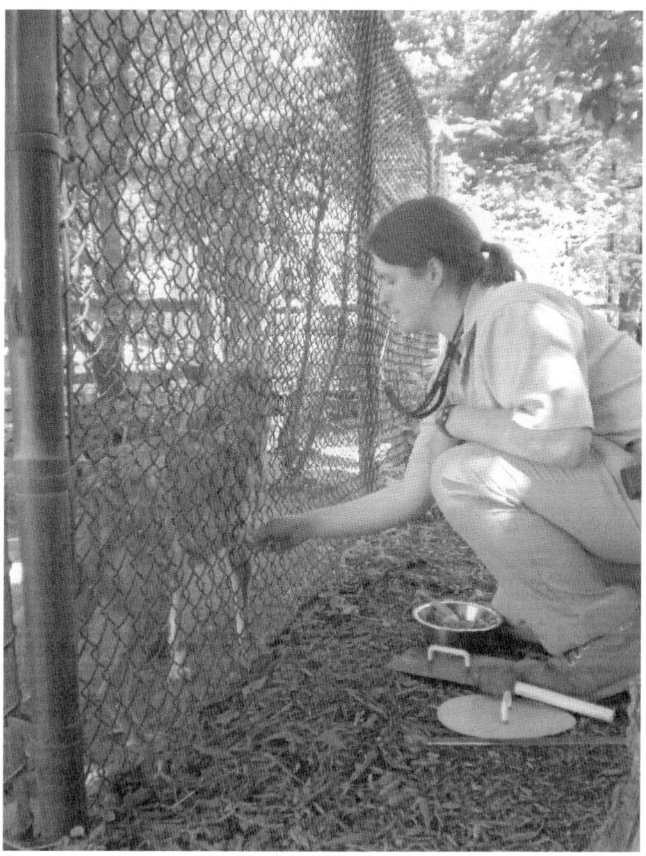

Kristi Sampillar and Tami Romejko

Sampillar inoculates a coyote through the fence. Above: Romejko, working in the Keeper Area of Raptors, trains an owl perched on her glove. Cosley Zoo rents space for birthday parties, themed around zoo exhibits. For instance, "Hoppy Birthday" features rabbits; "Buggy Boogy" features insects; and "Pony Pals" allows for rides on ponies. Many Cosley staff were influenced by celebrity zookeeper Jack Hanna, who writes, "Maybe you will want to work with animals one day. If you do, you will help other people learn about animals. I think that's the best job there is!" No educator or zookeeper at Cosley Zoo could disagree. (Courtesy of Wheaton Park District.)

DuPage Convalescent Center

Resident James LaNasa visits the chapel at DuPage Convalescent Center daily. Built in 1888, the Center began as a County Alms House for the indigent, its residents farming and overseeing dairy cattle, supporting themselves while providing food to the jail inmates. Eventually, the operation transformed into a nursing facility, offering care to the community. The center has since developed into one of the best equipped, professionally staffed treatment and rehabilitation facilities for the chronically ill in the State of Illinois. Since its inception, the DuPage Convalescent Center has maintained superior standards of professionalism. The facility holds 360 beds, with approximately 70 percent occupied by Public Aid recipients and 25 percent being under the age of 55 years. A visit to the center quickly reveals its efficient organization and the quality of care tendered to each resident. (Courtesy of DuPage Convalescent Center.)

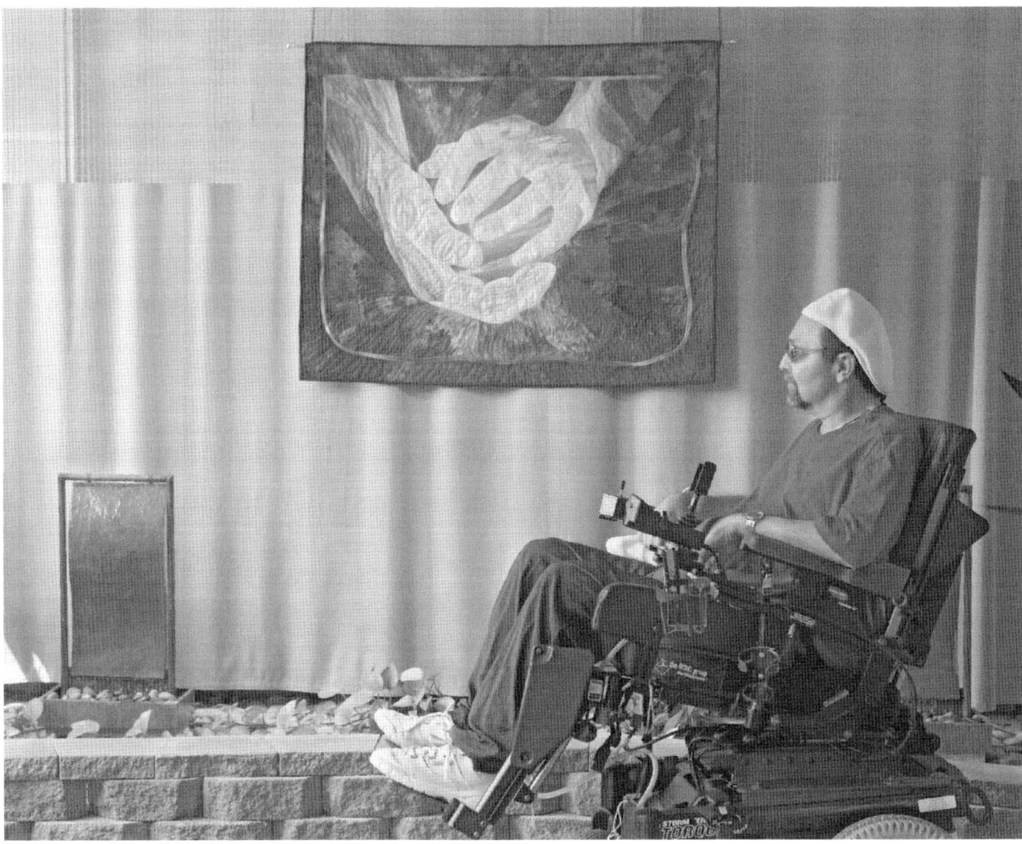

DuPage Convalescent Center Volunteers (RIGHT)

Assisted by Gina, resident Susan Dumo beautifies the world, painting a vase with a brush held in her mouth. DuPage Convalescent Center relies heavily on its volunteer workforce, who assist residents with completing crafts, escort them to appointments, and plan religious services. Volunteers also help with organizing birthday and holiday parties. Below: Another valuable resource is the use of animals, particularly dogs. According to Shauna Berman, manager of resident and volunteer services, residents with Alzheimer's are noticeably soothed by the presence of gentle animals and calming music. Bird cages and aquariums are also exhibited in the halls. Using "animal assisted visits" and other treatments, therapies, and activities, the center seeks to restore health, dignity, and hopefulness to its residents. (Courtesy of DuPage Convalescent Center.)

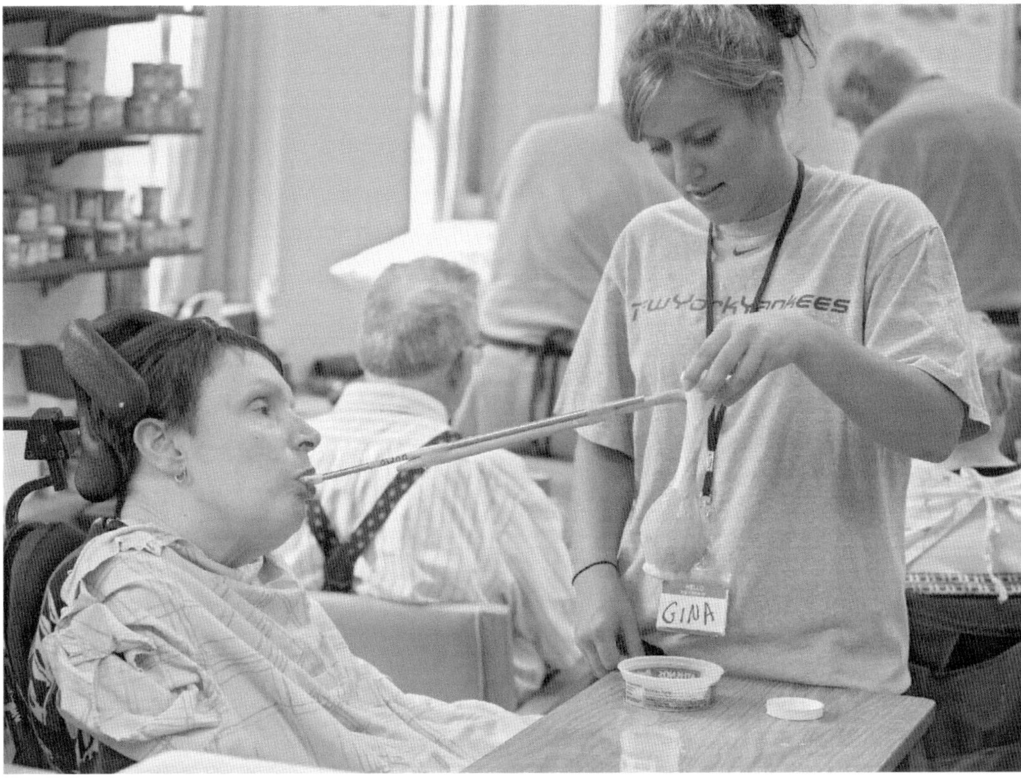
GINA

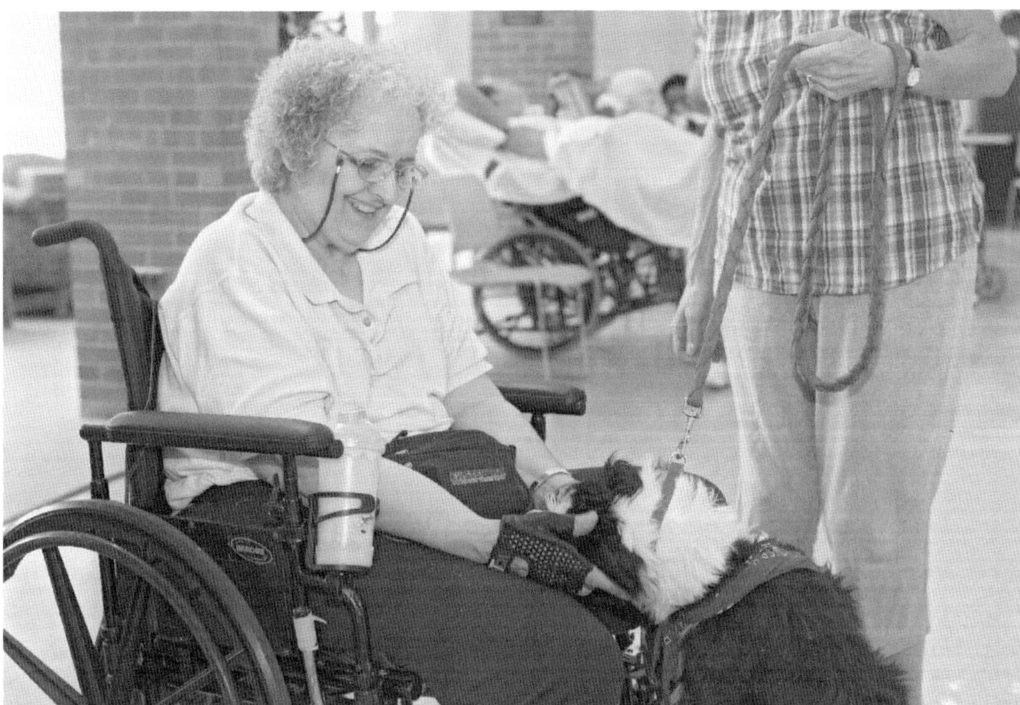

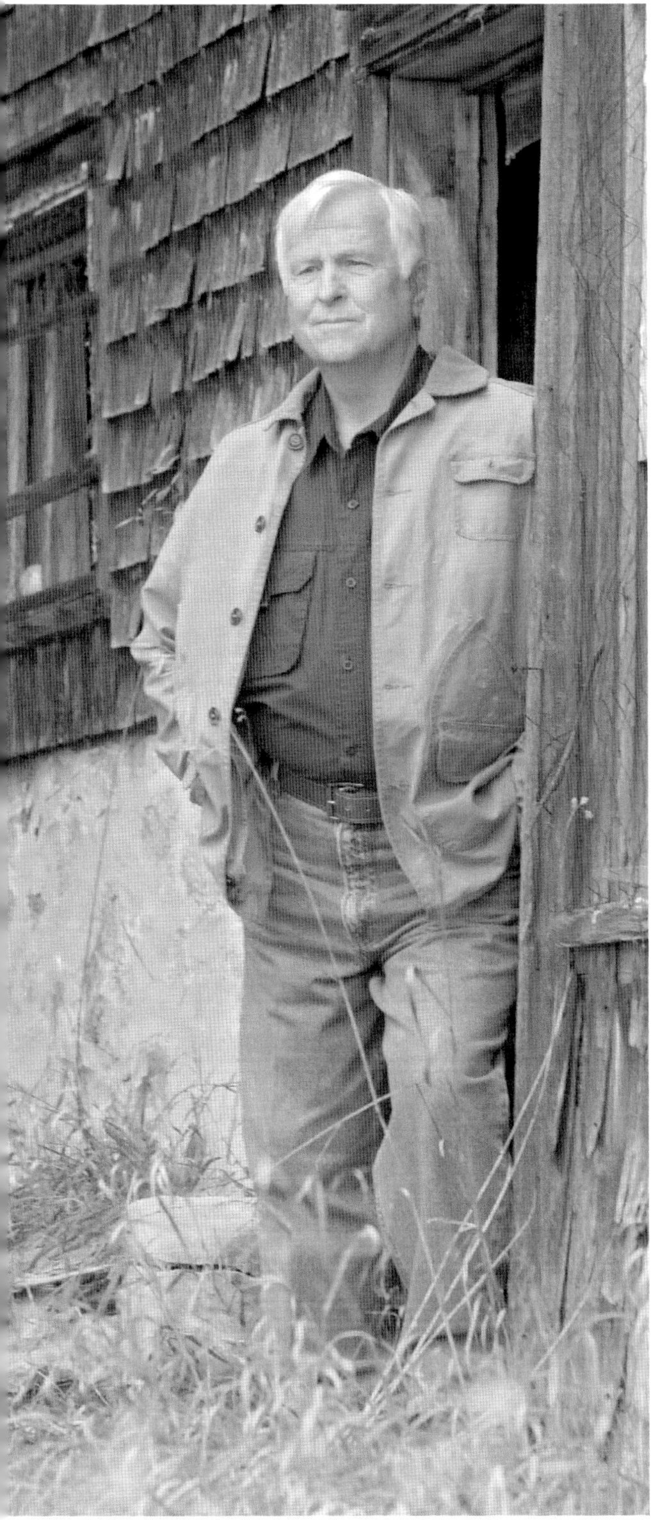

Josh McDowell

A young man named Joslin "Josh" David McDowell transferred in 1960 from Kellogg College in Michigan to Wheaton College. Adjusting to campus life with some difficulty, his time was occupied with studying or house painting. One day as he waited at a crossing gate near campus, he noticed a car speeding behind. The car barreled into him, pushing McDowell's vehicle onto the tracks at 45 miles per hour. Fortunately McDowell missed the path of the train. Though there was no visible injury, a sore neck indicated internal damage. Admitted to the college infirmary where he was confined to a cast and traction, he received a friendly visit from V. Raymond Edman, who stayed for two hours to pray with him. He later received a visit from Torrey Johnson, founder (with Billy Graham) of Youth for Christ, who encouraged him in his desire to preach. After recovering, McDowell and two friends met a visiting speaker named Bill Bright, founder of Campus Crusade for Christ. Joining the evangelist for coffee, Bright encouraged them to embrace the Spirit-filled life. Walking the streets of Wheaton, McDowell prayerfully considered these matters. But it was not until he discovered Bright's *Four Spiritual Laws* among his notebooks that he discerned clear direction; and so he finally committed. This decision provided the basis for his public ministry, wherein he would engage unbelievers through apologetic debates and exhort undecided believers to pursue the same dynamic empowerment that had revolutionized his own life. After Wheaton, he attended Talbot Theological Seminary, graduating magna cum laude with a master of divinity degree. In 1964, he joined the staff of Campus Crusade, and in 1991 he founded Operation Carelift (now called Global Aid Network), one of the largest humanitarian aid organizations in the United States. Among the 108 books he has authored or co-authored are *Right from Wrong, The Dad Difference,* and *The Last Christian Generation.* Still lecturing, he currently serves as president of Josh McDowell Ministries. He recently celebrated his 50th year in the ministry. (Courtesy of Josh McDowell Ministries.)

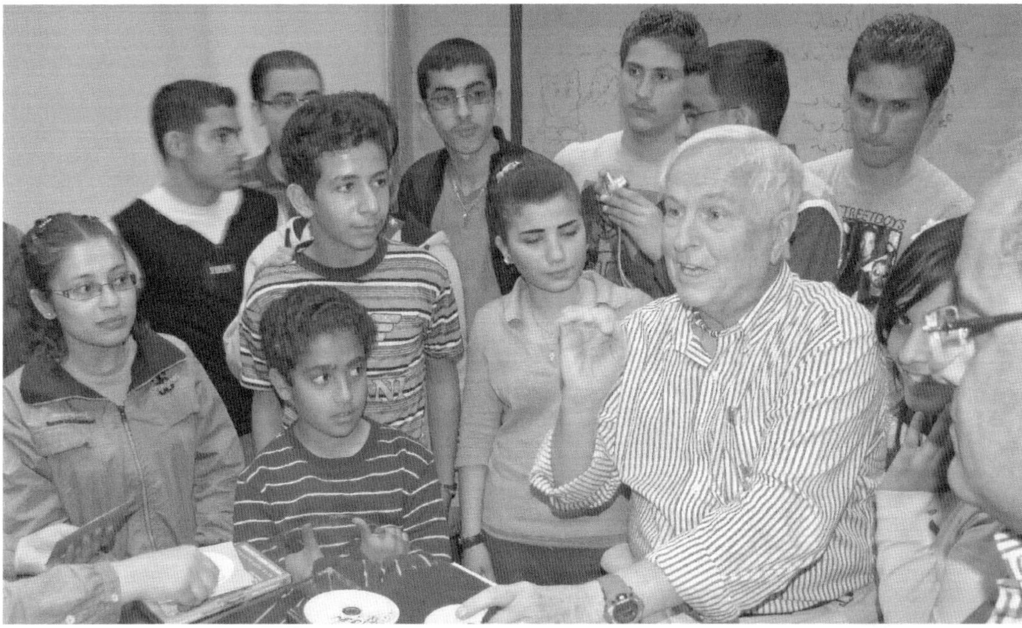

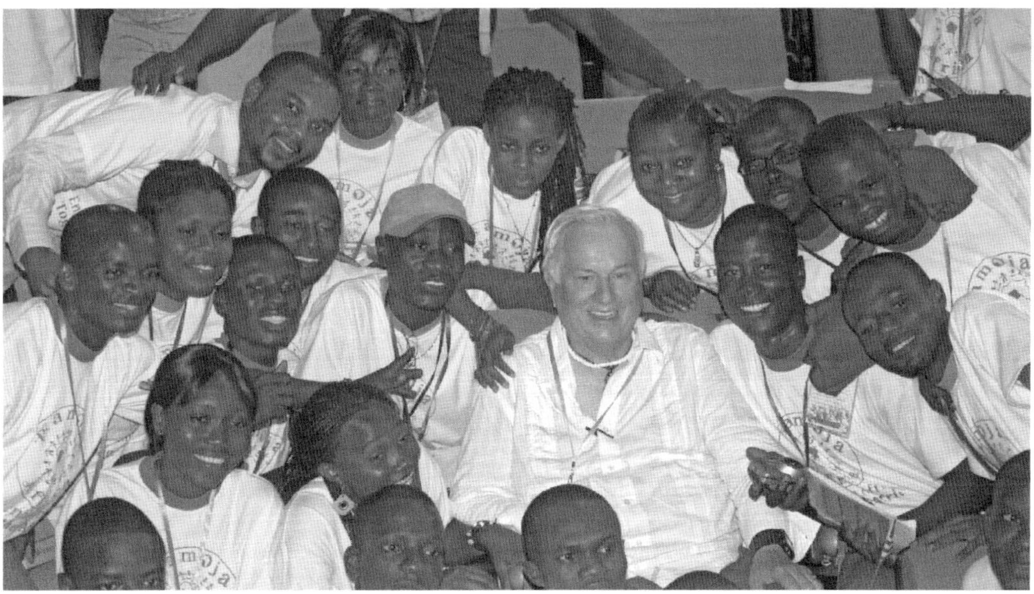

McDowell's Travels

As his body ages, McDowell seems to remain perennially young at heart, perhaps as the result of his frequent association with students. Visiting Lebanon (top), he signs copies of his "Bare Facts" DVD, which poses 43 of the top questions students ask about sex, love, and relationships, offering teaching, relevant statistics, entertaining anecdotes, and enlightening interviews with youth and medical experts. Above: African students gather for a photograph, showing their affection for McDowell. He is also known for his lectures on American college campuses, presenting reasonable arguments for the Christian faith, as contained in his books, *More Than a Carpenter* and *Evidence that Demands a Verdict.* (Courtesy of Josh McDowell Ministries.)

Card Ministry

From the strategic vantage of her keyboard, Lauren each week shares from the abundance of her heart, creating greeting cards for members of College Church who are sick, grieving, or have new babies. The cards include a Bible verse, a photograph, and a note from Lauren assuring each recipient of her prayers. Initially, she was surprised that recipients were so pleased to receive her cards that they sent her cards in return, frequently responding with this sentiment: "Of all the cards I received, yours meant the most to me." Lauren has been sending cards for about five years. (Courtesy of College Church.)

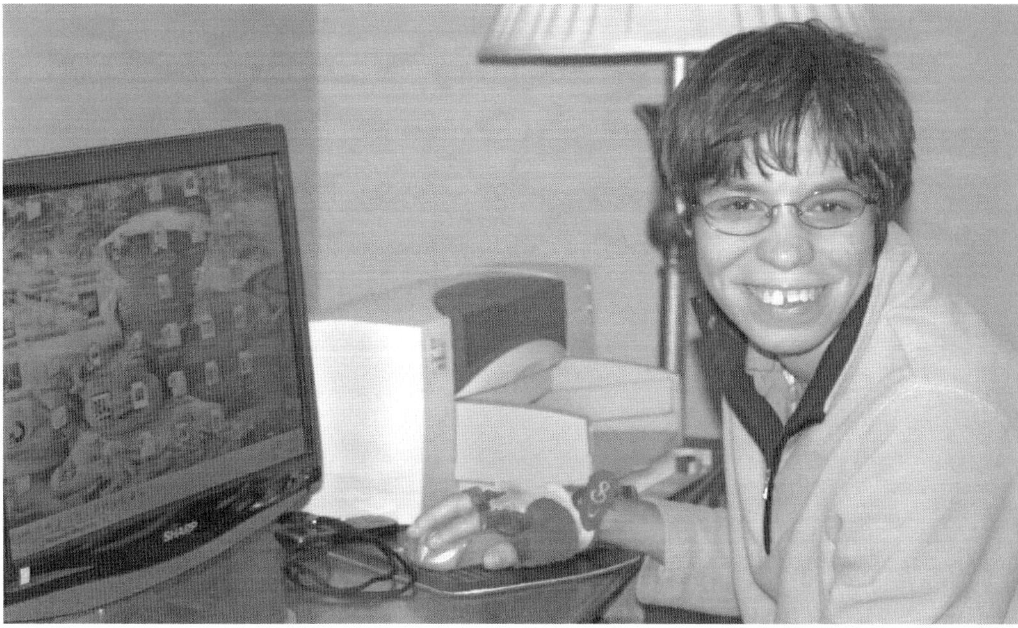

Frances Carothers Blanchard (RIGHT)

This silvery lady of kindly mien was for years the *grande dame* of Wheaton College and a celebrated citizen of the city. Dr. Charles Blanchard, second president of the school, had buried one wife due to heart disease when he married his second wife, Amanda Jane Carothers. But soon Amanda fell ill, as well; and consequently, her sister, Dr. Frances Carothers, an 1878 graduate of the college, departed a successful practice in Des Moines, Iowa, traveling to Wheaton to care for her. Armed with a degree from the University of Chicago, rare for females of the day, Frances Carothers offered skilled care, but her beloved sibling weakened and finally died. As Charles Blanchard and Frances Carothers exchanged letters of consolation, discussing loss and suffering, a romance slowly blossomed. "To leave a well-established and paying practice for the position of wife and mother to half a dozen growing daughters, is a momentous choice for an ambitious woman," she remarks, drolly using third person in her biography, *The Life of Charles Albert Blanchard*. They married in 1896 at St. Louis, a solid, happy match. Together they traveled to colleges and missionary institutes, lecturing and successfully fundraising on behalf of Wheaton College. On the promise of coming home after a journey she writes, "It seemed to the returning pair that, of all the places they had seen, their own dear Illinois and Wheaton were the most beautiful in the world." As the wife of the president, she played well her role as hostess, expecting the unexpected. "The home was a harbor . . . for students who came without having made proper arrangements," she recalls. "Many times when the family were about to sit down at the table, Mr. Blanchard would walk in with a stranger, give him a seat with us and ask that the proper dishes be set before him." For several years she functioned as the campus physician; historian Ruth Cording remembers the apprehension with which the giggling girls awaited their examination from the wife of the president. A woman of grace and authority, Frances Carothers Blanchard died on July 4th, 1947.

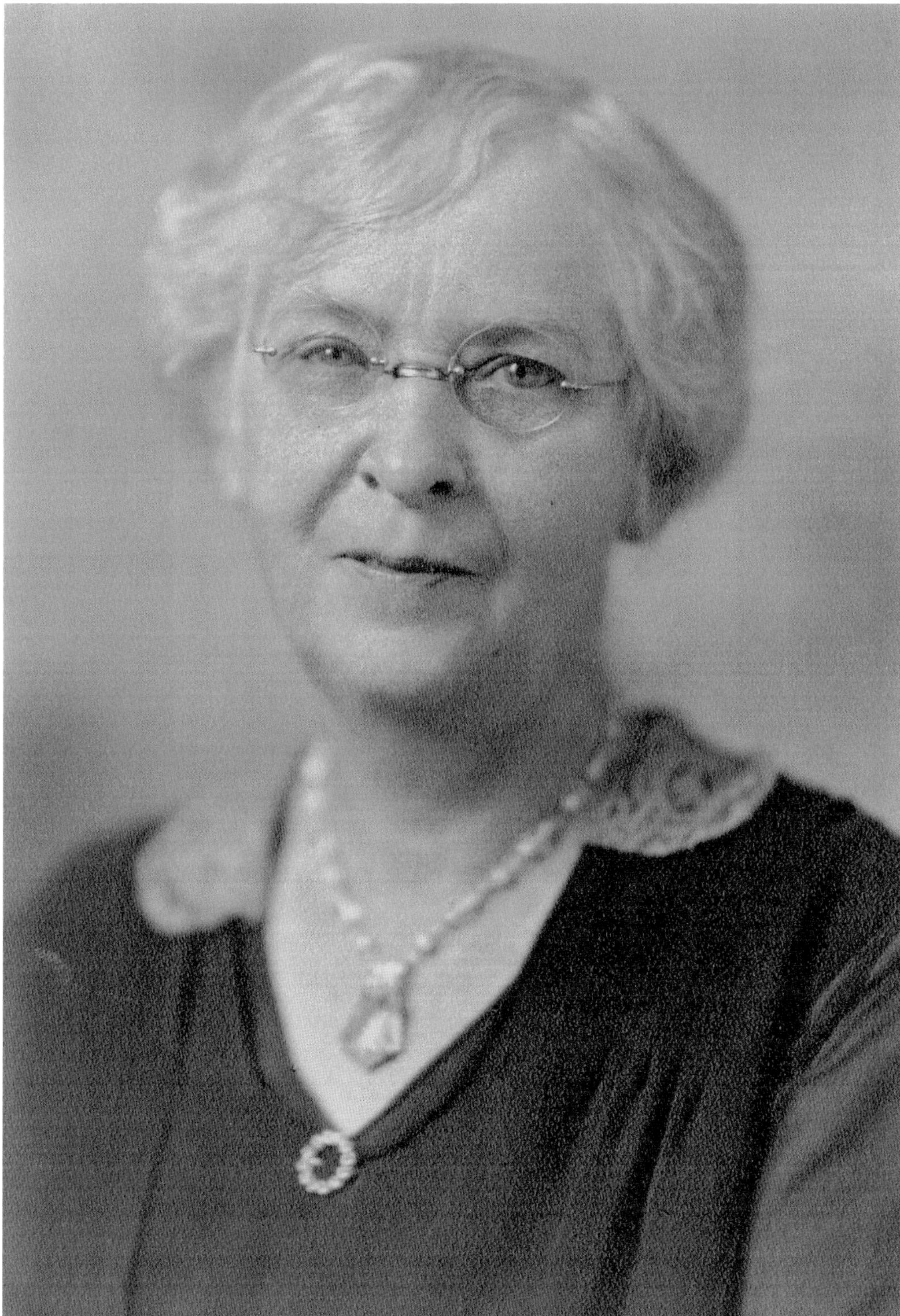

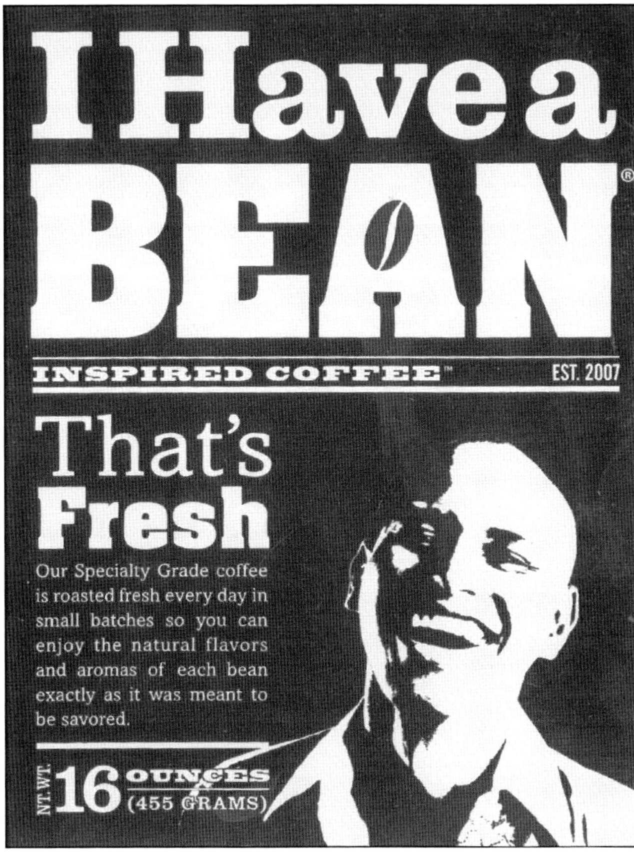

Second Chance Coffee Company

At a weekly breakfast meeting, Pete Leonard, Dave Scavotto, and Ron deVries dreamed up a way to blend a passion for roasting exquisite coffee with the desire to offer former offenders a second chance. That dream became a reality when the trio founded Second Chance Coffee Company and began roasting under the brand "I Have a Bean." The mission of the company was the catalyst that drove Leonard to create a unique coffee-roasting machine that enables anyone to produce perfectly roasted coffee. The "Bean Master 5000" hums almost nonstop at Second Chance's roasting plant in Wheaton. Not only does it enable the company to employ former offenders, the invention allows the company to make good on its obsession with freshness. Customers order coffee in the morning and receive expertly roasted beans in personalized bags that are individually signed and dated by the roaster the same afternoon. Providing customers with the finest coffee roasted the same day is what allows the company to advance the social mission for which it was created. Two of the founders have had relatives "in the system" and all could see the need for employers to offer jobs to those trying to turn their lives around. Second Chance Coffee Company also works with post-prison organizations that provide rehabilitation, counseling, mentoring, and life skills training. The company attempts to fulfill the mandate to "love your neighbor as yourself," positively impacting the spiritual, social, and economic condition of its employees, their families, and their communities. Indeed, the company is deliciously fragrant, both for its splendid coffee and the joy of its re-energized workers. And that aroma carries. As a guest of the executive chef of the White House, Leonard personally delivered seven pounds of "I Have a Bean" coffee to Cristeta Comerford, whom he met at the March of Dimes "Signature Chef" fundraiser in Chicago. Incidentally, the laughing man (nicknamed "Smiley") featured on the award-winning "I Have a Bean" package represents "everyman" and does not depict anyone in particular. (Courtesy of Pete Leonard.)

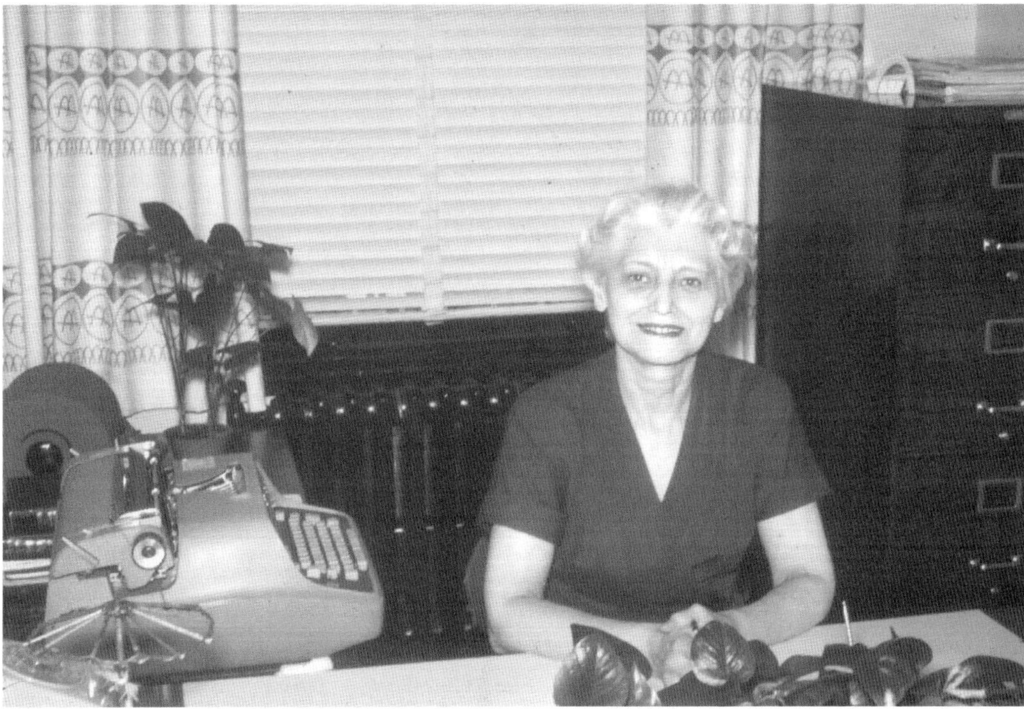

Bernice Storm

Storm, personal secretary to Ray Kroc, "founder" of McDonald's, sits in a 1960s-chic corporate office in downtown Chicago. Behind her hang custom-embroidered draperies sporting the original McDonald's arched "M" logo. On the filing cabinet in the corner sits a cardboard toy model of what was the original McDonald's restaurant in Des Plaines, Illinois. Storm resided for several years on Scott Street in Wheaton. (Courtesy of Chip Krueger.)

Charles and Victoria Kinnaman

Continuing an honorable tradition of supervising the family property on Seminary Avenue, Charles and Victoria Kinnaman, generous and conscientious, provide clean, comfortable, and operational housing for their tenants. Located near the amenities of Wheaton, the five-house complex offers the pleasantries of an old-fashioned neighborhood. Kinnaman occasionally exhibits a vehicle from his impressive collection of Model A and Ts, driving one each Sunday afternoon through downtown Wheaton.

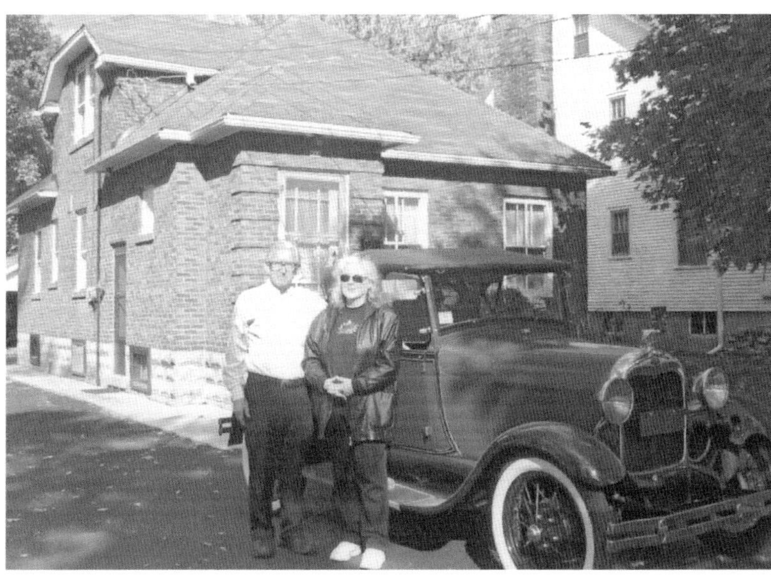

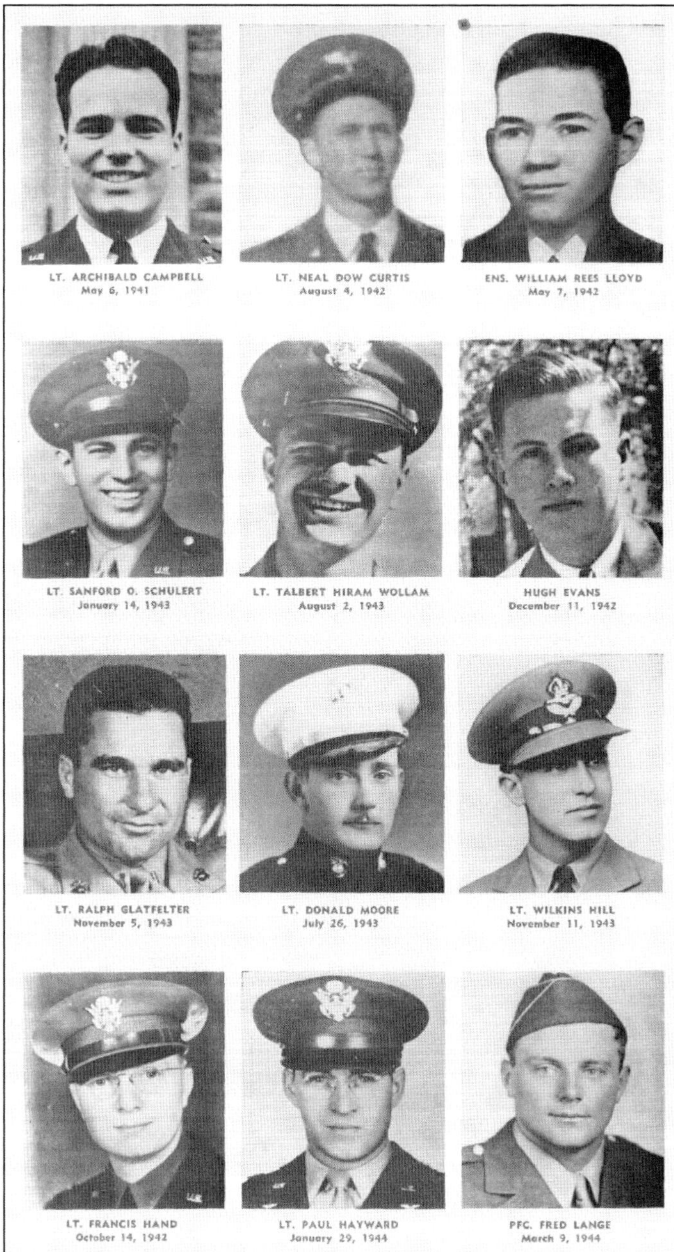

The Gold Star Men

Wheaton College graduates who "gave the last full measure of devotion" were prominently featured in a late 1940s mailing, intended to raise funds for a memorial. The text read: "These men once walked on Wheaton's campus, but not again. They didn't want to die, but they did and not without purpose. What they have given cannot be matched or described by sentimental expressions. A marble shaft or a bronze statue is hardly a suitable memorial for so large a sacrifice . . . But we like the idea of a 'memorial that lives.' . . . It will be the hub of student life, a memorial for the living . . . "

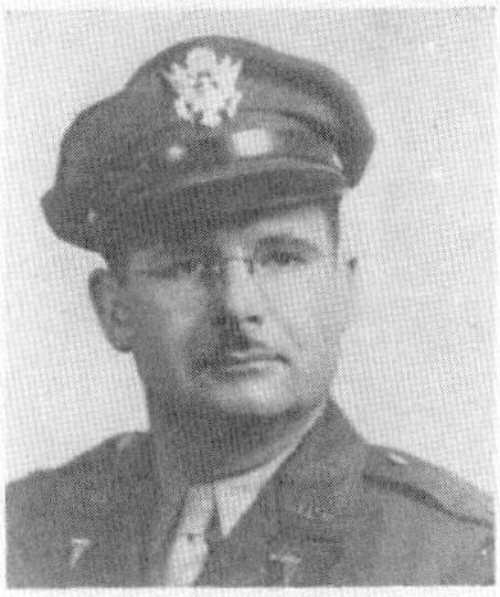

MAJ. ROBERT QUINE
July 19, 1943

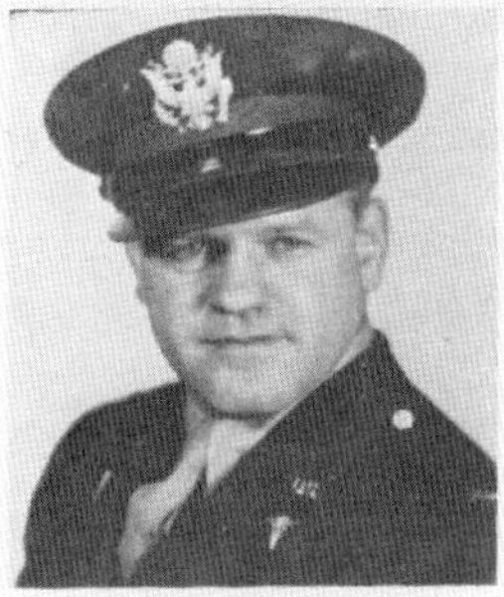

LT. OLIVER AUSTIN
July 3, 1944

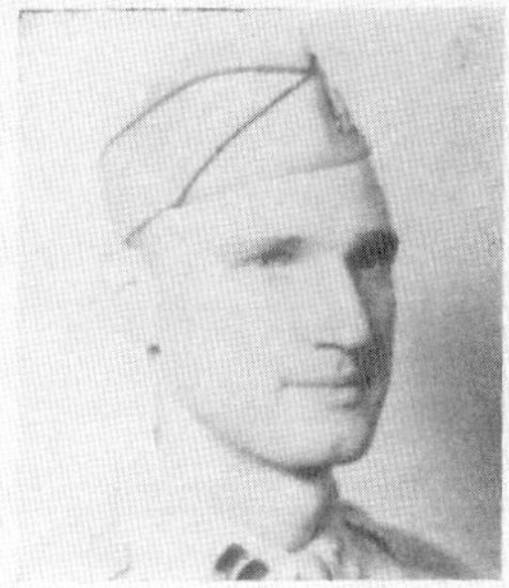

CAPT. WILBUR T. DAVIS
August 18, 1944

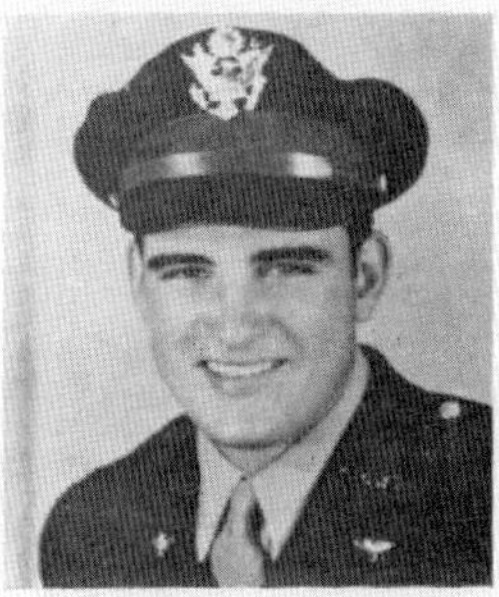

LT. ERNEST S. CONLEY
October 22, 1944

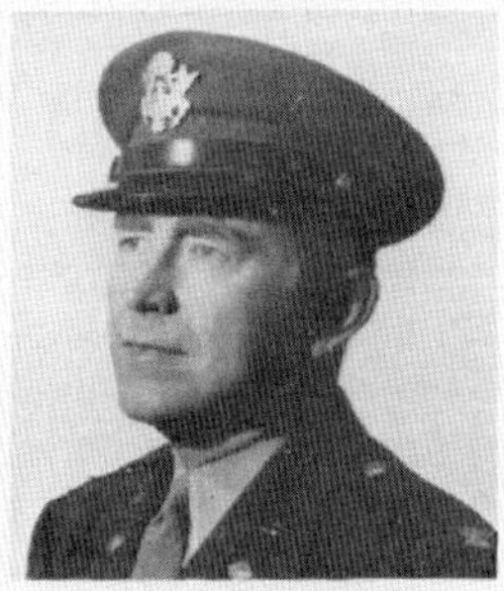

LT. COL. ROBERT ROBINSON
December 5, 1944

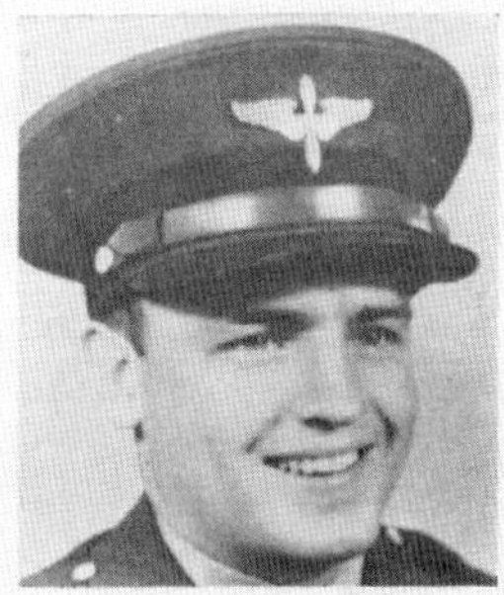

SGT. JAMES A. STUBBS
September 8, 1944

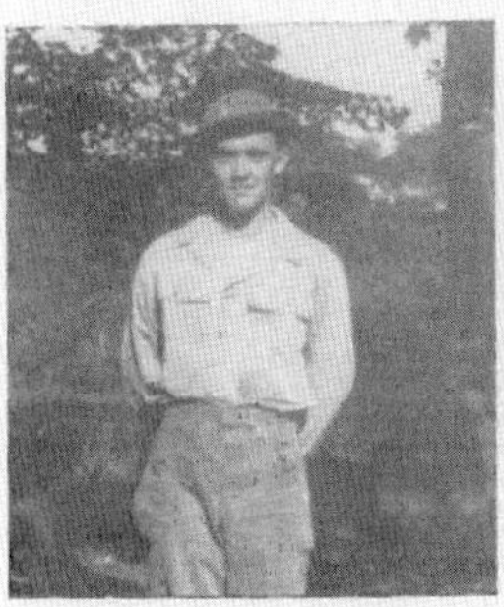

PVT. LEON I. HORNESS
December 3, 1944

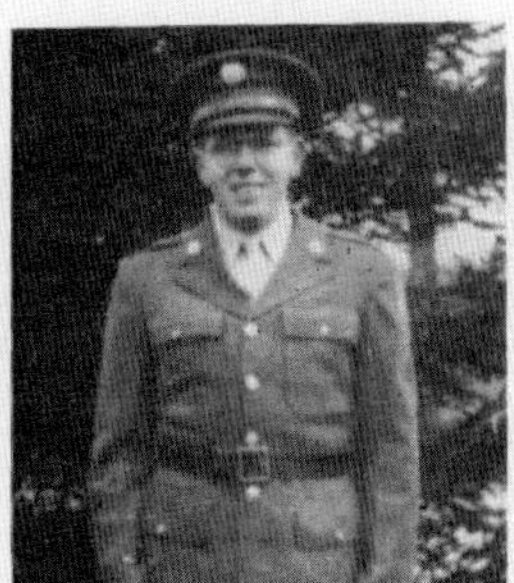

SGT. WILLIAM P. HARRO
December 14, 1944

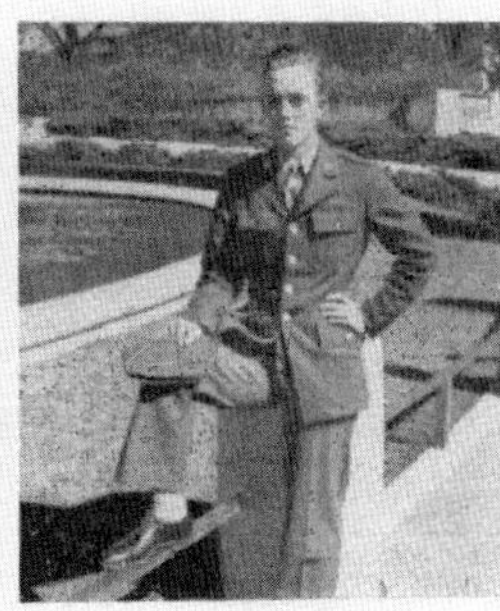

LT. PAUL MORTWEET
February 26, 1945

NO PICTURES AVAILABLE

SGT. JOHN FREEMAN
March 3, 1943

EARL WALKER
January 11, 1945

SGT. EDWARD C. KAUTZ
January 15, 1945

PVT. CHARLES E. STROTZ
December 5, 1944

RICHARD H. JOHNSTON
March 1, 1945

Missing in Action

FRED McGUIDWIN

GLENN READ

WILLIAM SWANSON

VERNON R. CUMBERLAND

JOHN K. DORSETT

JAMES MILMOE

VAN C. NALL

DONALD R. CANDY

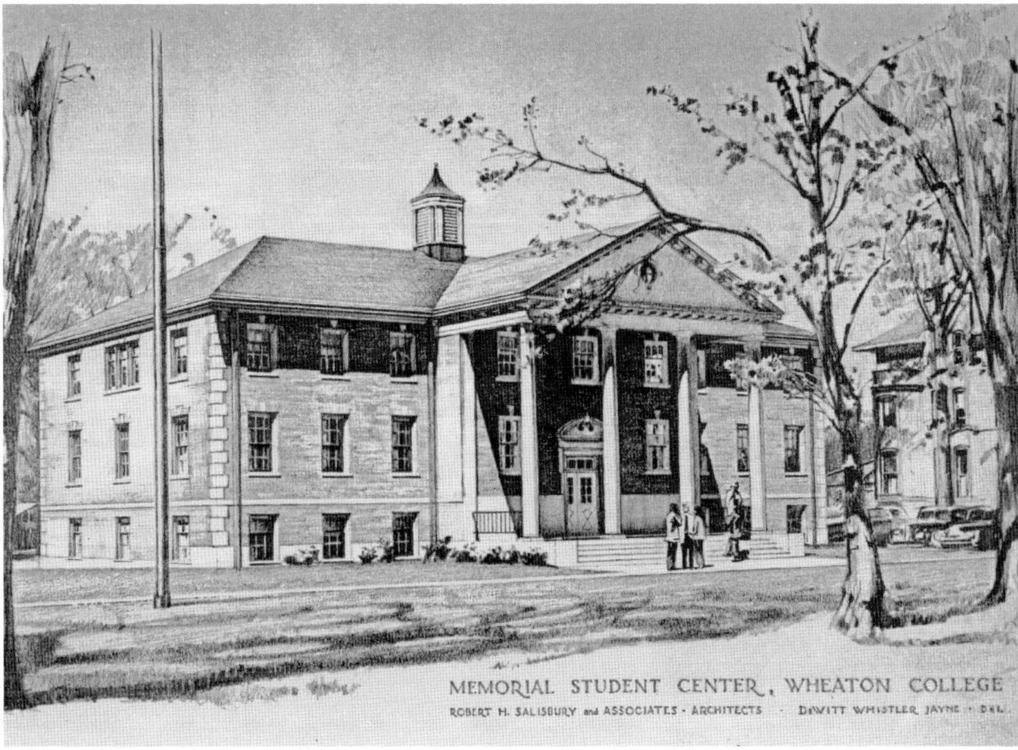

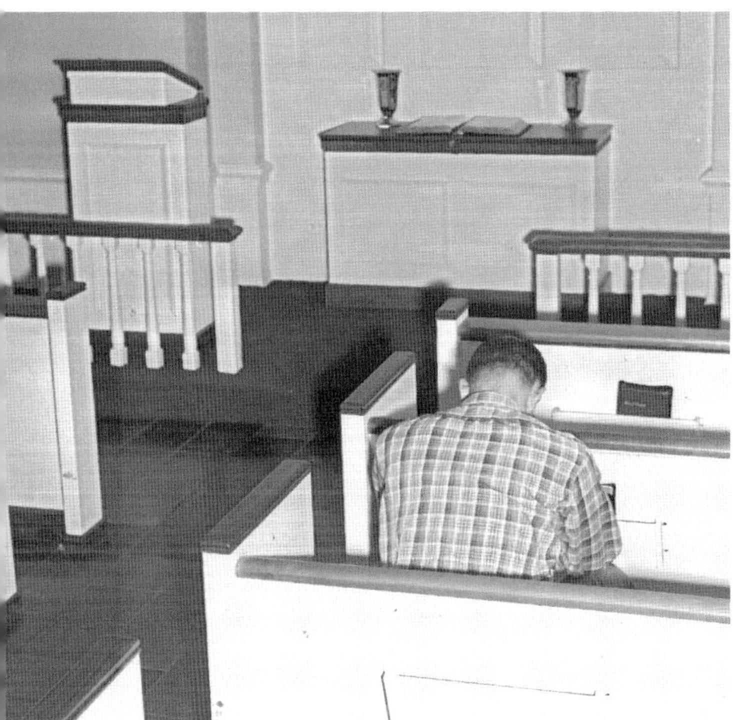

Memorial Student Center

As the result of 10 years of fundraising, the Memorial Student Center was at last opened in 1951. Though essentially an alumni project, responsibilities for its completion were shared by faculty and students. The structure housed a post office, lounge, art gallery, information desk, cafeteria, publications offices, and meeting rooms. Below: The Memorial Student Center contained the Gold Star Chapel, seating 36 persons, used primarily for private worship or weddings. Campus events were not scheduled for this room, leaving it available at all times. The center has been refurbished for the needs of a new generation, housing faculty offices, archival storage, and classrooms pertaining to political science. A plaque commemorating the Gold Star Men remains affixed to the wall of the foyer.

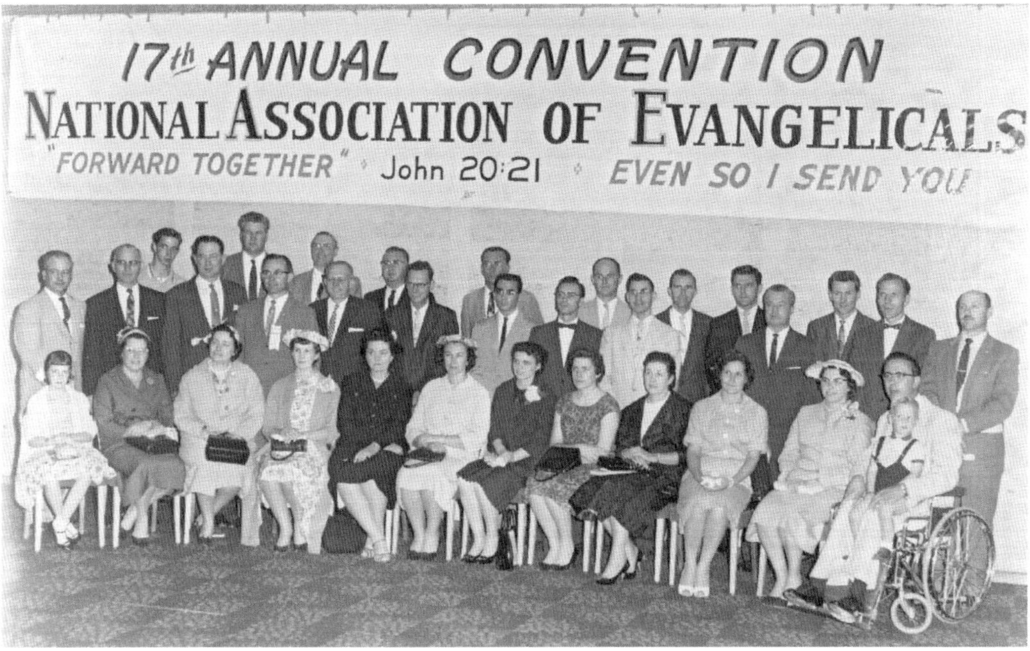

National Association of Evangelicals

The National Association of Evangelicals (NAE), founded in 1942, was established as a haven for conservative denominations facing the challenge of theological liberalism. It provided services that would enable them to more efficiently fulfill their stated missions. As the NAE grew, several ancillary organizations emerged, such as the National Religious Broadcasters, a chaplaincy program, the National Sunday School Association, and World Relief, assisting victims of poverty and disaster. As it solidified, the NAE became a platform for conservative politicians such as Ronald Reagan (below). Located for several years in Wheaton, the NAE is now in Washington, DC.

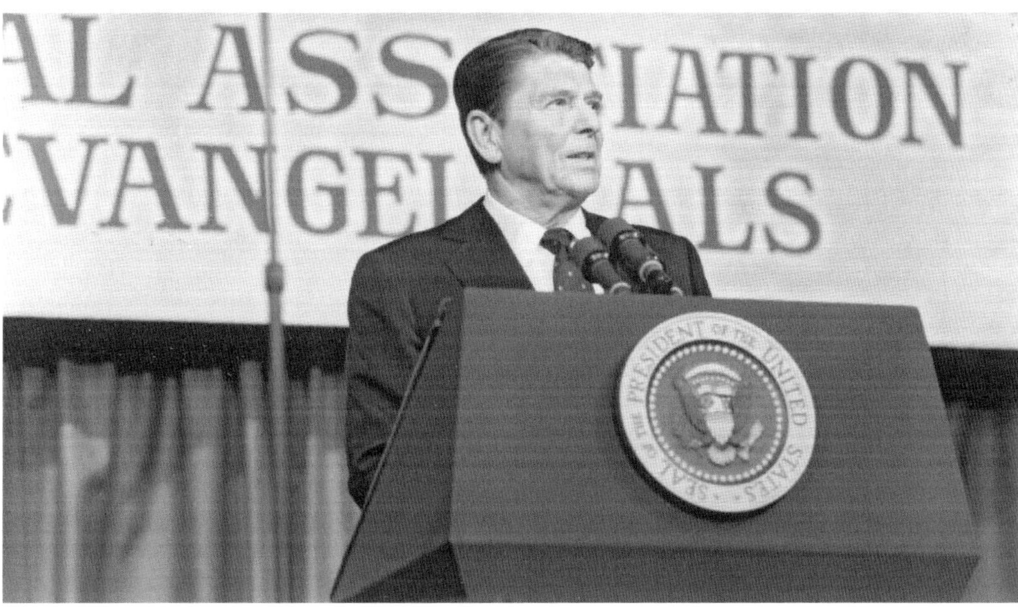

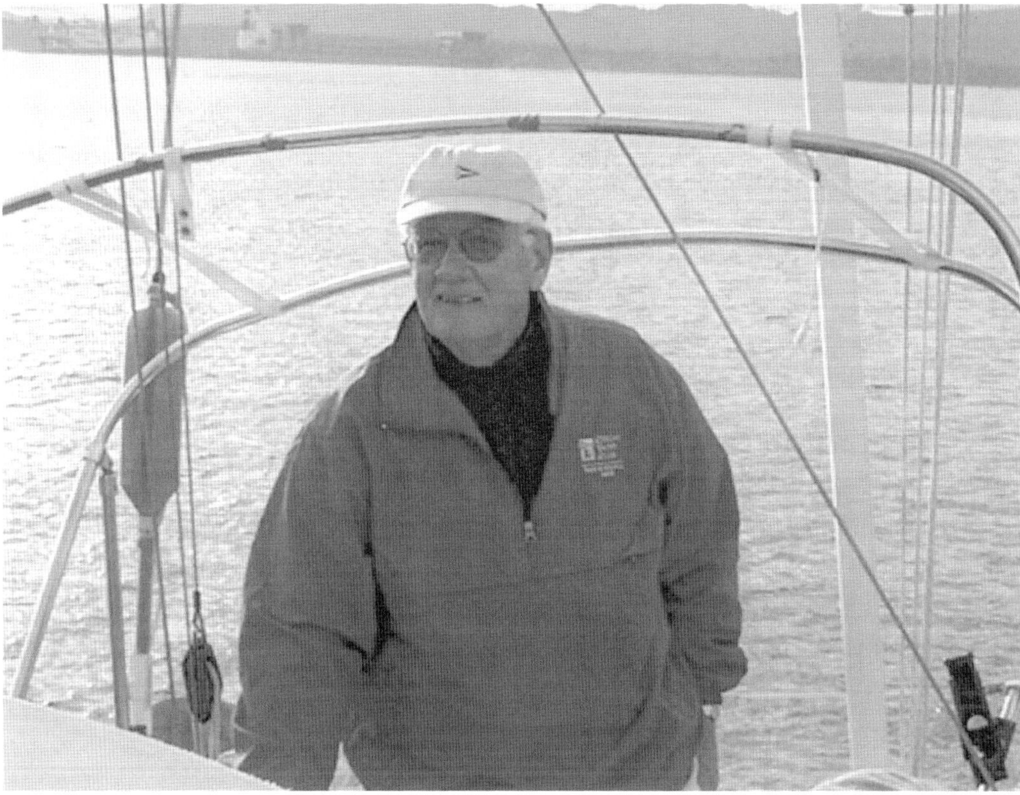

C. William Pollard
When not analyzing trends in business or in the boardroom, Pollard pursues other passions, including sailing. Over a 25-year period, from 1977 to 2002, he participated in the leadership of The ServiceMaster Company and served not once but twice as its chief executive officer. He also served as chairman of the board of ServiceMaster from 1990 to April 2002 and was elected chairman emeritus in 2002 when he retired from the board. He is currently serving as an advisor to the company. From 1972 to 1977, he served on the faculty and as a vice president of Wheaton College. In addition to his work at Fairwyn Investment Company and ServiceMaster, Pollard has served as a director of several public companies and a number of charitable, religious, and educational organizations. He currently serves as a director of the Central DuPage Hospital–Delnor Healthcare System, Illinois Children's Healthcare Foundation, The Drucker Institute of Claremont Graduate School, as chairman of the executive committee of the Billy Graham Evangelistic Association, and trustee emeritus of Wheaton College. Pollard is actively involved in addressing issues relating to ethics and the integration of faith and work. He is the author of the best-selling book, *The Soul of the Firm*, and also has written for or contributed to other books and magazines including "The Leader Who Serves" and *The Heart of a Business Ethic*. His newest book is *Serving Two Masters? Reflections on God and Profit*. Pollard also has been recognized by a number of educational organizations for his leadership in business, ethics, and corporate governance including receiving the Hesburgh Award for Business Ethics from Notre Dame, and recognition by Harvard Business School as an American business leader of the 20th century who helped shape the way people live, work, and interact. He was honored as one of corporate America's Outstanding Directors, and has received honorary doctoral degrees from Aurora University, Gordon-Conwell Theological Seminary, and Indiana Wesleyan University. Pollard is currently the chairman of Fairwyn Investment Company in Wheaton. He and his wife, Judy, have four children and 15 grandchildren. (Courtesy of C. William Pollard.)

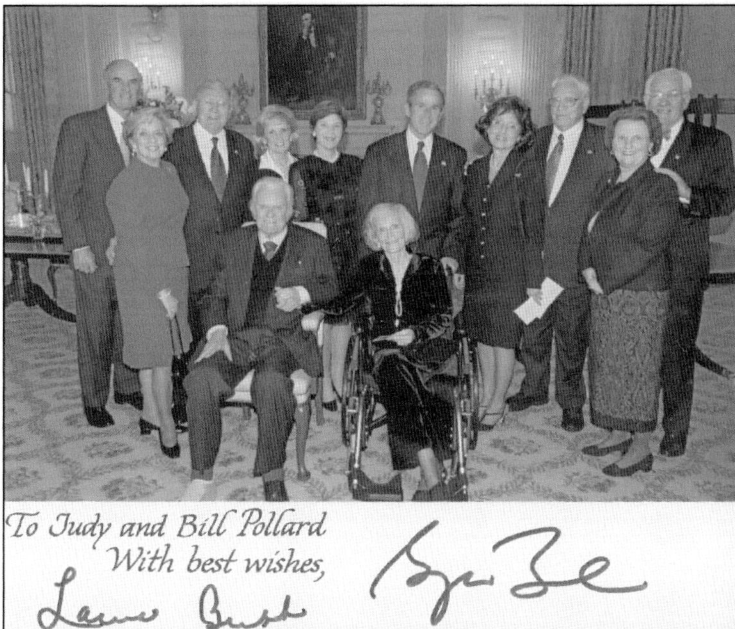

Pollard and Billy Graham

C. William Pollard and friends celebrate the birthday of Billy Graham, seated with Ruth Graham: (left to right) Graeme Keith, Gloria Keith, Cliff Barrows, Ann Barrows, Laura Bush, George Bush, Karlene Shea, George Beverly Shea, Judy Pollard, and C. William Pollard. Below: As chairman of the executive committee of the Billy Graham Evangelistic Association, Pollard frequently chats with the evangelist regarding aspects of his international ministry. In his autobiography, *Just as I Am*, Graham gratefully acknowledges Pollard among others who have offered "wise counsel and practical experience" toward the maintenance of the BGEA. Business correspondence, evangelistic films, campaign posters, and other material relating to Billy Graham's crusade career is available to researchers at the Billy Graham Center on the campus of Wheaton College. (Courtesy of C. William Pollard.)

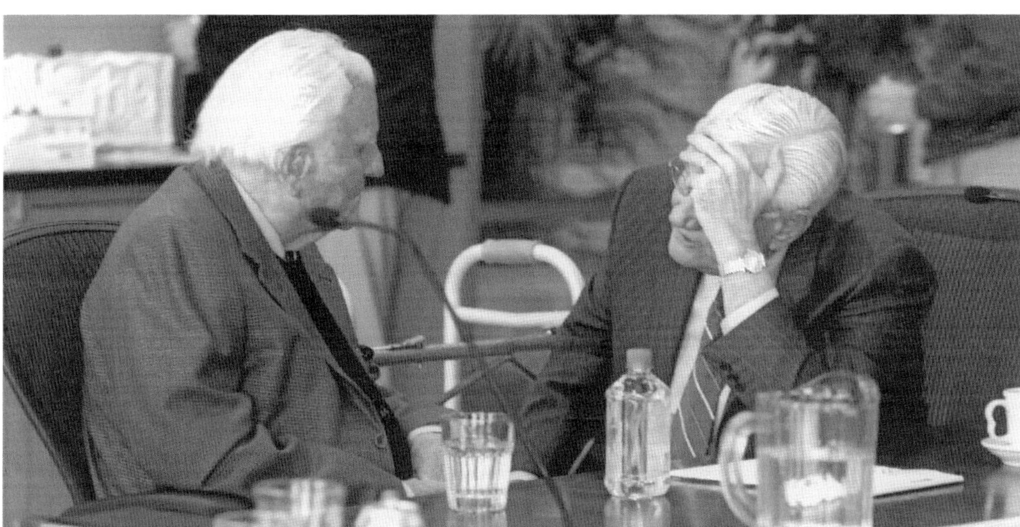

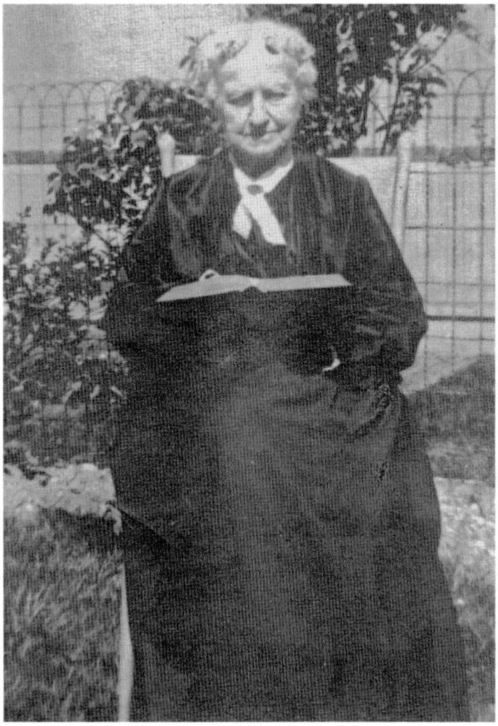

Emma Dryer

Charles Blanchard, Wheaton College president, wrote a book in 1913 on prophetic issues, dedicating it to Emma Dryer, "the friend who first opened my mind to the Dispensational Teaching of the Word of God." Blanchard first met her while serving as pastor at Moody Church in Chicago. Dispensational theology proposes a sudden "rapture" and a seven-year Tribulation period. This approach to biblical prophecy influenced many evangelicals toward accelerated activity in missions.

H.C. Thiessen

Henry Clarence Thiessen was teaching New Testament Literature and Exegesis at Dallas Theological Seminary when he was hired by Wheaton to implement its graduate school in 1937. Thiessen's *Systematic Theology* further advanced dispensational theology for many years at Wheaton, and laid the groundwork for not only Hal Lindsay's *Late, Great Planet Earth,* but also the popular *Left Behind* series by Jerry Jenkins and Tim LaHaye. He died in 1947.

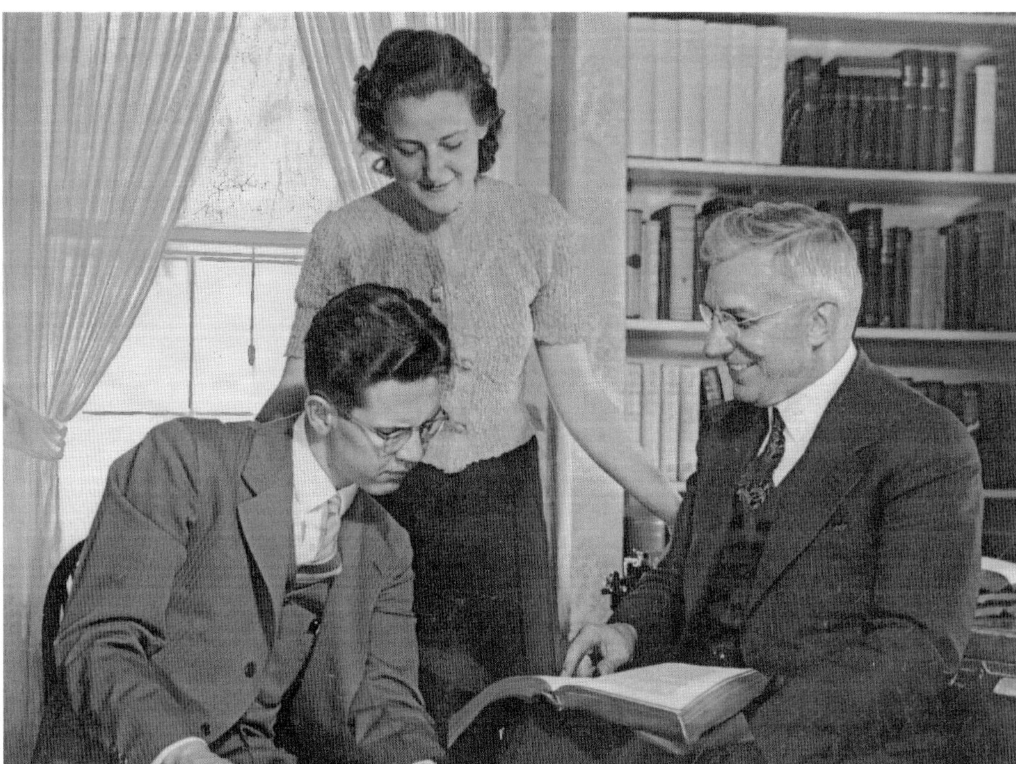

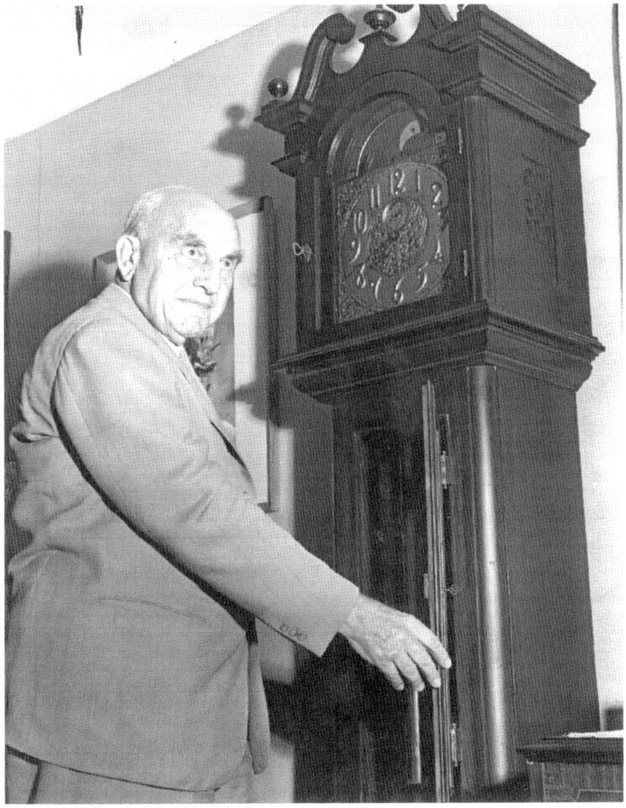

Herman Fischer

As far as Wheaton College administration was concerned, the buck stopped with Fischer, chairman of the board of trustees, who held the position for a remarkable 43 years. Fischer was one of 12 children born to Herman A. Fischer Sr., who instructed math at the college for 50 years, and Julia Blanchard Fischer, daughter of Jonathan Blanchard, first president of Wheaton College. After graduating, Fischer taught mathematics for two years at Wabash High School in Indiana before enrolling at Harvard Law School, receiving his JD in 1908. Returning to Chicago with his license, he practiced for 65 years with the firm Campbell, Clithero, Fischer and Guy. Dr. Charles Blanchard, second president of Wheaton College, shortly before his death in 1926, proposed that his nephew, Herman, be appointed as a trustee. A year later he was elected chairman, heading the board until his retirement in 1970 when it awarded him a plaque stating that he had "demonstrated uncompromising fairness and integrity, shared unusually wise counsel, manifested consideration for varying viewpoints and showed exemplary faithfulness to Jesus Christ and the cause of higher education." Fischer exhibited durable leadership elsewhere, as well. From 1932 to 1953, he served as president of Gary-Wheaton Bank, continuing as chairman of its board until 1966. He led as officer and director of the Cuneo Press from 1919 to 1973, and was a member of the board of InterVarsity Christian Fellowship and also the Billy Graham Crusades. For relaxation, he enjoyed membership at the prestigious Union League Club and the Chicago Golf Club. A lifelong bachelor, he died in 1974 at age 91. Billy Graham sent condolences: "There was a glorious reunion in Heaven when Herman Fischer swept through its glorious gates. His powerful leadership was possibly the greatest single factor that kept Wheaton College spiritually balanced, financially sound with academic excellence during the last half century. All of us who have benefited from Wheaton's influence owe him an enormous debt. Please convey to his personal family and to the Wheaton family my appreciation and thankfulness for the life of Herman Fischer."

Raymond P. Fischer

Raymond Fischer possessed a mind both meticulous and imaginative. Born the youngest of 12 in the house in which his grandfather, Jonathan Blanchard, died, he attended Wheaton College and Pomona College in California, before matriculating to Harvard Law School. His degree equipped him for a 15-year practice with Campbell, Clithero and Fischer, located on La Salle Street in Chicago. Ending his legal career in 1941, he then served as executive vice president of the Cuneo Press, president of Combined Paper Mills, director of the National Tea Company, and sat on the Chicago advisory board for the Salvation Army. Retiring from the paper business, he established Associated Consultants of Wheaton, Illinois. He was a licensed lay leader in the Episcopal Church, and belonged to the Chicago Golf and Union League clubs. While in prep school, Fischer mailed a submission to Harriet Monroe, the formidable founder and editor of *Poetry* magazine. Shortly thereafter, ever scouting for fresh talent, she invited him to visit her office to discuss improvements. Monroe had been pivotal in publicizing the work of Carl Sandburg, Wallace Stevens, and Ezra Pound. Fischer's corrections were deemed acceptable and his first publication, "A Year," appeared in 1922. "A regret regarding *Poetry*," he recalls, "is that I was unable to attend a white tie dinner which the magazine gave for William Butler Yeats to which I was invited but did not go, because the dress suit of an older brother was several sizes too large for me." His disappointment probably lightened when *Poetry* again accepted his work in 1924, then in 1929, and again, 55 years later, in 1984. His verse collection, *An Aged Man Remembers April*, is dedicated to Monroe, "who showed me that both inspiration and revision are essential." In 1987, Fischer assembled four decades of research and published *Four Hazardous Journeys of Jonathan Blanchard*, chronicling his grandfather's antislavery escapades during the Montana Territory gold rush. Fischer and his wife, Marita, had one daughter. The aged poet-lawyer-businessman was the last surviving grandson of Blanchard when he lay down his pen forever at age 89 in 1990.

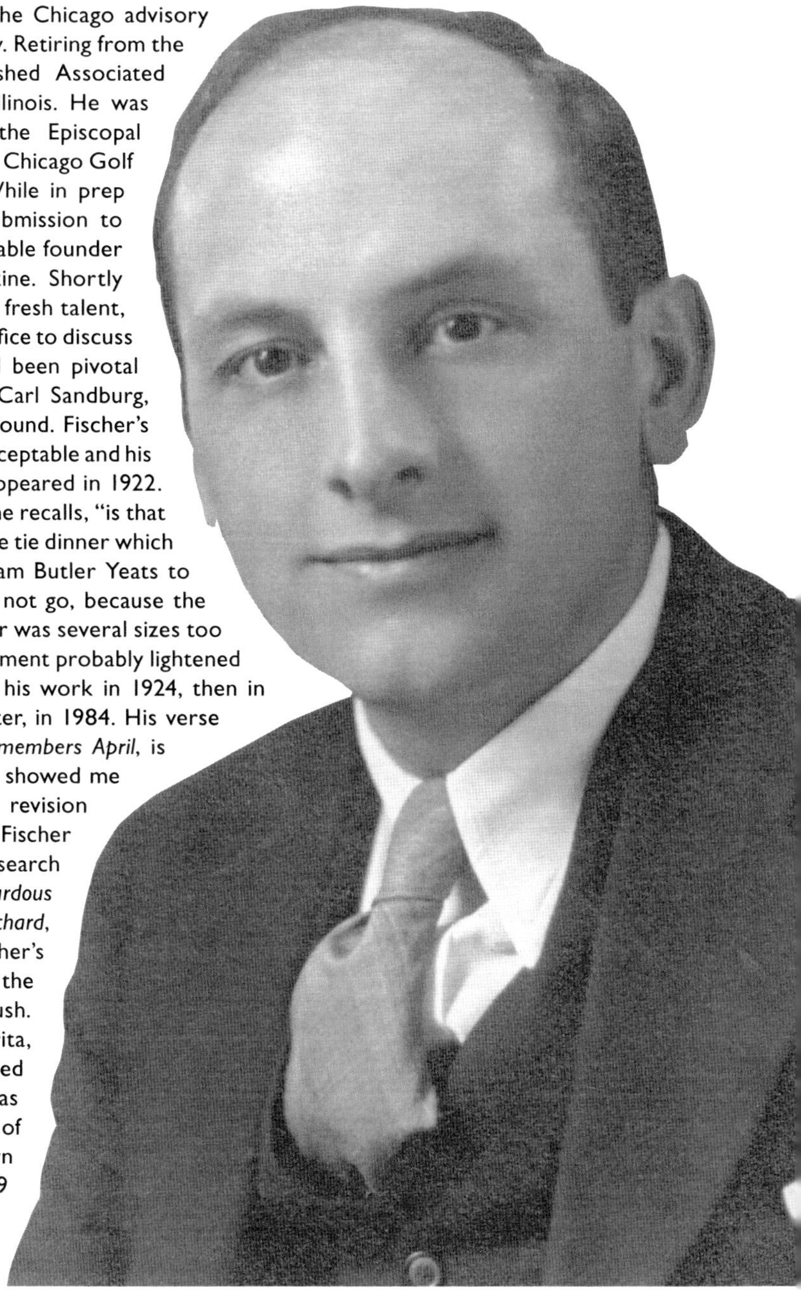

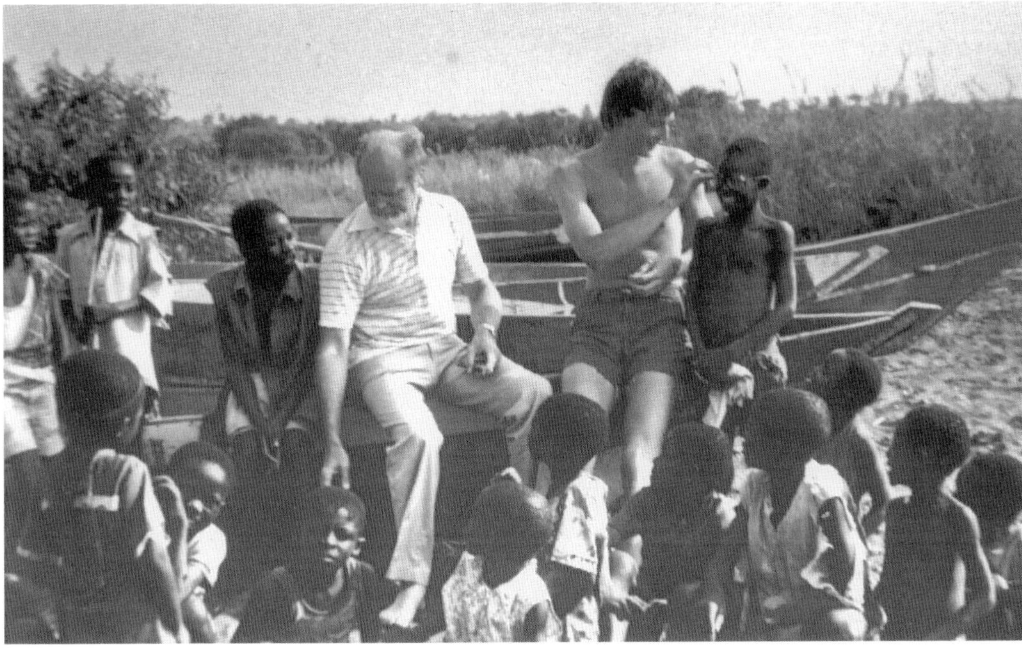

HNGR
Distressed about world hunger, two Wheaton College professors in 1974 created a Third World study curriculum called HNGR (Human Needs and Global Resources Program) with Wayne Bragg appointed as director. Its objective is to raise awareness on campus of the needs of global society. Interns spend months overseas, serving the community in which they reside. Here Bragg and a student visit locals in the field. HNGR is currently led by Dr. Paul Robinson.

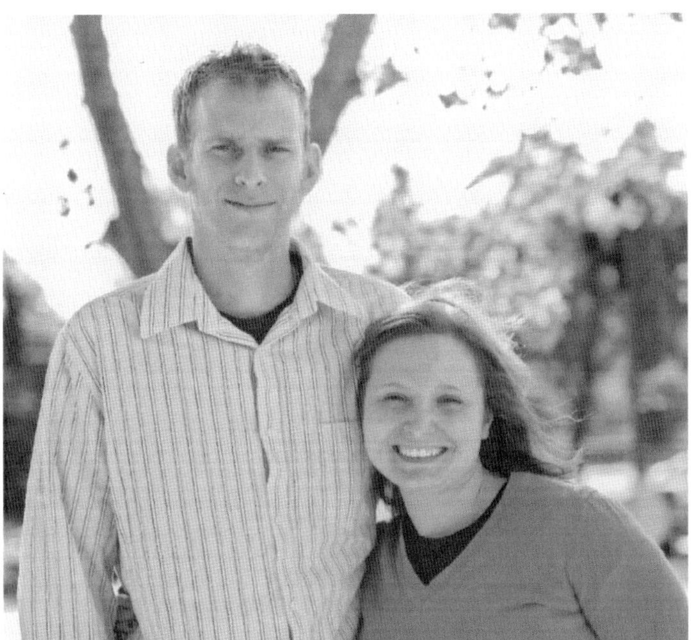

Jason and Charisa Krieg
Residing in Wheaton near a busy intersection and the train station, the Kriegs often encounter needy visitors seeking material help. On many occasions, Krieg has stopped while driving to help the homeless, providing financial assistance or organizing temporary living arrangements. In addition, the Kriegs are generous, gracious hosts, often inviting friends to their comfortable apartment. (Courtesy of Bethany Chapel.)

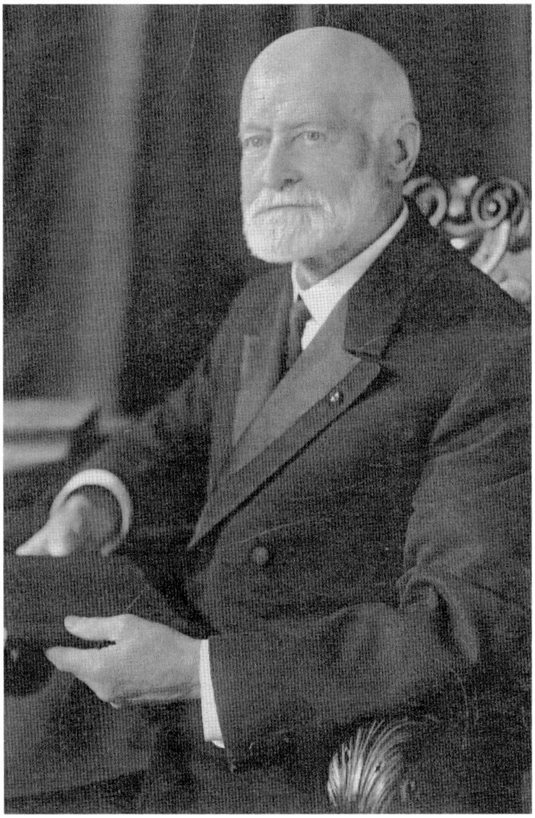

Anson and Adelaide Hemingway

Novelist Ernest Hemingway had little use for Christianity, but his paternal grandparents, Anson and Adelaide, gladly professed the faith and attended Wheaton College. Anson and two brothers fought in the Civil War, but only he survived. After military service, Anson attended Wheaton College for two years. Deeply influenced by D.L. Moody, he went on to serve as general secretary of the Chicago YMCA for 10 years. He then established a real estate business in Oak Park, Illinois. Hemingway married fellow Wheaton student Adelaide Edmonds, who graduated in 1867. They had four sons and two daughters. Passionate about the outdoors, Anson presented his grandson, Ernest, with a 20-gauge shotgun for his 10th birthday, perhaps a harbinger of the writer's adventurous life—and sad death, killing himself with a shotgun in 1961. Anson died in 1926 at 82.

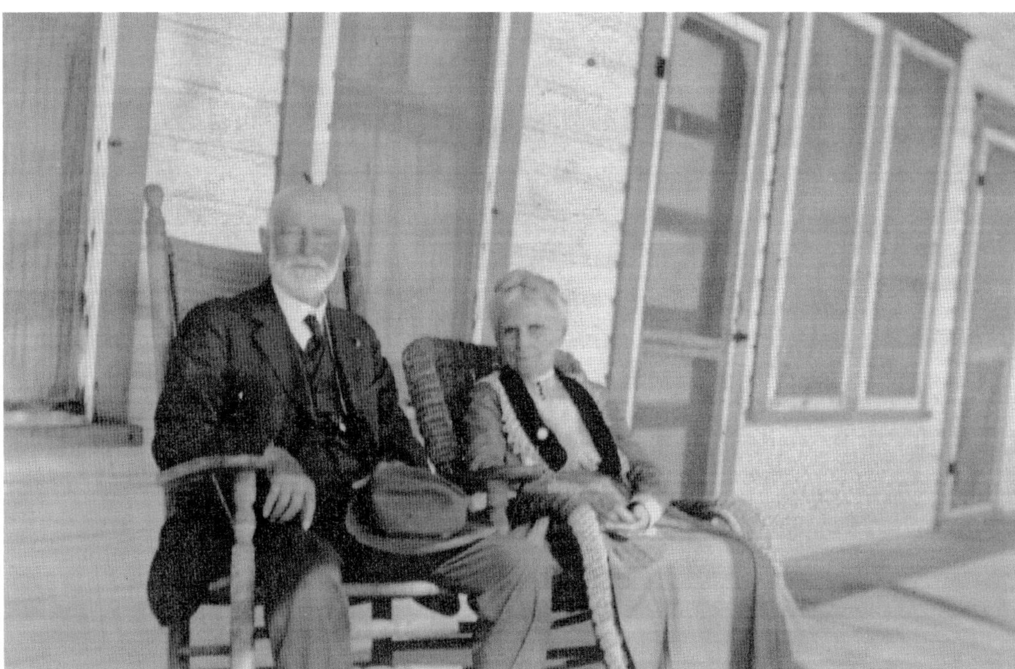

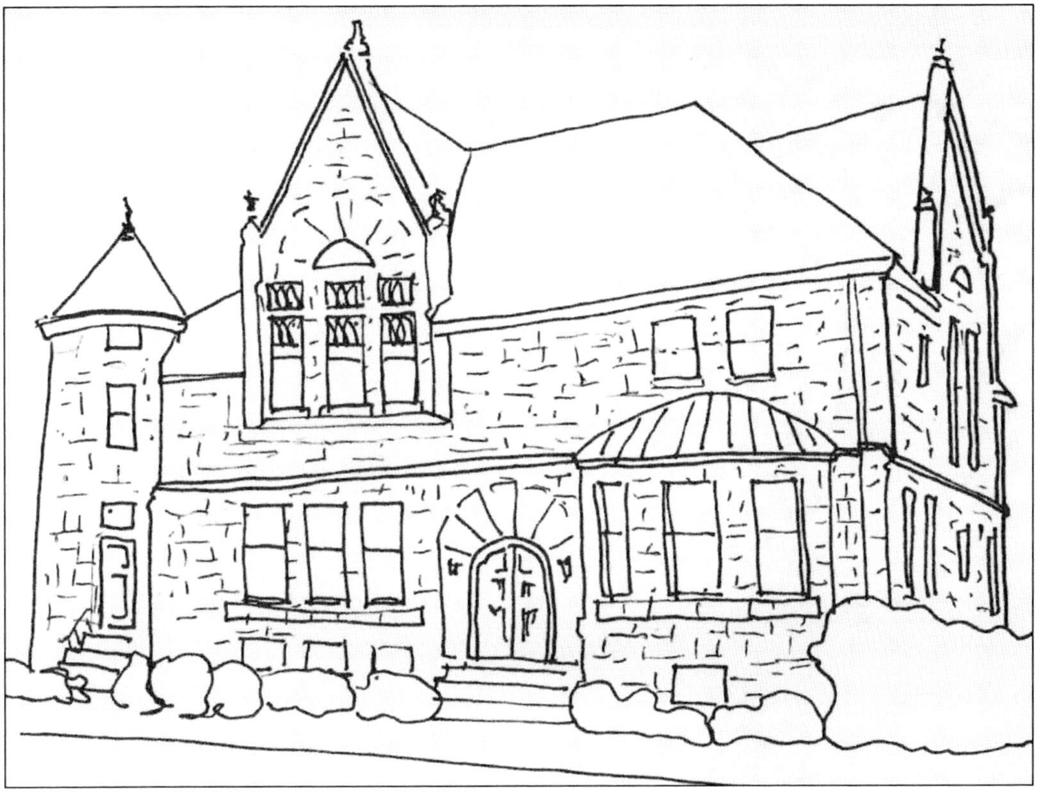

DuPage County Historical Museum
A time machine stands at 102 East Wesley Street in Wheaton. Unlike the sinister contraption from H.G. Wells's novel, this portal does not whirr with spinning wheels and blinking lights. Instead, stately and stationary, it beckons curious visitors into its stonemasoned elegance, stained-glass lobby, and high-ceilinged corridors. The museum is housed in what was formerly known as the Adams Memorial Library, erected in 1891 by John Quincy Adams, a relative of Pres. John Quincy Adams, as a gift to Wheaton in memory of his wife, Marilla Phipps Adams. Designed by Charles Sumner Frost in the Richardsonian Romanesque style, it was added to the National Register in 1981. Sumner also designed Navy Pier and the Maine Pavilion at the 1893 World's Fair. In the 1960s, the DuPage County Historical Society recognized the availability of the building as a more spacious library was being erected. The DuPage County Historical Museum opened in 1967 with Margaret Adams Dunton as its first curator. It is the only institution dedicated to the collection, preservation, and interpretation of the material culture documenting the county of DuPage, Illinois. The collections represent artifacts amassed by the DuPage County Historical Society since 1929 as well as artifacts acquired by the museum since its founding in 1965. Staff, volunteers, and interns utilize the collections as well as loans from private donors and other institutions to create both permanent and temporary exhibits for the community. The two permanent exhibits focus on the general history of DuPage County and the importance of the railroad in DuPage. The exhibit includes an H.O. Gauge Model train with over 2,000 feet of track. Built and designed by the DuPage Society of Model Engineers, this exhibit earns the museum its nickname, "the train museum." A wide range of educational opportunities are planned for the surrounding community outside of regular exhibits. Programs such as tours, lectures, workshops, and summer camps on historical topics are regularly included in the calendar. The museum currently operates under the savvy, capable curatorship of Sara Arnas. (Drawing by Marcia Gray Martin; courtesy of Marcia Gray Martin, Chip Krueger, and Barbara Hall.)

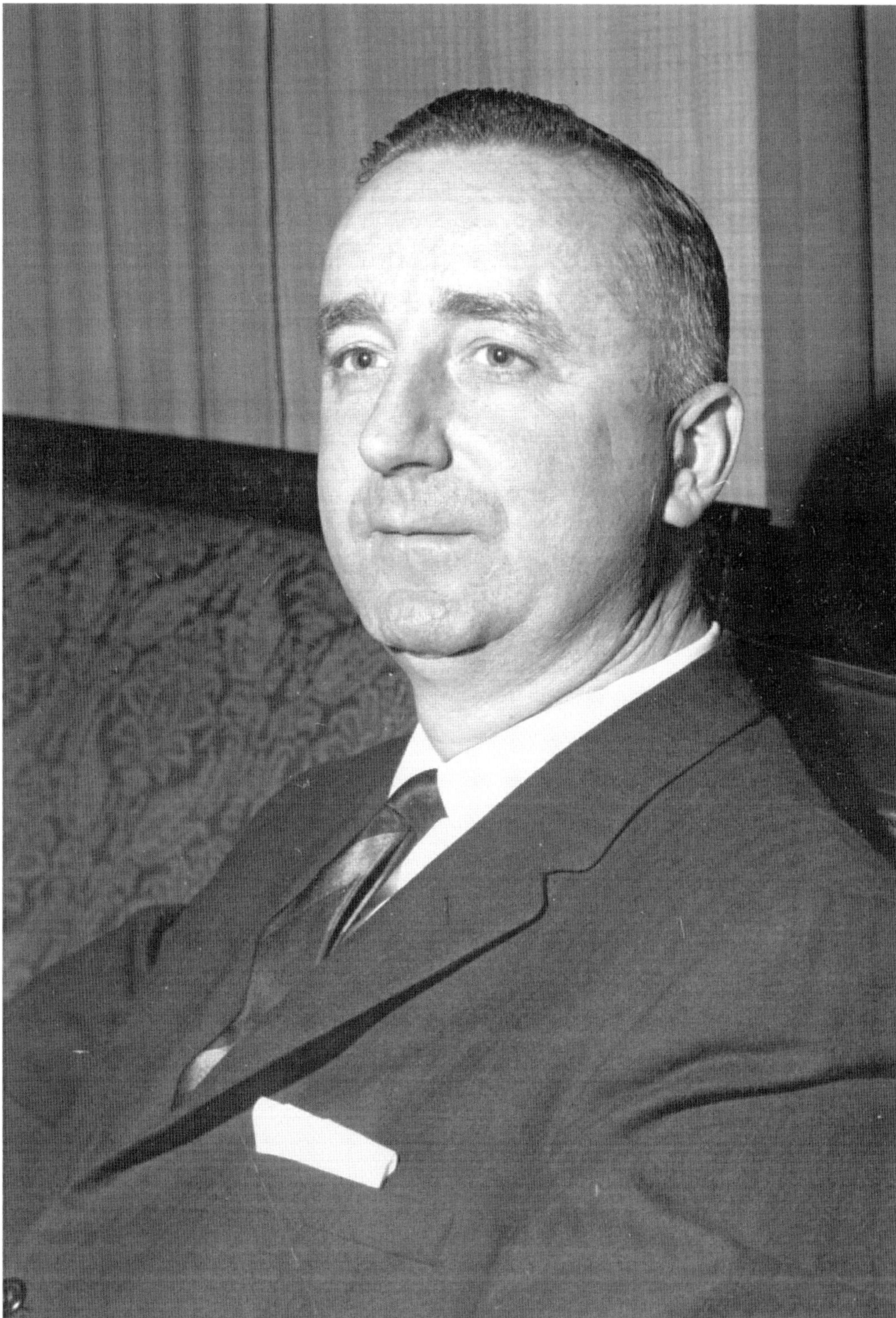

Edgar C. Bundy (LEFT)

A strident opponent of left-wing politics, Bundy was one of the supremely colorful personalities inhabiting Wheaton. A retired former staff intelligence officer in the Air Force, serving in every major theater of operations during World War II, he was also chief of research and analysis, headquarters intelligence, of the Alaskan Air Command after the war. He testified frequently as an expert witness in both open and executive sessions of both houses of Congress and state legislatures. An ordained Southern Baptist minister, Bundy preached at conferences and churches across America. Opposing the incursion of theological compromise and radical leftism, he spoke on hundreds of radio and television talk shows, debating such figures as Bishop James A. Pike and spokesmen of the Communist Party. He was a member of the Mayflower Society, the Order of Founders and Patriots of America, the Sons of the American Revolution, the American Legion, the Military Order of the World Wars, the Veterans of Foreign Wars, and was past president of the Miami Beach Symphony Orchestra. For decades, he and his wife, Lela May, resided in the Jesse Wheaton home, built in 1838, given to them by a Wheaton family member as an inheritance. At their home, the Bundys entertained doctors, attorneys, and politicians. They had no children, but Lela May worked alongside her husband in his endeavors, including raising German shepherds, which they often brought into their offices at the right-wing Church League of America. As president of the organization, "Major Bundy" (as he preferred) maintained a far-reaching mailing list for the distribution of his newsletter and books. His roommate in officers' training school was Sen. Lloyd Bentsen, and during drill exercises he marched with actor Clark Gable. Bundy's collection of books, maps, and file cards was occasionally used by the FBI for research. World-traveled and widely connected, he enjoyed friendships with powerful conservative voices like Robert Taft, William F. Buckley, and Ronald Reagan. Bundy, single-minded, fearless, and irascible, was a Cold War warrior who undoubtedly loved his country and did not deviate from his principles. He died in 2008 at 93.

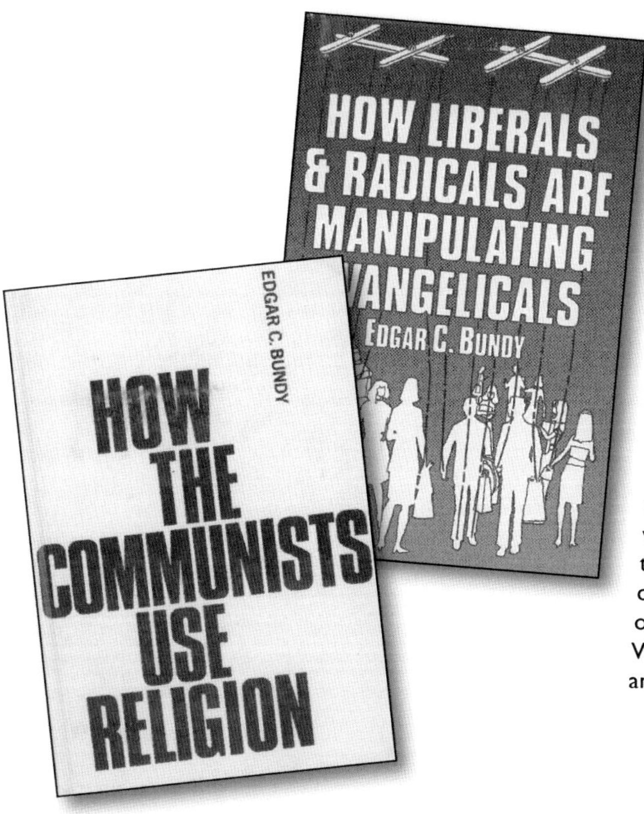

Bundy's Books

Bundy perceived that certain evangelical leaders and institutions had been co-opted by unfriendly forces through the slow, steady poison of compromise. In books such as *How Liberals and Radicals are Manipulating Evangelicals* and *How the Communists Use Religion* he presents his exposé of their tactics, chronicling the evangelical drift toward liberalism and Communism. "Great moral damage has been done to the United States as a result of this neo-evangelical compromise," he writes. "We can only pray, further, that the hour is not too late for the bringing of the United States of America, and other nations which remain in the Free World, back to the God of their fathers and founders."

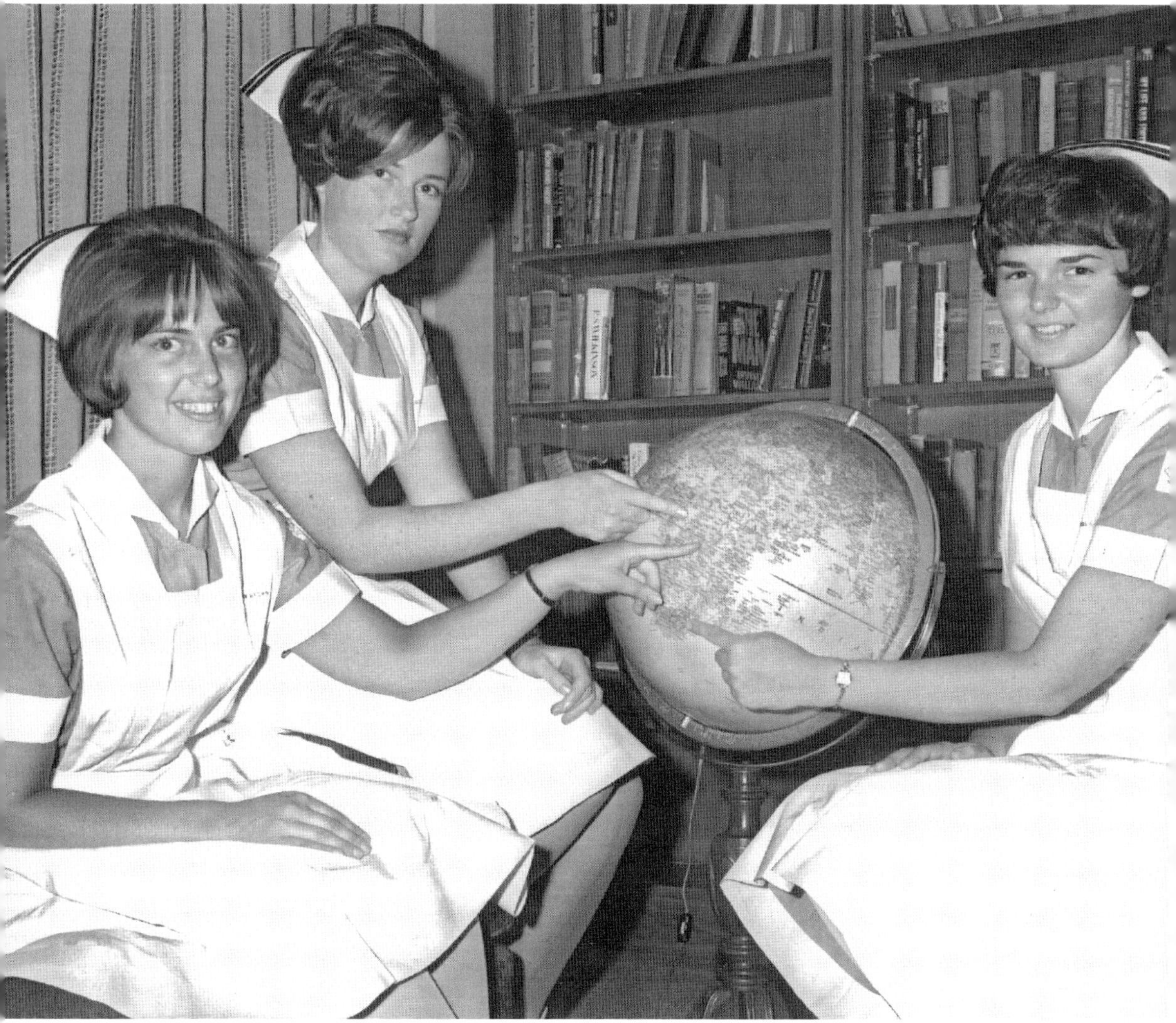

West Suburban School of Nursing

Wheaton College in 1946 joined with West Suburban Hospital in Oak Park, combining college courses with a professional nursing program. The hospital provided facility and staff for the three-year program, while the college was responsible for academic studies as well as the final two years of the integrated course. Qualified graduates could elect to continue studying on the Wheaton campus for two more years for a bachelor of science degree, allowing the candidate to complete professional training and a college education in five years. College faculty served as part-time faculty at the nursing school. Student nurses, recruited from all over the world, were encouraged to join campus social activities. A bus shuttled them between college and hospital. These nurses are probably pointing to their place of origin, or perhaps their desired locations for service.

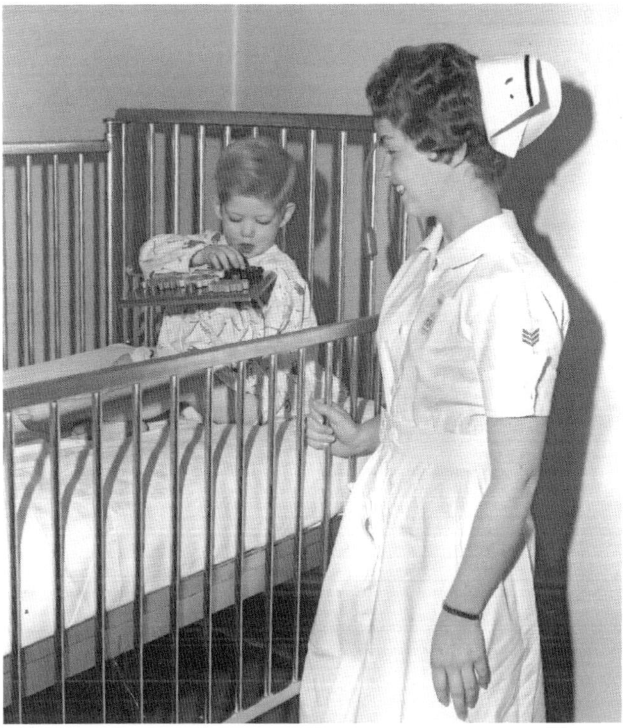

Graduating Nurses

An unidentified West Suburban nurse visits a young patient, happy with his toy. West Sub nurses were reputed boy-chasers on campus, but they denied the accusation. As the program progressed, fewer nurses transferred to Wheaton. After nearly four decades, the program was discontinued, though Wheaton still offers pre-health professions courses. Below: Graduating nurses, resplendent in white uniforms, walk the commencement exercise at Wheaton College. "A nurse learns the harsh realities of the sick in a way that a casual visitor to a hospital ward cannot appreciate," states the 1963 Wheaton College *Tower* yearbook. "She knows the unglamorous part of nursing, but most of all, she knows the satisfaction of helping others—the joy of giving. Nursing. A profession. But to be a nurse—a way of life."

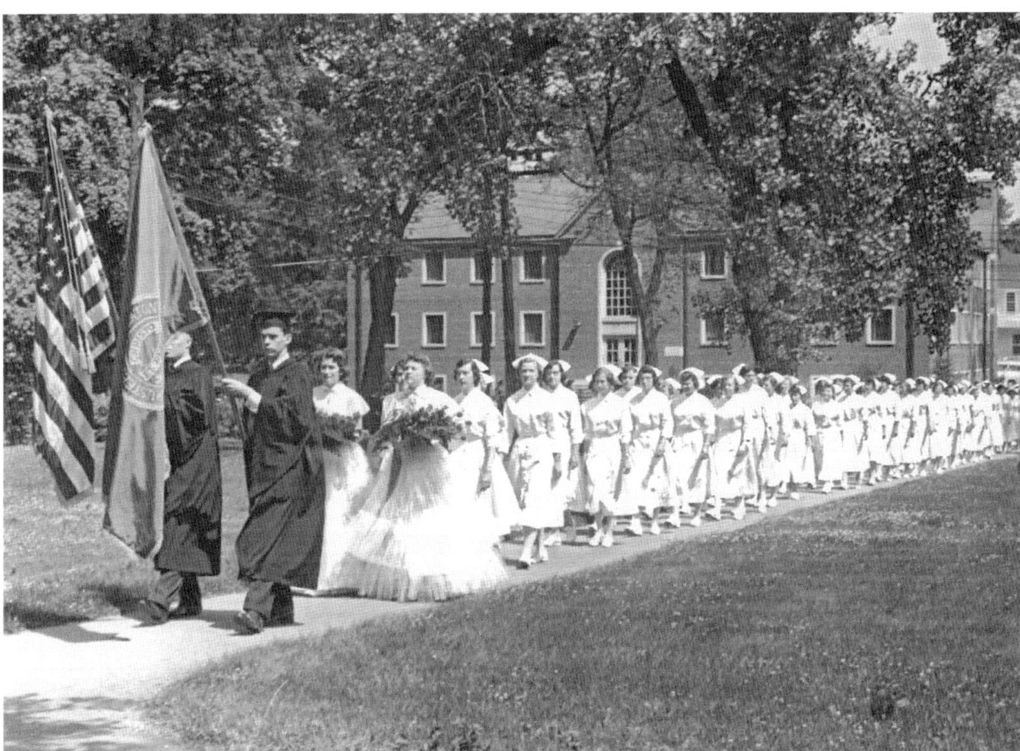

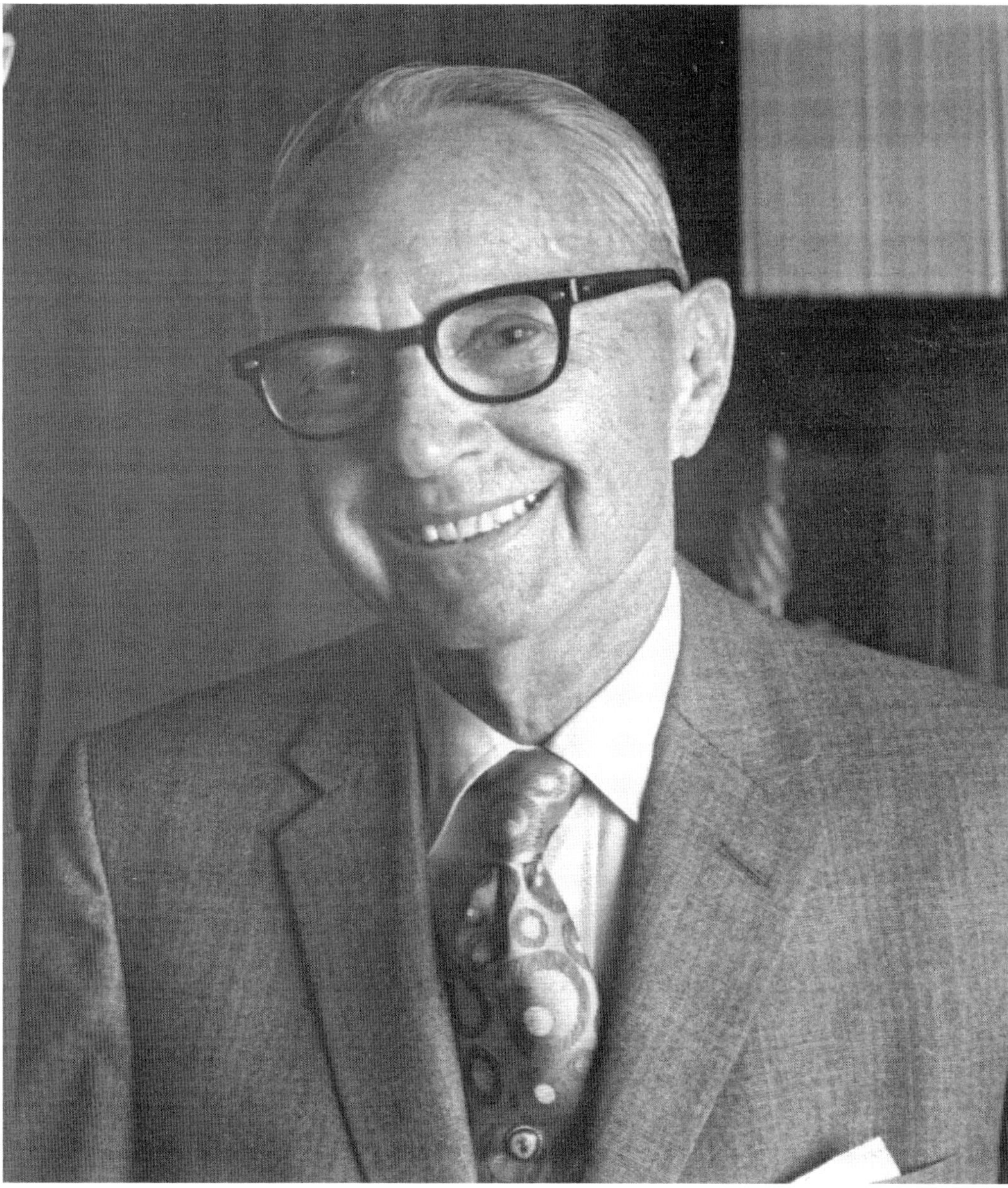

Marion Wade

As Dr. Clyde Kilby of Wheaton College assembled the collection of primary and secondary manuscripts pertaining to C.S. Lewis, J.R.R. Tolkien, Dorothy L. Sayers, G.K. Chesterton, Charles Williams, George MacDonald, and Owen Barfield, he determined more space was required. And so Marion E. Wade, founder of ServiceMaster, and his wife, made a substantial monetary gift. After his death, the Marion E. Wade Memorial Fund was established by his associates. In 2001, a new building was constructed, purposely resembling a structure that might be seen on the campus of Oxford University, the revered institution so closely associated with Lewis and Tolkien. In addition to housing manuscripts, the center displays Tolkien's desk, Lewis's desk, and a wardrobe owned by Lewis, presumably an inspiration for *The Lion, The Witch and the Wardrobe.*

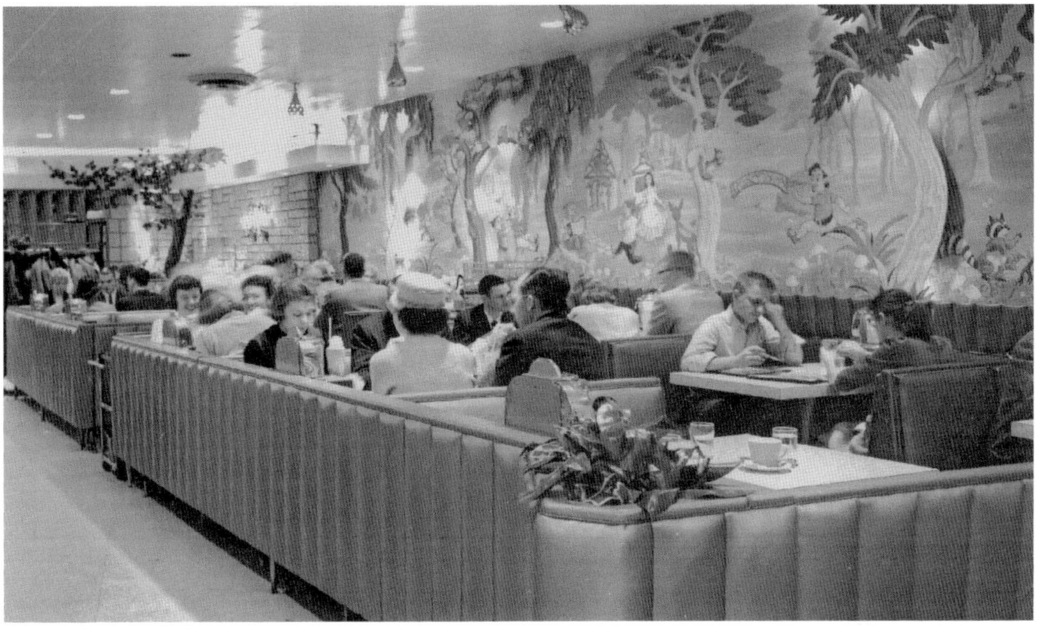

Seven Dwarfs Restaurant

The Seven Dwarfs Restaurant seems nearly as perennial as the fairy tale itself. For decades, it has provided the comforts of the cozy, independent diner, a dying breed of business lost to the influx of generic fast food establishments. The mural depicting Snow White and the Seven Dwarfs still graces the wall. The interior has not greatly changed since this shot was taken in the late 1950s.

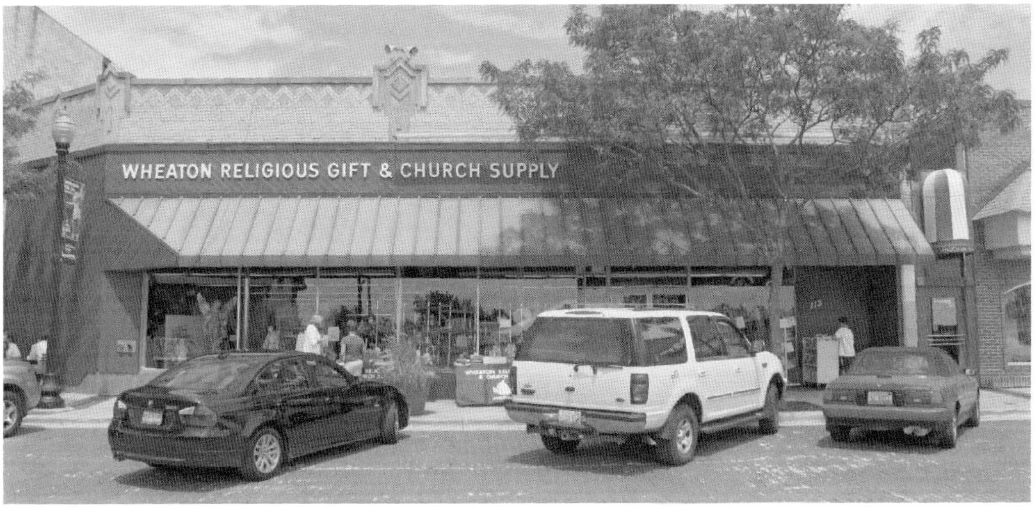

Wheaton Religious Gift and Church Supply

Wheaton is typically associated with Protestantism, but there is a sizable Catholic population. For over 40 years, Wheaton Religious has supplied liturgical churches in Wheaton and all Chicagoland with books, communion supplies, altar candles, altar wine, communion breads, tabernacles, candlesticks, albs, deacon supplies, clergy shirts, and more. The spacious store is managed by the convivial, competent brothers, Phil and Joe Taschetta. (Courtesy of Phil Taschetta.)

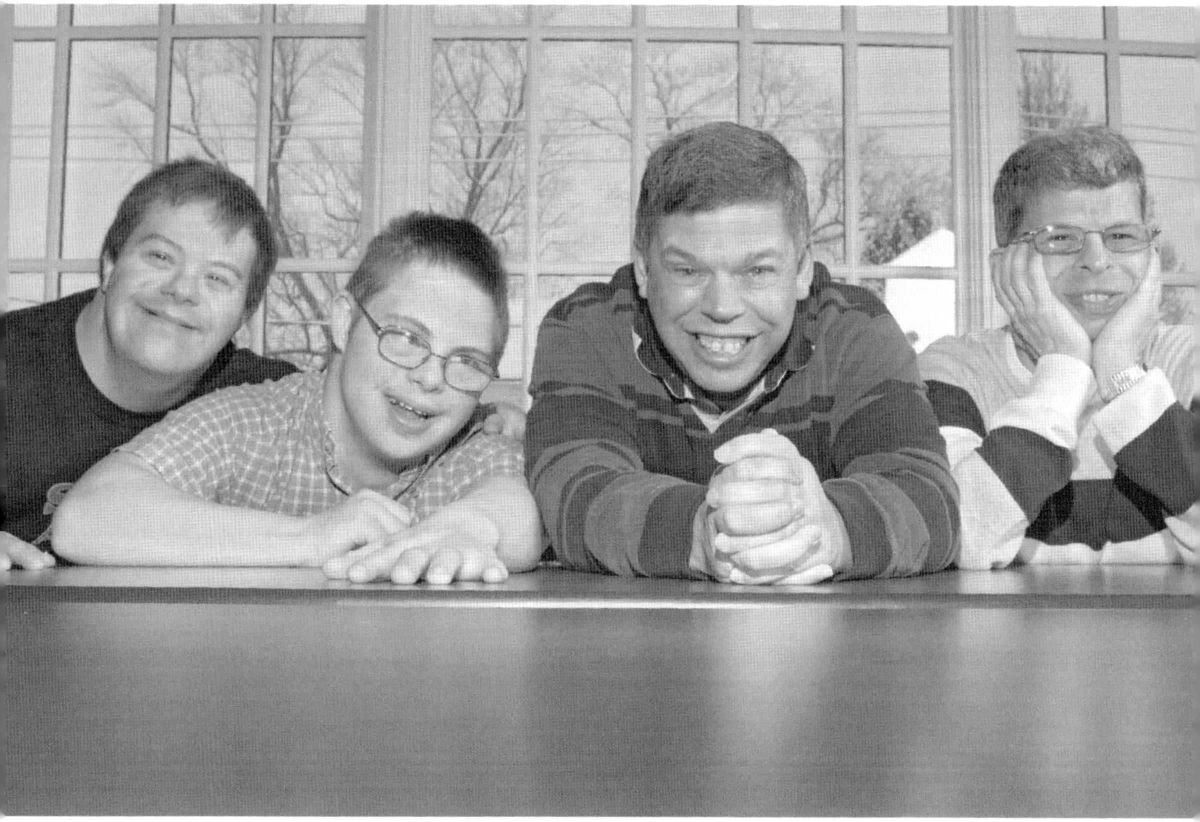

STARS

A ministry of College Church, STARS (Seeking Always to Reflect the Savior), serves children and adults with intellectual and developmental disabilities. Special needs children are included in all children's ministry programs whenever possible. The Sunday morning program offers Bible classes taught by trained volunteers who use a multisensory approach to teaching. Each month STARS hosts a support group for parents and other caregivers. Participants enjoy a meal while guest speakers address specific needs. Teen and adult STARS enjoy "Friday Night Fun," a recreational program with a home-cooked meal, gym activity, crafts, and a table game. "Support on Saturdays" provides a time for parents to drop off their special needs children under the age of 14 and their siblings. These children and their siblings enjoy songs, crafts, games, and a Bible story. The ministry also provides volunteers who visit homes and assist with family needs. Through the "Hangin' with a STAR" program, STARS who are 16 and older are paired with students to attend various events. STARS also learn music, including hand bells, choir, and the autoharp, and are provided with opportunities to perform in the community. STARS Family Services is an extension of the STARS Disability Ministry. The goal is to establish supportive living arrangements in a home-like atmosphere for participants in the STARS ministry. The first home, Washington House, opened in June, 2011, with residents Tim, David, John, and Gary (above). They hope to open more homes. Dawn Clark, director of disability ministries, says, "As I have directed the STARS ministry, I have been constantly reminded that individuals with intellectual and developmental disabilities are an important part of the body of Christ. I have watched them share their lives and faith in open and honest ways. They desire to serve others with the gifts that God has given them if only we will give them a chance. Our church needs the STARS and their families as much or more than they need us." Displaying humility and charming gusto, the STARS shine bright; and those fortunate enough to benefit from their guileless love receive an incalculable gift. (Courtesy of College Church.)

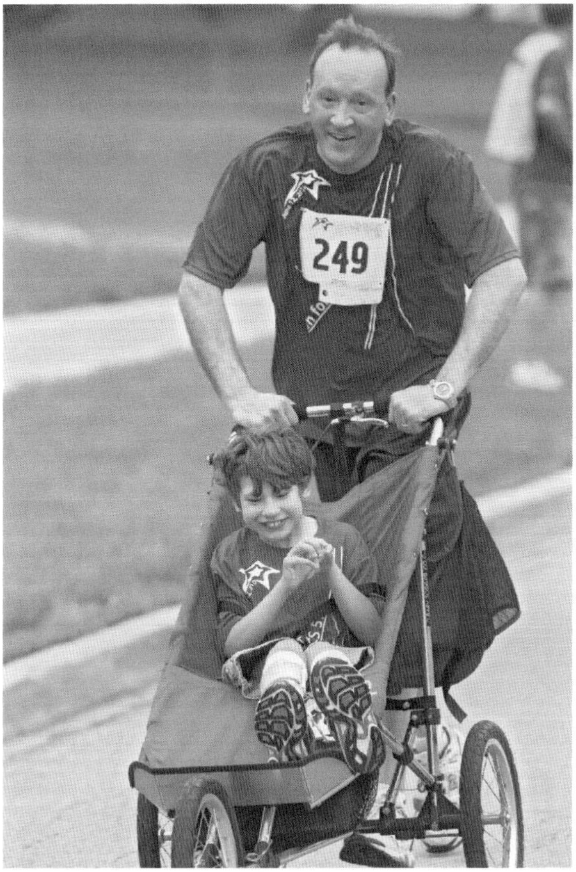

Run for the STARS and STARS Christmas Pageant
David Lyon, running, pushes his delighted son, Peter, who has cerebral palsy, in "Run for the STARS." Each June, College Church sponsors the 5K run, with proceeds from the race providing STARS families with camp scholarships and other supportive services. The STARS also produce a calendar, highlighting in photographs their activities throughout the year, including trips to camp, baptisms, picnics, or sporting events. Below: Kim plays a sheep in the annual STARS Christmas pageant at College Church, a highlight of the year. STARS performers delight audiences as they act their parts with charm, enthusiasm, and great conviction. (Courtesy of College Church.)

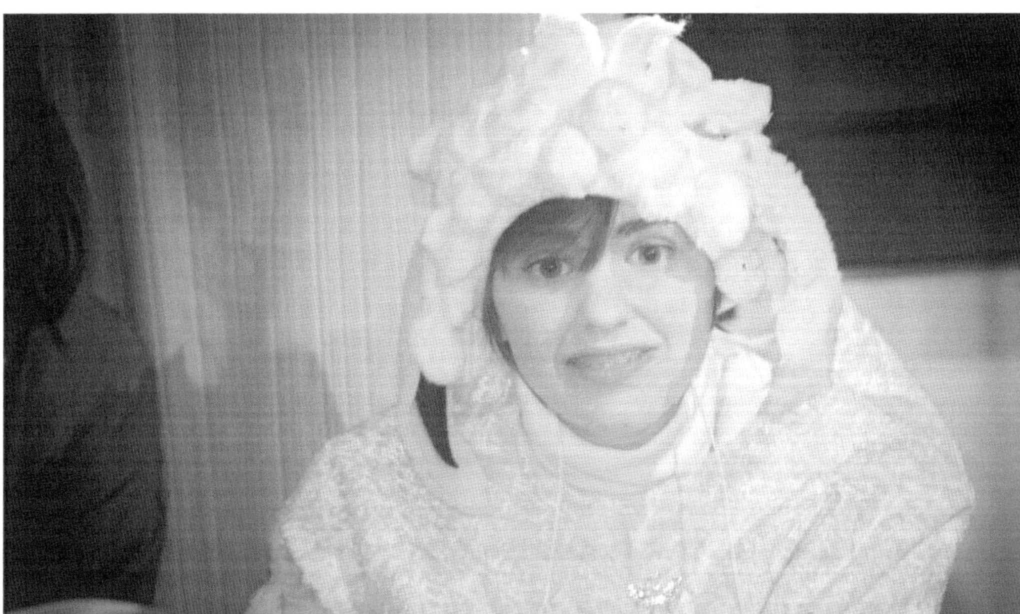

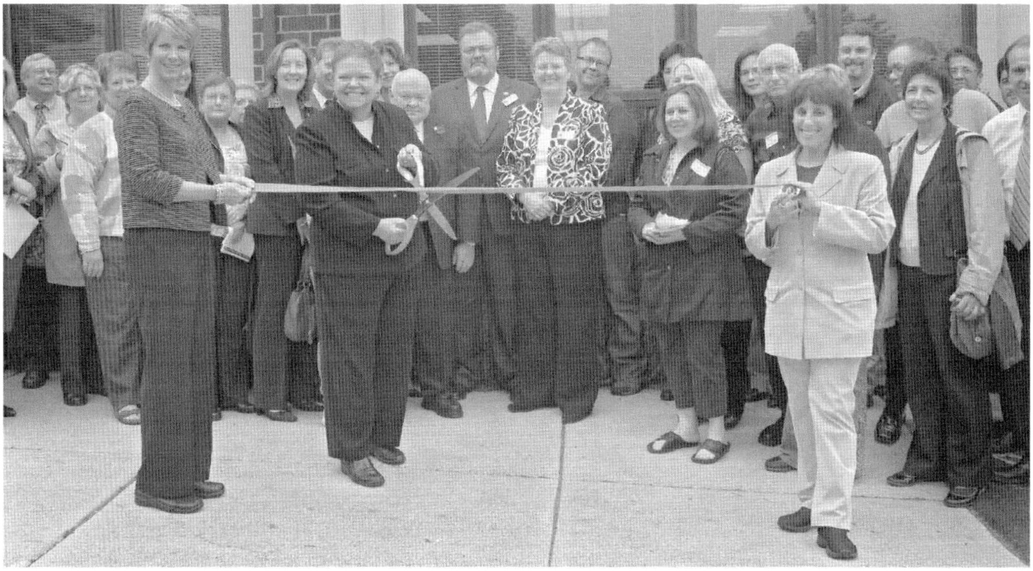

DuPage PADS

Carol Simler, executive director for DuPage PADS, cuts the ribbon at the opening of the renovated client service center. "Public Action to Deliver Shelter. "Though Wheaton and DuPage County are associated with wealth, varying circumstances create poverty and dislocation. Homelessness occurs due to substance abuse, mental illness, trauma, or the vicissitudes of the current poor economy. Through education, supportive services, and financial training, DuPage PADS empowers its clients to implement genuine change. The organization provides overnight housing through a network of churches and volunteers, offering food, safety, and shelter. Recently Mike DeMeritt of Wheaton collected $20,000 for the DuPage PADS, soliciting donations for his running during the Kettle Moraine 100 race in Wisconsin. DeMeritt represents the level of commitment offered by the PADS volunteers. (Photographs by MarianKrausPhotography.com; courtesy of DuPage PADS.)

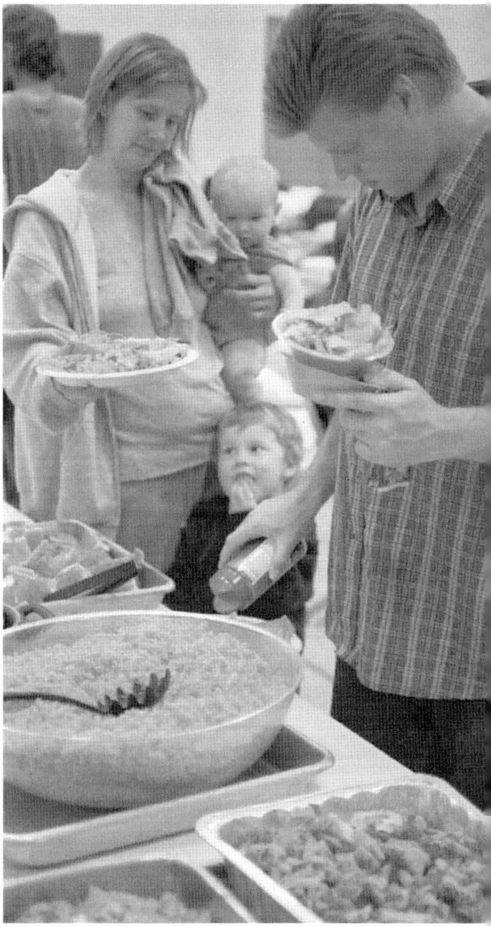

DuPage PADS Employment Program and Dining

A mother and baby engage services at the DuPage PADS. The Employment Program trains men and women for gainful vocational activity, assisting with resume preparation and job searches. DuPage PADS partners with College of DuPage for on-site GED classes and tutoring. Volunteer job coaches also assist clients with remaining successfully employed. Below: A family dines on a warm, balanced meal at DuPage PADS. (Photographs by MarianKrausPhotography.com; courtesy of DuPage PADS.)

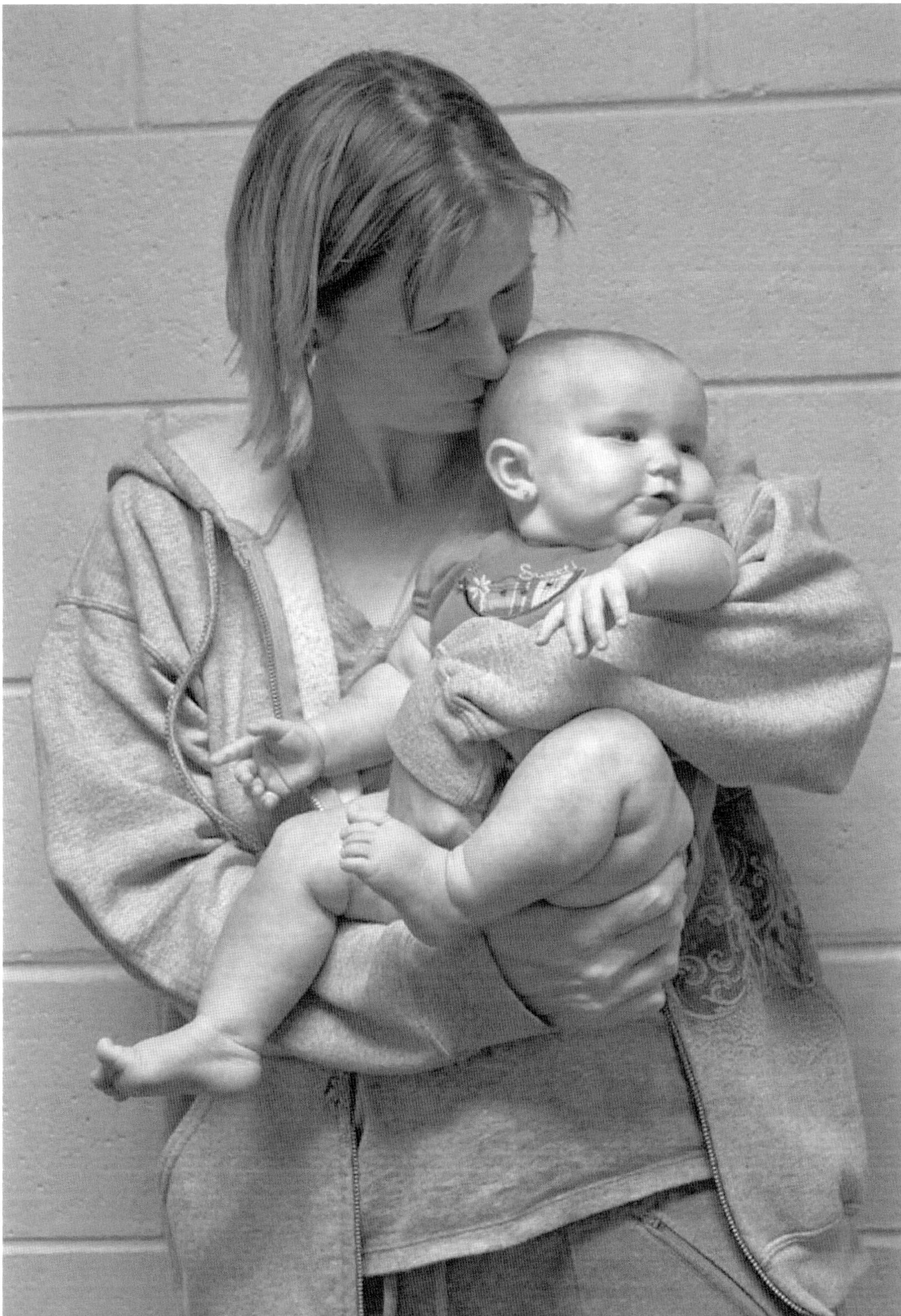

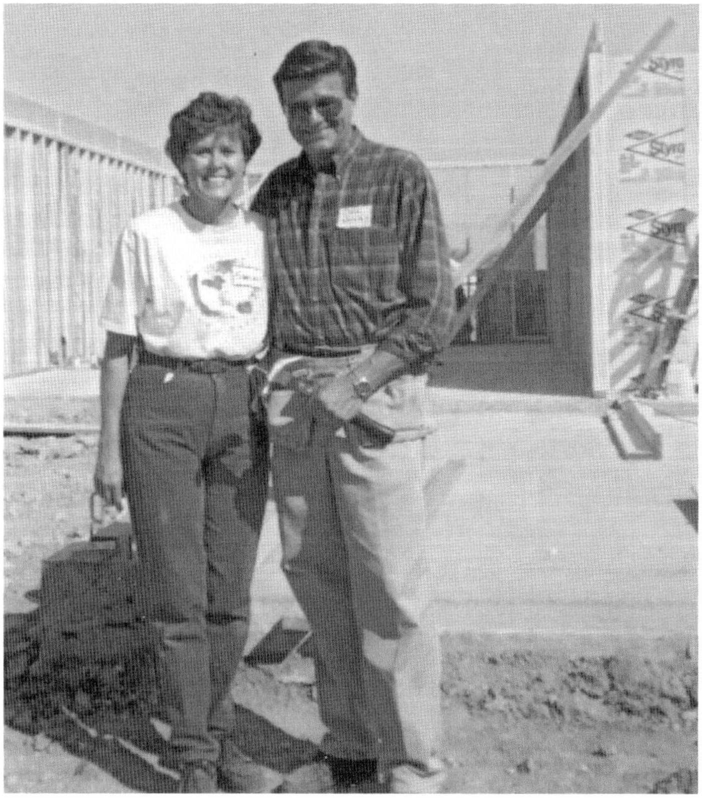

Dick and Florence Nogaj

After 30 years in the engineering field, Dick Nogaj ("no-jay") sold his firm, RJN Group, Inc. Since youth, he had pursued fairness and equality, and eventually joined the civil rights movement, marching, praying, and singing with Martin Luther King Jr. Later, with his wife, Florence, he founded the RJN Foundation, a charitable organization seeking to provide resources and financial assistance to not-for-profit programs focusing on areas of human services. "Florence and I were both blessed with talent, resources and the drive to make a difference in other people's lives," he writes. Continuing their desire to serve, the Nogajs in 1995 founded DuPage Habitat for Humanity, allowing limited-income families to purchase affordable homes in the county. To learn about the organization, they visited Americus, Georgia, where they were trained in building construction and met Millard Fuller, founder of Habit for Humanity. They also met Pres. Jimmy Carter, who endorsed Habitat for Humanity International. For the next few years, Nogaj and his team planned and built several homes in DuPage County, often wrangling with village governments and courts, encountering soaring victories and bitter defeats. Vacationing in Florida, the Nogajs read about destitute migrant workers in Immokalee, near the affluence of Naples. Intrigued, they visited and were horrified at the conditions. Here Nogaj saw an opportunity to design a community like the old-fashioned Chicago neighborhood in which he grew up, emphasizing better wages, affordable housing, and education. The Nogajs then founded Harvest for Humanity, its mission to empower individuals, families, and the surrounding community to implement necessary changes and improvements in Immokalee. Called the "Jubilation Development," the revitalized community now offers better wages, home ownership, and opportunities for education. The community features homes with welcoming porches, safe parks, and sidewalks. Self-described "full-time volunteer servants," the Nogajs as a couple demonstrate impressive "synergy," a combined energy, respect, and sense of mission. Dick and Florence Nogaj divide their time between Wheaton and southwestern Florida. (Courtesy of Dick and Florence Nogaj.)

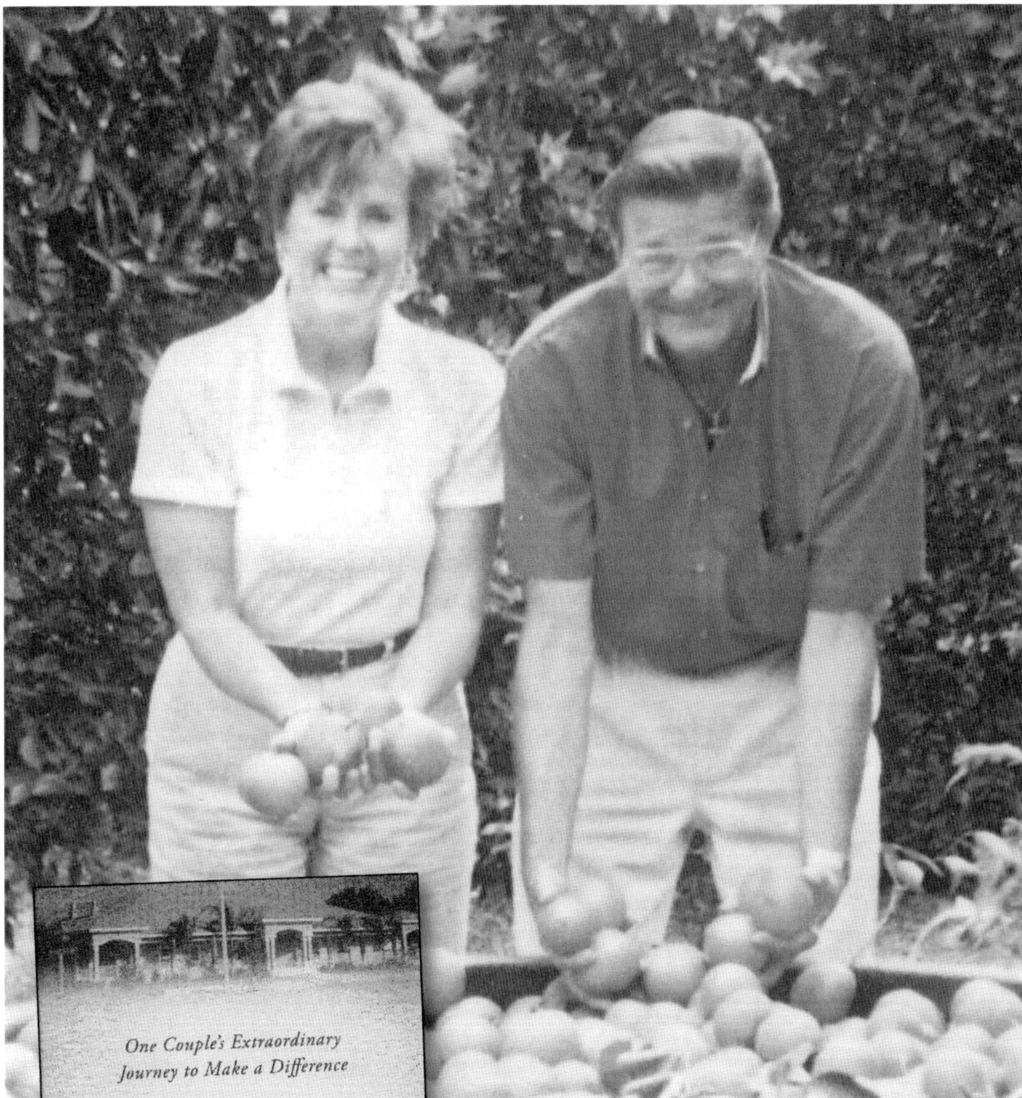

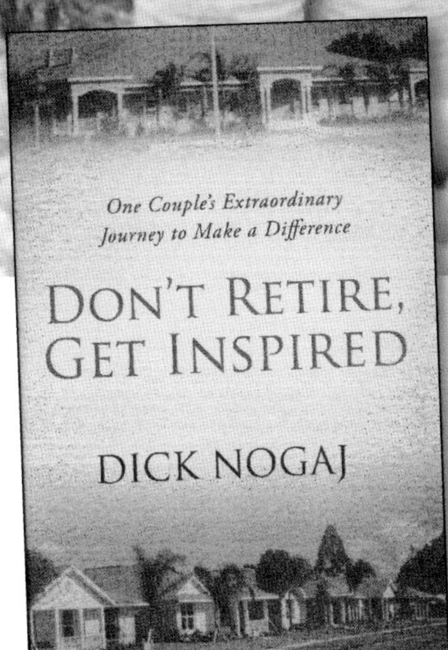

Don't Retire, Get Inspired

Dick and Florence Nogaj enjoy sun and success in Immokalee, Florida, where the Jubilation Development thrives. Left: Nogaj tells the story of his courtship with Florence, Habitat for Humanity, Harvest for Humanity, and Jubilation in his memoir *Don't Retire, Get Inspired.* It is dedicated to Florence: "You have helped me be a better person, and your steady, encouraging love and willingness to enter into a spiritual partnership with me enabled us to take this special risk-filled journey to make a difference in the lives of others. You have my care and respect, and you are my love." (Courtesy of Dick and Florence Nogaj.)

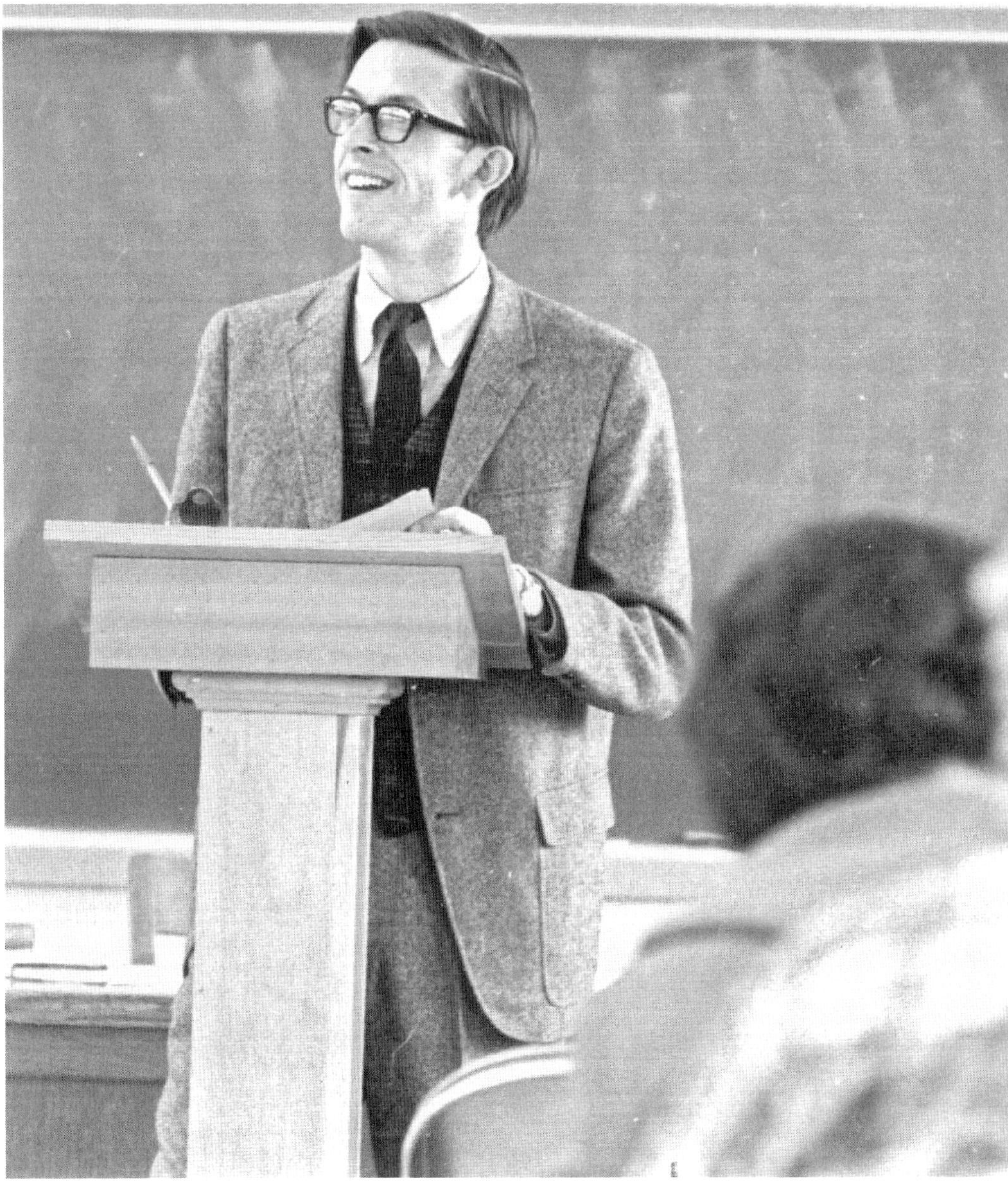

John Alexander

Teaching at Wheaton College in the late-1960s, philosophy professor John Alexander gained a reputation as a troublemaker, eloquently speaking against social injustice and the Vietnam War. He and his wife, Judy, had started a magazine called *Freedom Now* (which later became *The Other Side*), banned in the college bookstore. After leaving Wheaton, Alexander moved to Philadelphia and founded Jubilee Crafts, marketing Third World handcrafts while describing conditions in less-privileged countries to North Americans. In 1976, he founded Jubilee, Inc., its objective "to encourage and give technical and financial assistance to holistic ministries around the world that promote evangelism, development and justice." He was the author of two books, *Your Money or Your Life* and *The Secular Squeeze*. For the last 11 years of his life, he served as pastor of the Church of the Sojourners in San Francisco. Alexander died in 2001.

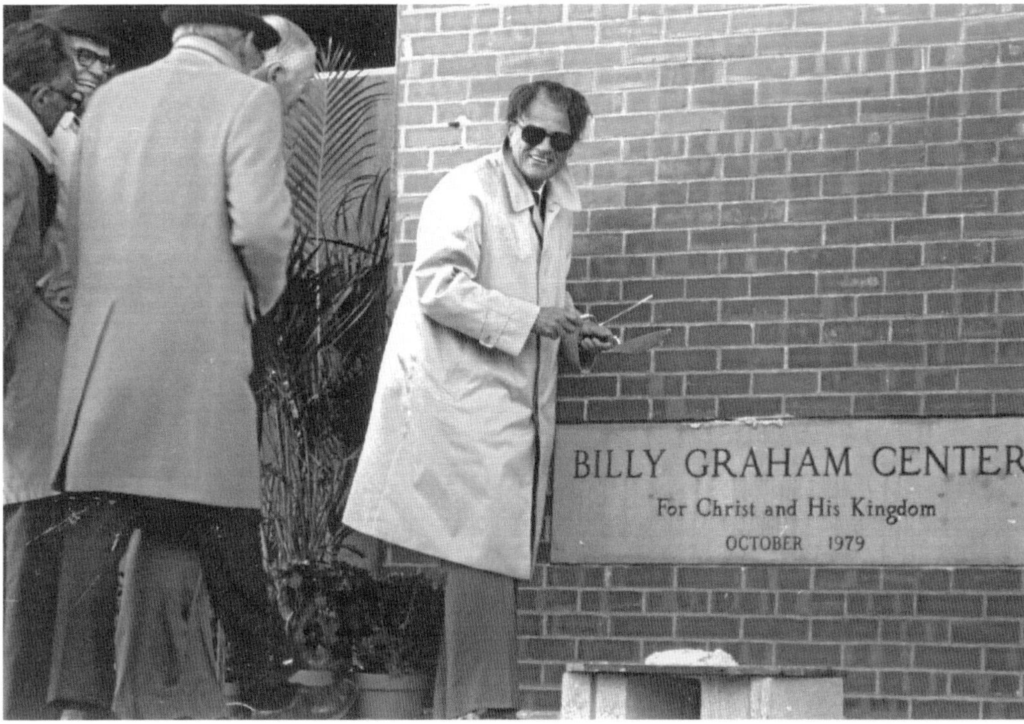

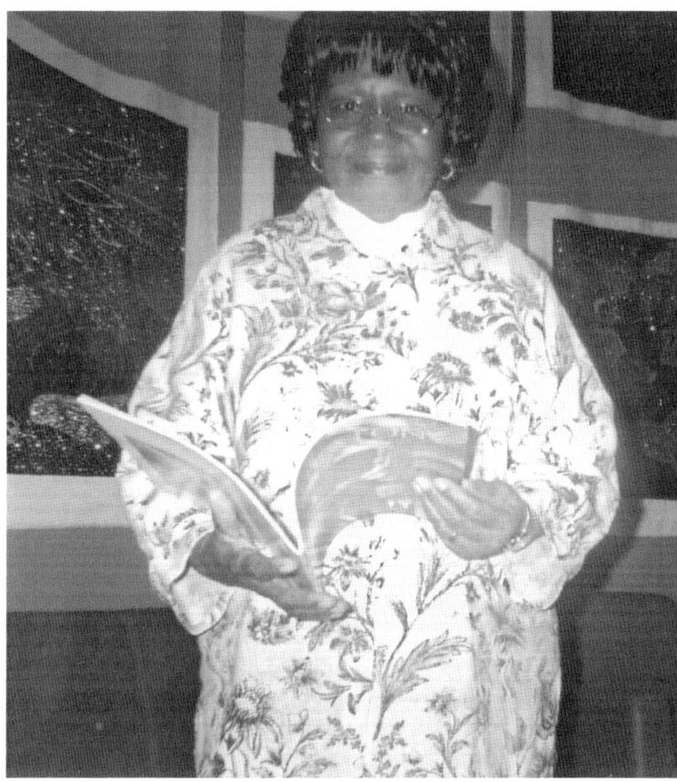

Billy Graham
A 1943 graduate of Wheaton College, evangelist Billy Graham has visited his alma mater on several occasions throughout the decades. At the 1980 dedication, he applies a bit of concrete to the cornerstone of the edifice that bears his name. Within are offices, classrooms, an auditorium, and the graduate school. On the first floor is a museum exhibiting Graham's evangelistic career and the history of American Protestant Christianity.

Norma Whitt
The gracious lady greeting visitors in the lobby of the Billy Graham Center is Norma Whitt, receptionist and guide since 1996. Displaying unfailing humility and kindness, Whitt often hears heartfelt reactions from guests as they finish touring the museum and art gallery. When a young man in the graduate program was asked about his greatest influence at school, he unhesitatingly cited Whitt as *numero uno.* (Courtesy of Norma Whitt.)

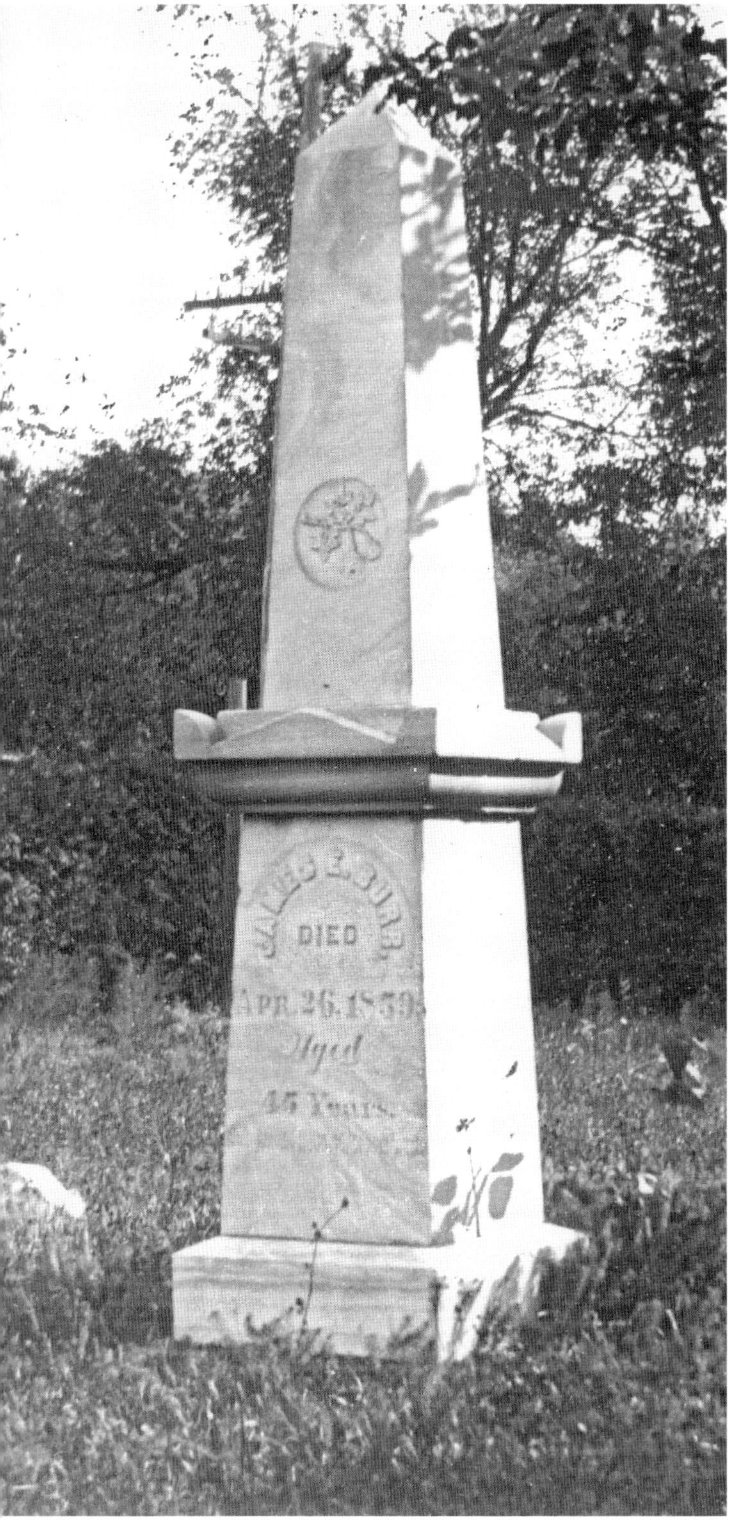

James Burr

This tombstone marks the only grave on the campus of Wheaton College. Its occupant, James Burr, was an ardent abolitionist who assisted runaway slaves at the Adelphia Theopolis Mission Institute in Quincy, Illinois. He received five years hard labor in the Missouri State Penitentiary as a result. Dying in 1859 of consumption contracted while incarcerated, Burr had requested to be buried on soil "untrampled by the slaver." And so he was brought to Wheaton College, nationally renowned for its battle against slavery. For years, the grave was marked by an obelisk, which suffered the vicissitudes of vandalism and weathering, in addition to the fact that it spooked girls in nearby Williston Dormitory. Burr's plot is now marked by a boulder affixed with a bronze plaque. Burr's grave is a somber reminder of the heavy price paid for freedom.

William Osborne (RIGHT)

Osborne, a freed slave, attached himself in 1865 to the 117th Illinois Infantry Regiment, which won the battle for Mobile. He was brought to Atlanta, Illinois, by Col. Jonathan Merriam, who provided for him until he enrolled in the college preparatory course at Wheaton College in 1869. Osborne, the first black president of the Beltonian Literary Society, was known for his melodious singing and skilled oration. After graduating, he served pastorates in Montana, Missouri, Washington, and Nebraska. He was a bishop in the African Methodist Episcopal Church. Osborne died in 1932. In 1987, Wheaton College students formed the William Osborne Society to promote self-identity and self-awareness among African American students.

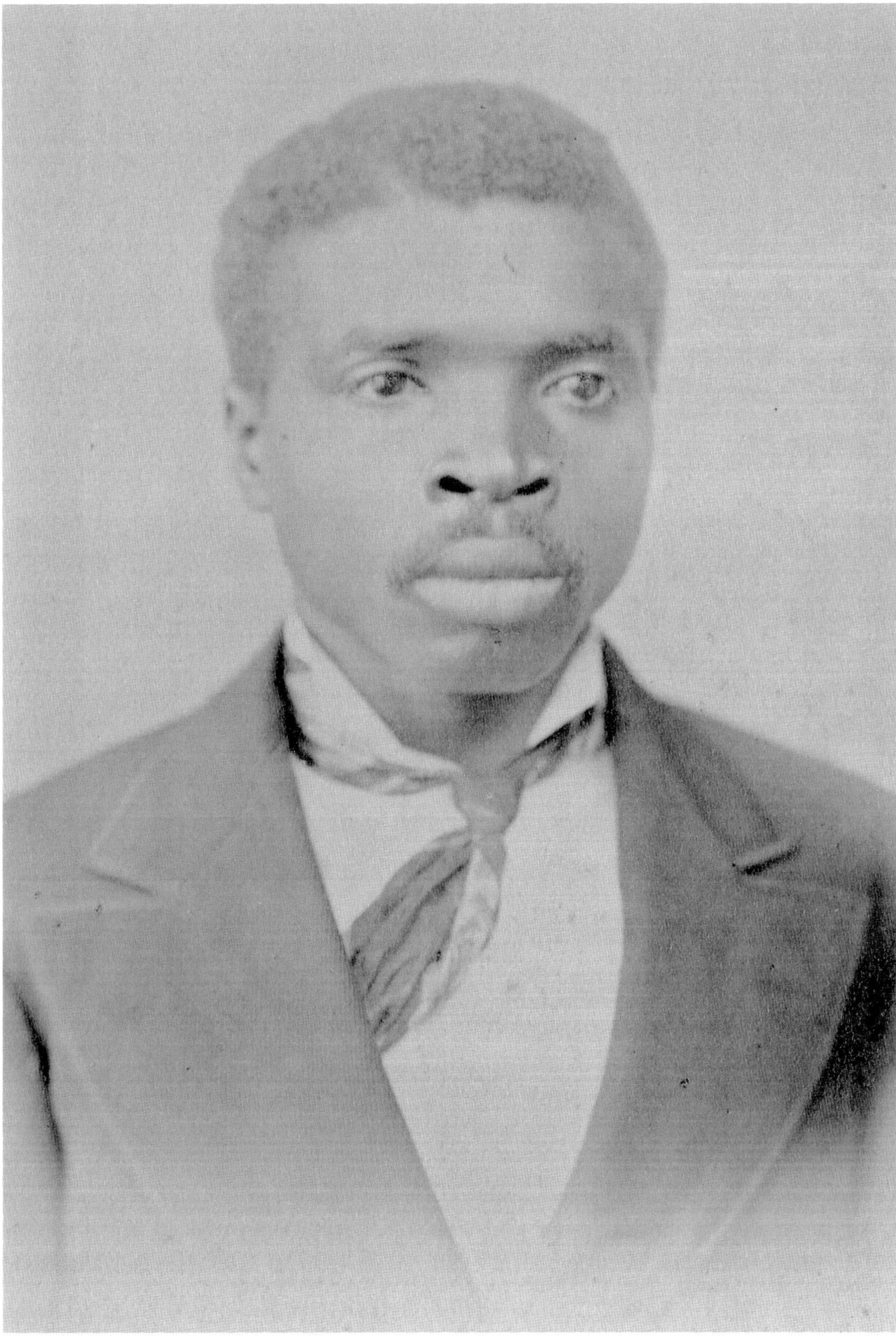

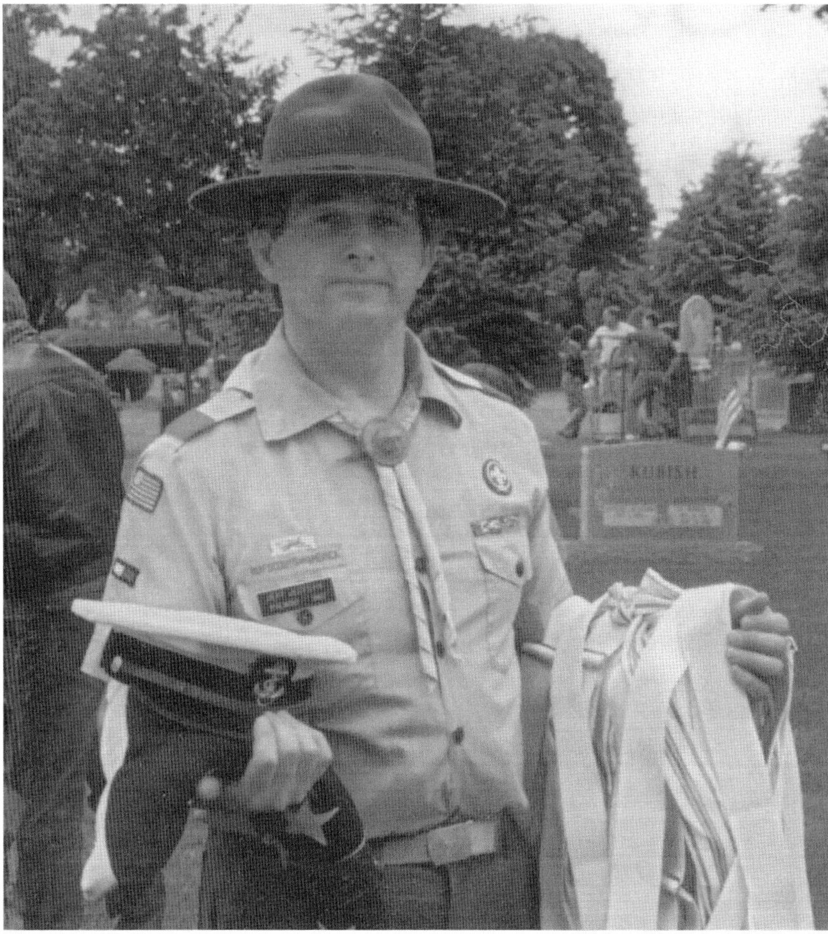

Frank E. Jeffers

After a Memorial Day parade and ceremony at the cemetery, Troop 23 scoutmaster Frank "Jeff" Jeffers collects the color guard items and straps used by the scouts to carry the flags. British general Robert Baden-Powell, founder of the scout movement, desired that his organization live honorably and leave the world better than it was found. Jeffers is committed to advancing this principle to his troop. Surveying the years of his service, it is difficult to estimate the number of boys he has influenced. As a youth, he was a scout in Troop 23 and is among a small majority of men who remain in the organization as a leader. Jeffers has been involved with scouting since he was a Cub Scout. Modeling conscientious leadership, he is known for never raising his voice or embarrassing a boy. Rather, he expertly guides his scouts to become trustworthy, principled men. One scout from Troop 23 remarks, "Mr. Jeffers was always one of the quiet guiding forces in our troop. He was always watching and would occasionally talk to a group of boys (or on rare occasions one in particular) reminding them to live up to their full potential. That might mean talking to boys about immature or hazardous activity and reminding them that they should be a better example; pointing out a necessary task that is being ignored. His quiet reminders were gentle and powerful, and boys often heeded his lessons in the future without prompting." At one scout's Court of Honor, Jeffers presented the Eagle Charge. The scout honored at this event is typically responsible for its organization, and Jeffers was requested by the scout to deliver the charge. The men who are asked by the scouts to participate in their Courts of Honor are the pillars of the troop leadership. When not occupied with scouting, Jeffers is an attorney with offices in Wheaton. (Courtesy of Augie Fackler.)

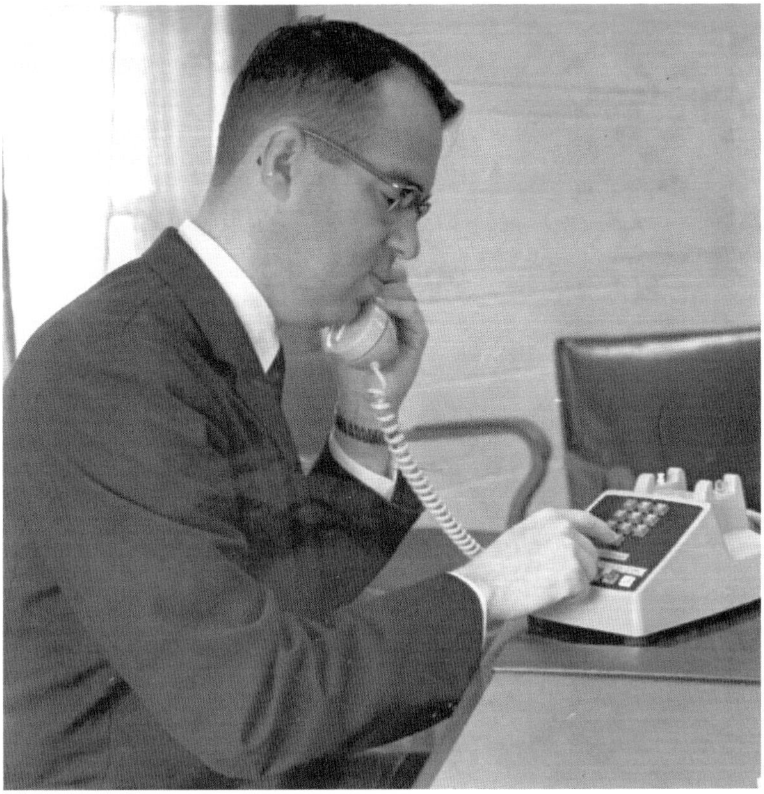

Ray Smith

As both editor of *Telephone Engineer & Management* and president of the Wheaton College Alumni Association, Smith is privileged in 1965 to dial the first TouchTone phone call in Wheaton, placing it to none other than fellow alum Billy Graham. Born in warlord China and raised in Hawaii, Smith—known as "Scribe"—insists Wheaton has held first place in his heart for the past 61 years. Entering Wheaton College in 1950, Smith served as the Crusaders' sports correspondent for the *Wheaton Daily Journal*. His crisp game reports and lively "Observations" column earned him the school's sports information director post. "Ray's six years set our 'gold standard,'" remembers Coach Lee Pfund. "His innovative promotion helped produce six All-Americans and scores of all-conference athlete votes in the 1950s." During decades of campus volunteerism, he co-founded the athletic Hall of Honor and led the booster club, served 20 years as an advisor of Honey Rock Camp, edited *Alumni* magazine, and today pens *Inside Wheaton* for 4,000 e-readers. Smith was honored with the school's Lifetime Friendship Award. As for his "day job," he enjoyed a distinguished 36-year career with companies or offices based in town: Hitchcock Publishing, Brookhill, HBJ Publications, and Advanstar Communications. As the nation's senior telecommunications technology journalist, he was editor and then publisher/vice president of business-to-business journals. Assignments to over 35 countries climaxed representing the US telephone industry at the opening of the American Embassy in Beijing in 1979. He was invited by the People's Republic of China to organize three trade and seminar missions. In semi-retirement, Smith as RHS Media Consulting has been a press liaison for the International Engineering Consortium. Smith was honored to serve for six years active and reserve duty in the US Army. He and the former Lillian Weaver of Glen Ellyn (a great-great granddaughter of founder Jonathan Blanchard) have two children (grads of Wheaton-Warrenville High and Wheaton College) and four grandkids who attended Wheaton Academy and Wheaton North. "I can't lose rooting for all of them," Smith chuckles. (Courtesy of Ray Smith.)

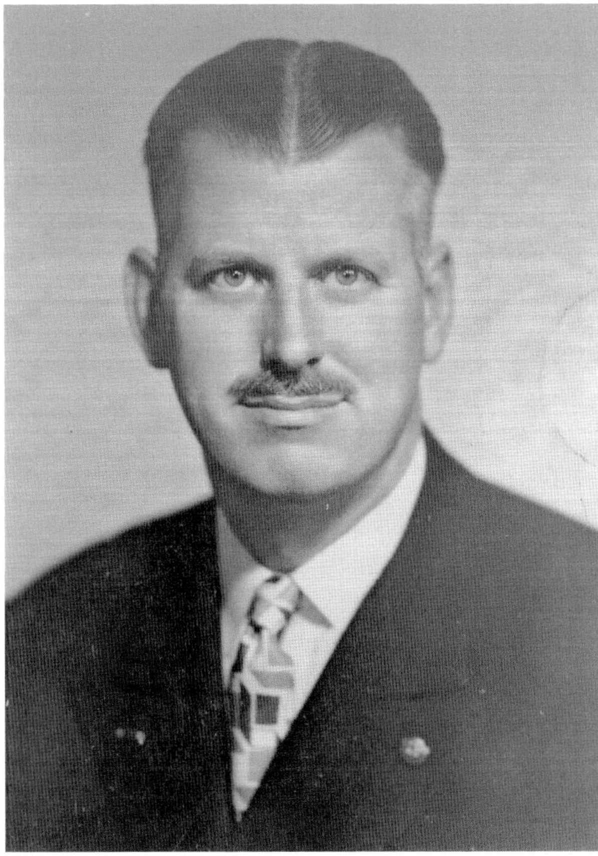

W. Wyeth Willard

Among the extraordinary individuals who have contributed to the soul of Wheaton College, few were more seasoned than Willard. Graduating from Brown University and Princeton Theological Seminary, Willard had already distinguished himself as an author, businessman, camp founder, and pastor before volunteering as a chaplain during World War II. Ministering to needy soldiers, he landed in 1943 with the 2nd Marine Division at the battle at Guadalcanal, and was awarded the Legion of Honor Medal for his service to them during the battle at Tarawa in the Gilbert Islands. According to one report he was "credited with serving more consecutive days under constant enemy fire than any chaplain in the history of the U.S. Navy and Marine Corps." In 1944, he was awarded the Legion of Merit, the Navy's highest honor. Lieutenant Willard's wartime chronicle, *The Leathernecks Come Through*, brought him national fame, and in February 1944, he was invited by Wheaton College to deliver its midwinter evangelistic services. So impressed were staff and students with the heroic 39-year-old that it was decided to hire him as director of evangelism and assistant to Pres. V. Raymond Edman. Moving his family from Cape Cod to Wheaton, Willard settled into his responsibilities. "It was easy to be loyal to Dr. Edman," he writes. "As we daily walked together across the campus for the college chapel worship services, he would greet a hundred students and call them by their first names. . . . He loved them all as though they were his sons and daughters . . ." Edman tasked Willard with writing the first history of the college, *Fire on the Prairie*. In 1951, the self-described "old goat of 46 years," seeking to sharpen his reasoning skills, departed Wheaton to study law at Northwestern University, earning his JD. But the pulpit called Willard from law, and he returned to the ministry as pastor in Barnstable on Cape Cod. In 1960, he was called to a church in Massachusetts, where he served for 22 years before retiring. His memoir, *Confessions of a Minister*, appeared in 1975. He died in 2000 at 94.

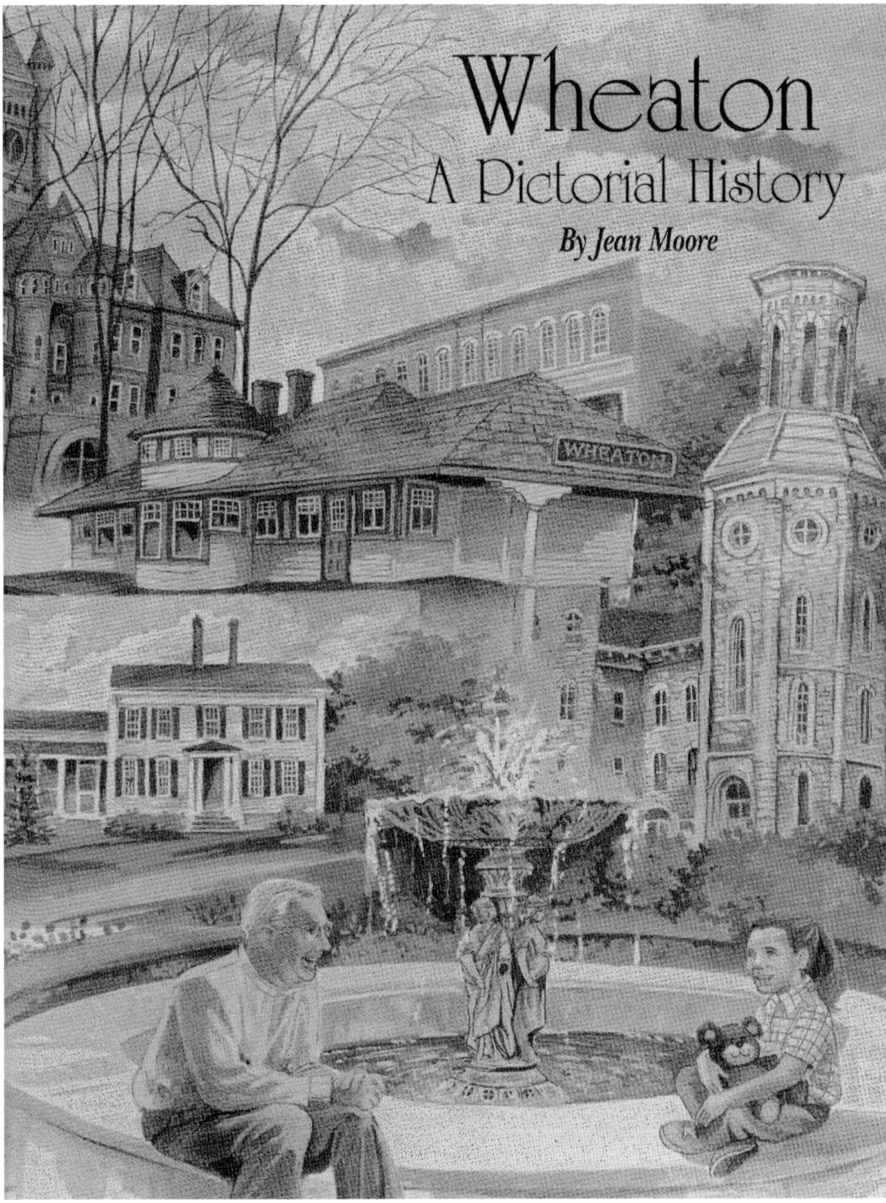

Jean Moore

The royal historian of Wheaton and DuPage County, Moore, journalist and newspaper executive, designed and raised funds for prominent history exhibits, particularly the Pioneer Wall at the DuPage Heritage Gallery. She was past president of the DuPage Press Association, founder of the Suburban Press Club, and wrote local histories, including *Wheaton: A Pictorial History* and *From Tower to Tower: A History of Wheaton, Illinois*, containing riveting reminiscence from old-timers. "There are few communities in the nation which can compare with Wheaton . . . in sending forth giants to do battle in the world," she writes. "Some of these persons have been lifelong residents . . . while others are here for only a brief period of time . . ." Her diligent fact-gathering laid the groundwork for all further local history research. Her husband, Ace, was an associate producer for Mutual of Omaha's *Wild Kingdom*. Moore died in 2010.

Larry Ward

Known as "the man who probably has looked into more hungry faces than any other man," Ward's compassion was genuinely as wide as the world. A tireless advocate for the homeless and starving, he graduated from Wheaton College with high honors in 1949. After several years editing magazines and books, Ward served as vice president of World Vision and held other administrative positions before founding "Food for the Hungry" in 1971. Driven by his tireless Christian charity for the impoverished, Ward directed earthquake relief in Nicaragua; distributed food in Honduras; led the "mercy ship" operation for the exodus of thousands of Vietnamese from Saigon; and established "Hope Village" for 1,100 refugees in Weimar, California. Constantly engaging logistical issues, he led multiple innovative programs, stressing appropriate technology, utilization of renewable energy sources, and emphasis on urban and desert agriculture. In 1981, his alma mater, Wheaton College, awarded him its Distinguished Service to Society Award, recognizing outstanding professional accomplishments. The ceremony featured videotaped greetings from Robert H. Schuller, Pat Robertson, Jerry Falwell, Oral Roberts, and Jimmy Swaggart. That evening he also received a plaque from "The League of Families" honoring his efforts on behalf of American MIAs (Missing in Action) in Vietnam and Laos. After Ward retired in 1984, Ronald Reagan named him an "Honorary Ambassador to the Hungry World," writing, "Your good works, your sincerity and your consistent and constant message shine as a beacon of hope that mankind can be noble and good." Ward then advocated on behalf of the hungry in Australia, Japan, Canada, and the United States. His tendency was to cut through red tape and directly tackle frontline relief in the sore spots of the world. He died in 2003.

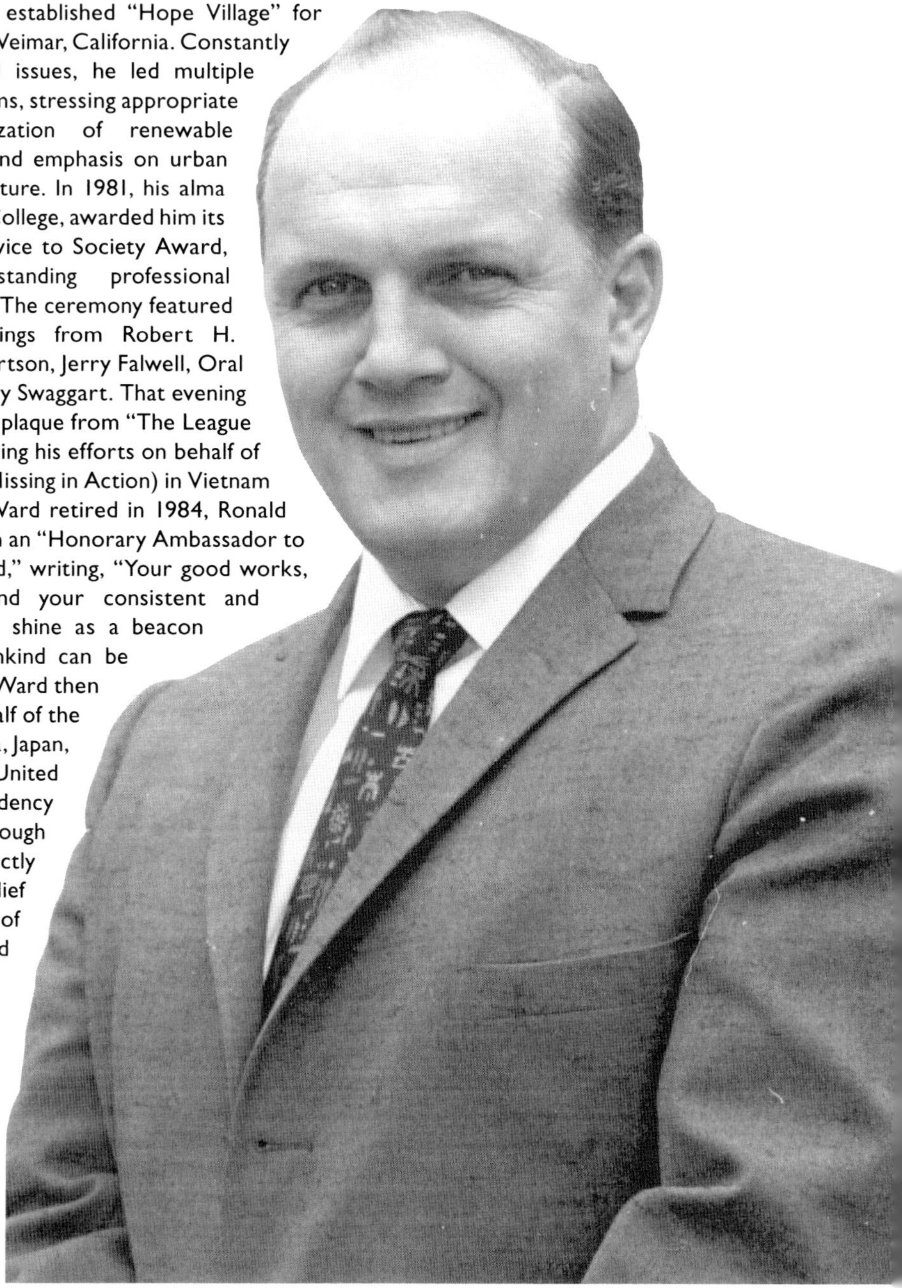

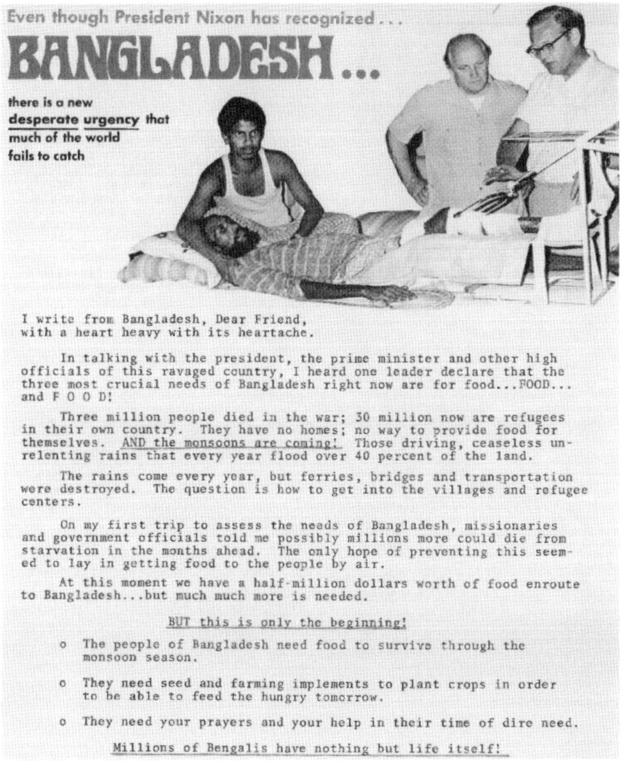

Even though President Nixon has recognized . . .

BANGLADESH...

there is a new **desperate urgency** that much of the world fails to catch

I write from Bangladesh, Dear Friend, with a heart heavy with its heartache.

In talking with the president, the prime minister and other high officials of this ravaged country, I heard one leader declare that the three most crucial needs of Bangladesh right now are for food...FOOD... and F O O D!

Three million people died in the war; 30 million now are refugees in their own country. They have no homes; no way to provide food for themselves. AND the monsoons are coming! Those driving, ceaseless unrelenting rains that every year flood over 40 percent of the land.

The rains come every year, but ferries, bridges and transportation were destroyed. The question is how to get into the villages and refugee centers.

On my first trip to assess the needs of Bangladesh, missionaries and government officials told me possibly millions more could die from starvation in the months ahead. The only hope of preventing this seemed to lay in getting food to the people by air.

At this moment we have a half-million dollars worth of food enroute to Bangladesh...but much much more is needed.

BUT this is only the beginning!

- The people of Bangladesh need food to survive through the monsoon season.
- They need seed and farming implements to plant crops in order to be able to feed the hungry tomorrow.
- They need your prayers and your help in their time of dire need.

Millions of Bengalis have nothing but life itself!

Food for the Hungry
In a "Food for the Hungry" newsletter, Ward reports his trip to Bangladesh and solicits support. "Food for the Hungry was formed out of the recognition that bodies must be kept alive," he writes, "so that souls can be saved." Below: The humanitarian lifts anchor on a mercy ship mission to Vietnamese boat people in the South China Sea, 1980. Whenever discouraged at the magnitude of his mission, Ward reminded himself with this simple logic: "They die one at a time, so we can help them one at a time." His inspring story is told in *This Poor Man Cried* by Norman Rohrer.

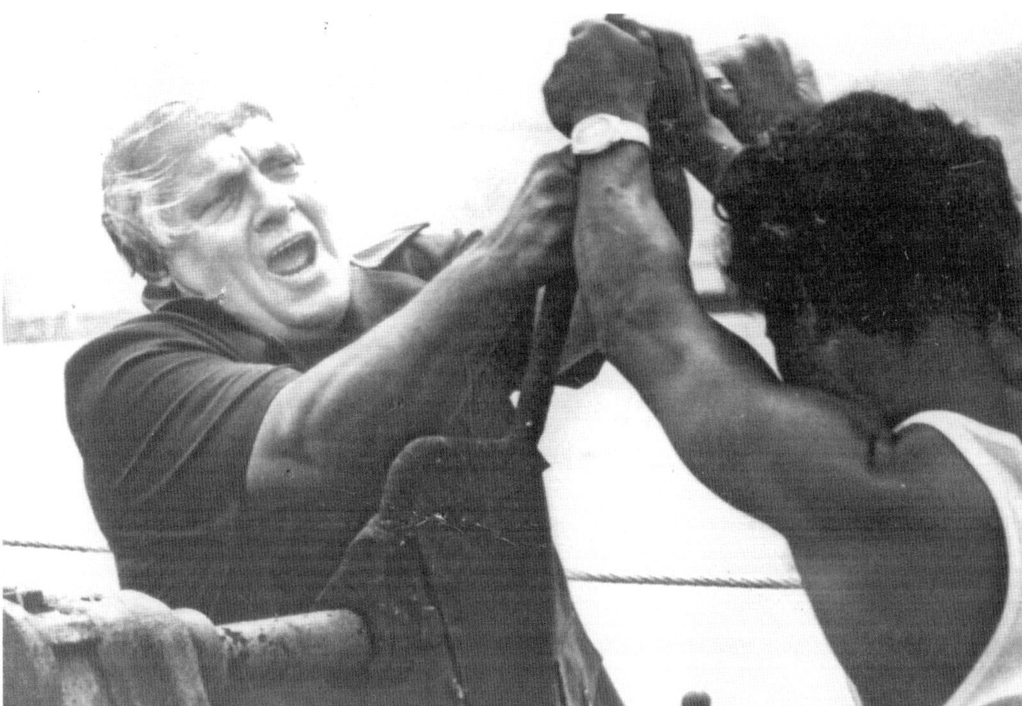

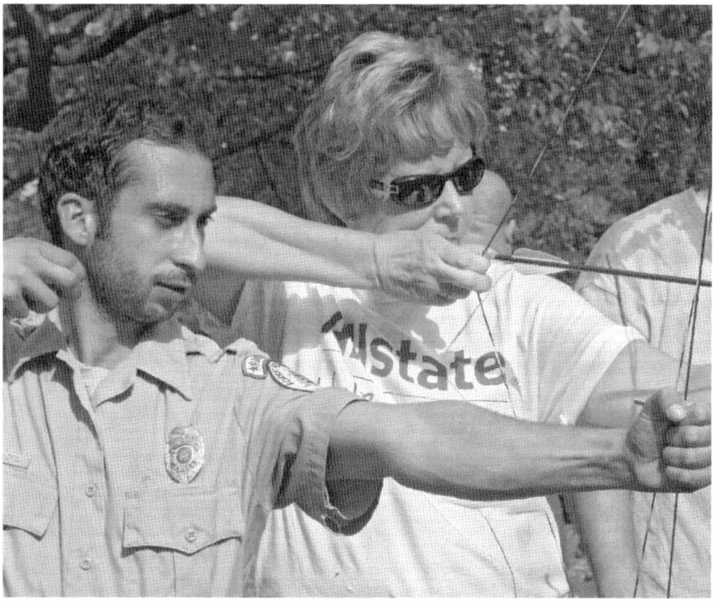

Ranger Dan Touzious, Forest Preserve District of DuPage County
Touzious provides introductory archery instruction to a forest preserve visitor. The district is constructing an archery and recreation complex at Blackwell Forest Preserve in Warrenville, funded by a grant from the Open Space Lands Acquisition and Development Program. The complex, which will open during spring 2012, will feature three archery ranges, a picnic shelter, a fishing pier, and a paved trail. (Courtesy of the Forest Preserve District of DuPage County.)

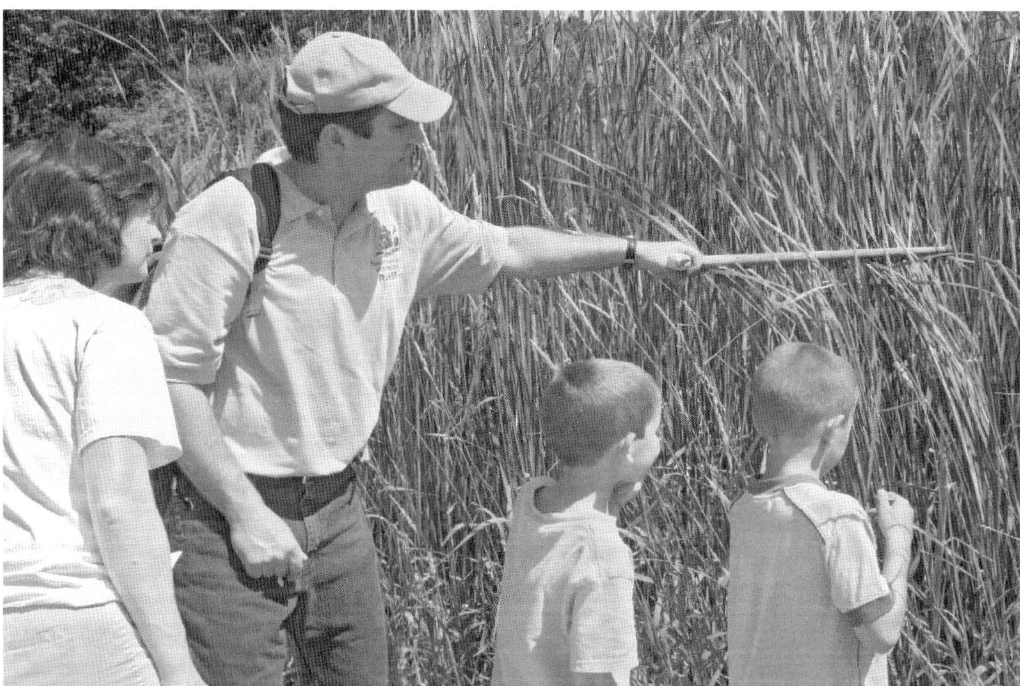

Ranger Ray Soszynski
Soszynski leads a trek off the beaten path to discover native wildlife in a DuPage forest preserve. The Forest Preserve District of DuPage County was established in 1915 when voters cast ballots to preserve woodlands. The district continues to serve the county through its mission "to acquire and hold lands for the purpose of preserving the flora, fauna and scenic beauty for the education, pleasure and recreation" of citizens. (Courtesy of the Forest Preserve District of DuPage County.)

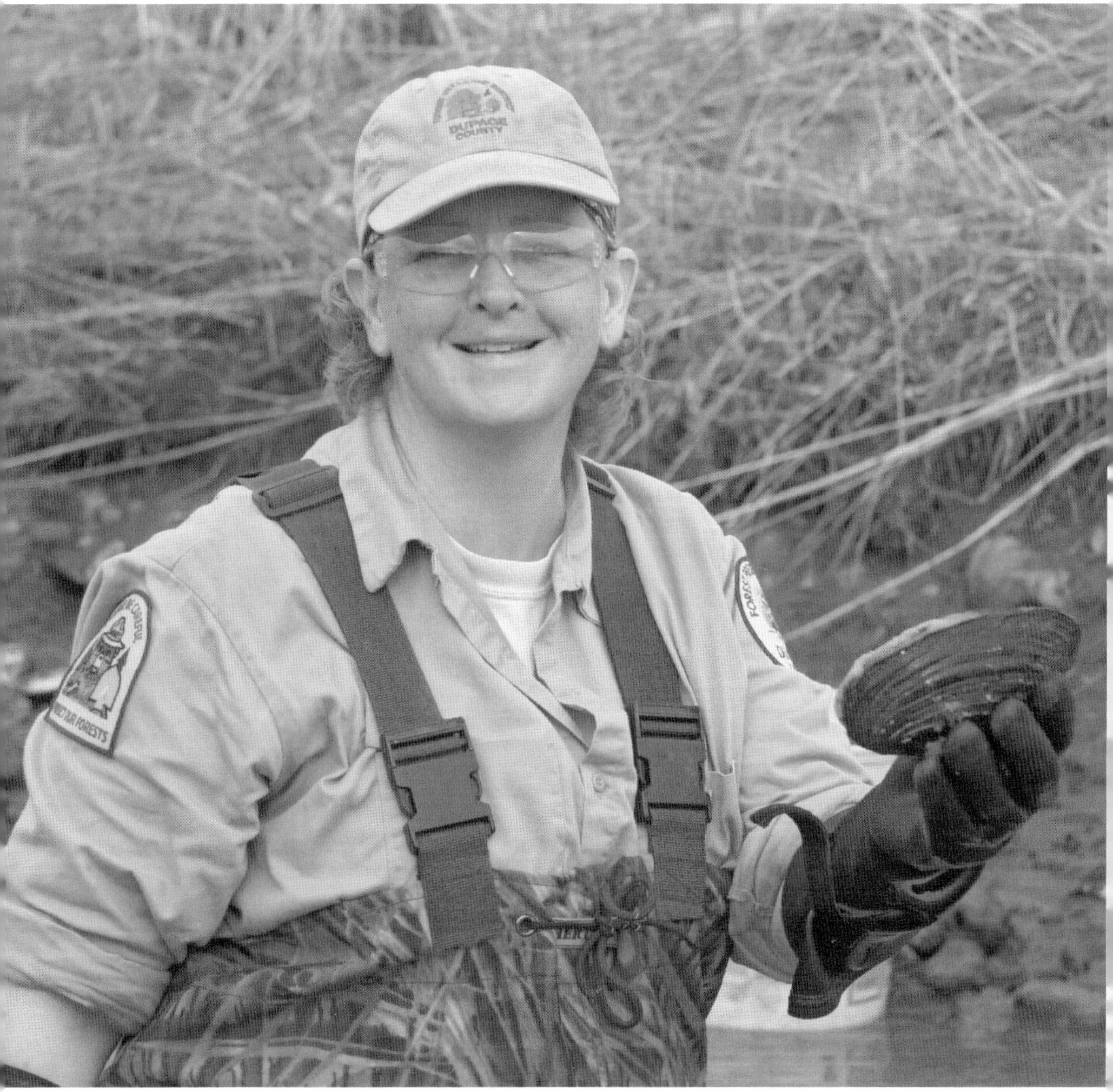

Kathy Pulte

Forest Preserve District natural resource management technician Kathy Pulte relocates a giant floater *(Pyganodon grandis)* mussel during the Spring Brook meander project at Springbrook Prairie Forest Preserve in Naperville. The two-mile stream restoration project created a meandering channel, restored natural functions, improved water quality, and enhanced habitat along the waterway. The district's Natural Areas Management Program promotes ecological conditions that sustain and preserve native plant and animal communities. As part of natural area management, district staff and volunteers work to remove invasive and exotic vegetation, propagate native plant species and, in some cases, reintroduce native wildlife in some of the county's high-quality natural areas. The district is steward to over 25,000 acres at 60 preserves and one state park. (Courtesy of the Forest Preserve District of DuPage County.)

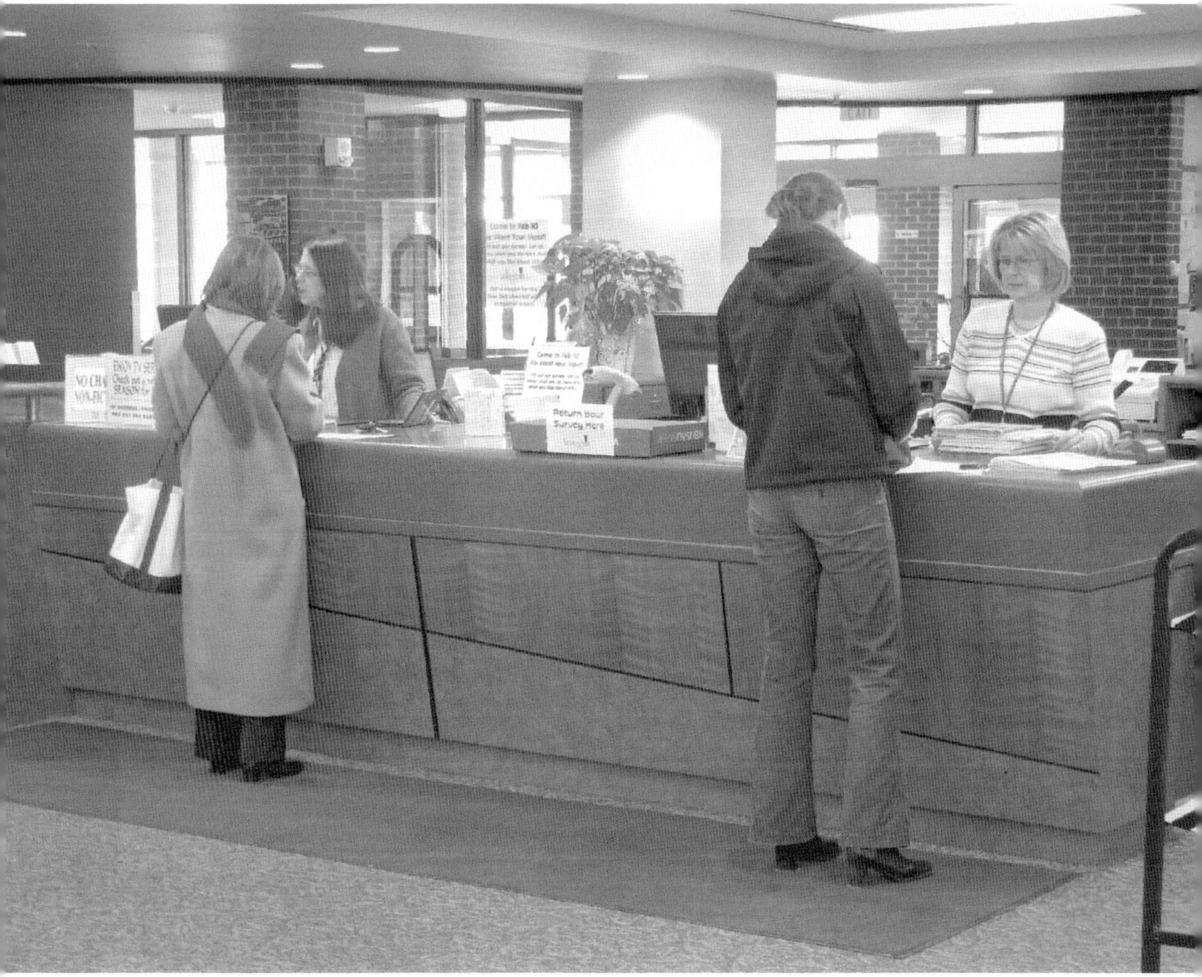

Wheaton Public Library
Circulation staff Laurel Kiburg (left) and Sue Spreenberg (right) check out materials for patrons. "Librarians are the secret masters of the world," says science fiction writer Spider Robinson. "They control the flow of information. Don't anger them." No sensible citizen would dream of angering the magnificent custodians of world knowledge at Wheaton Public Library. Approachable and knowledgeable, the Wheaton Public Library staff is expert in leading a reader to the right book, or the researcher to the appropriate resource. Perhaps more than any other institution, the library provides the heart and soul of Wheaton. (Courtesy of Wheaton Public Library.)

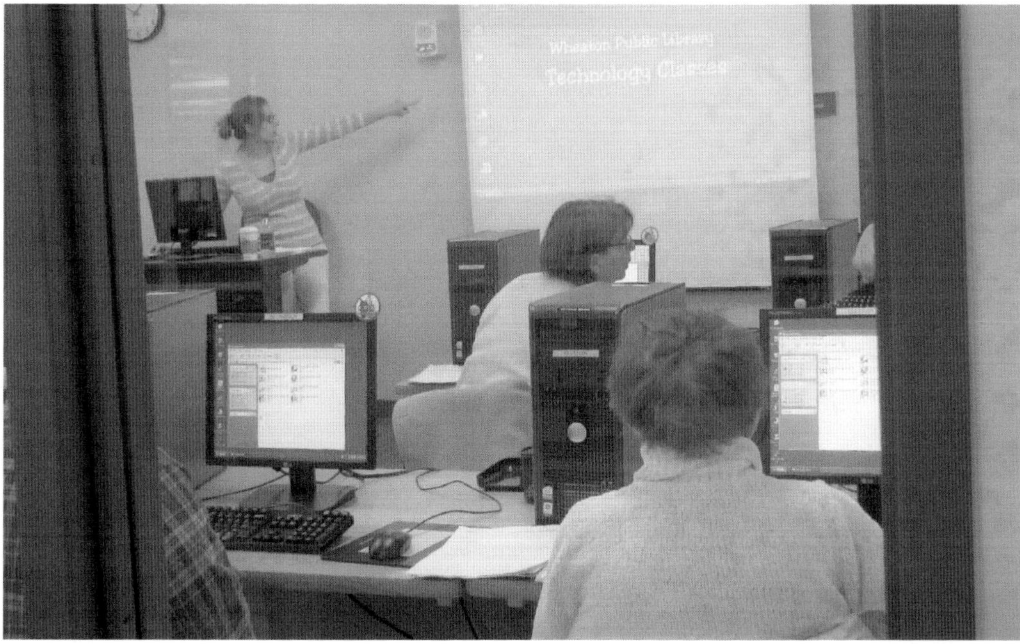

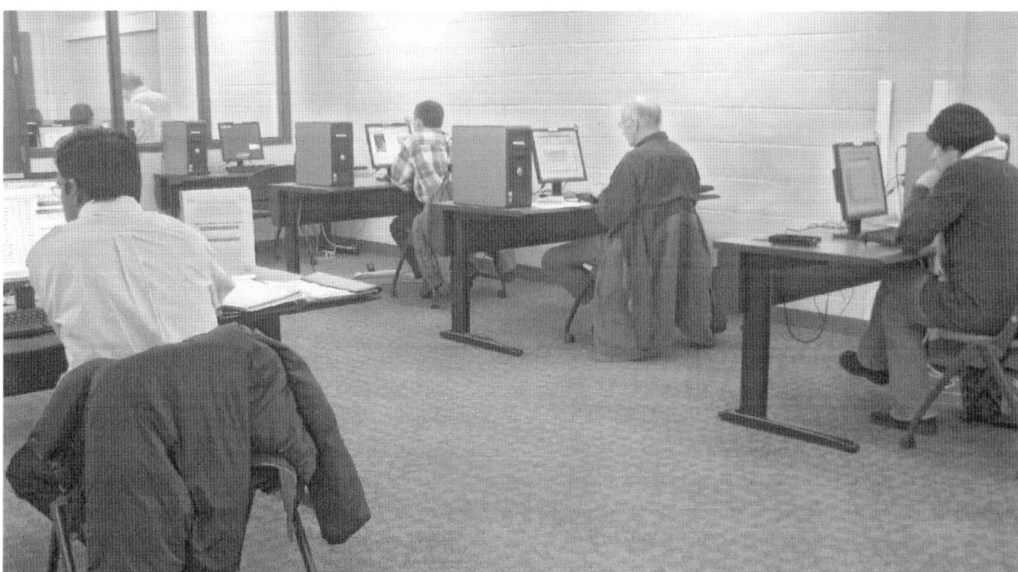

"Smart Classroom"

Information technology librarian Eileen Crowley instructs a class in Internet usage in the "smart" classroom on the second floor of Wheaton Public Library. The recently expanded building hosts concerts, book discussions, and a genealogical section pertaining to DuPage County, Wheaton, and the Civil War. The kids' section on the lower level offers games for preschool and grade school, and homework help, including databases featuring maps, periodicals, and dictionaries. The library also hosts an array of programs and events, including an opportunity for children ages two to five, accompanied by an adult chaperone, to join a naturalist from Lincoln Marsh to hear a nature-themed story and participate in a related craft or activity. (Courtesy of Wheaton Public Library.)

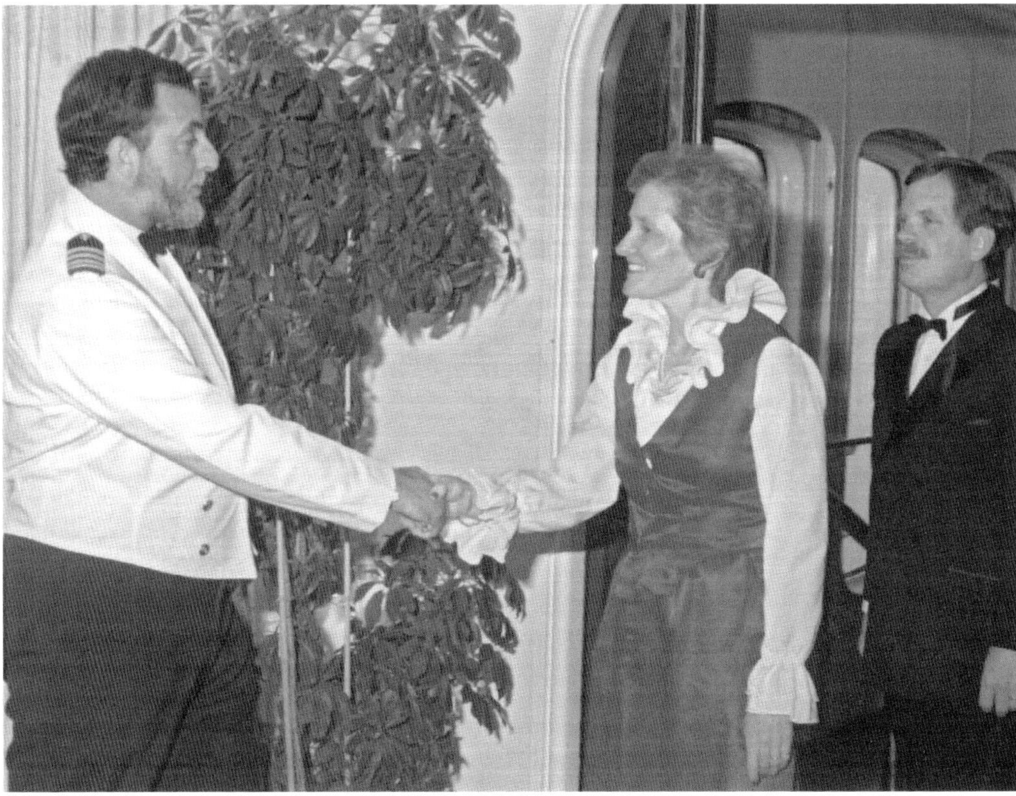

William and Mary Anne Phemister

The captain of the *Queen Elizabeth II* in 1984 welcomes aboard William Phemister, a featured concert pianist on three transatlantic crossings, and his wife Mary Anne. As the result of their globetrotting, the Phemisters are frequently asked, "Where next?" William Phemister, a graduate of the Juilliard School, the Ecole Normale de Musique (Paris), and the Peabody Conservatory, where he received the doctor of musical arts with conductor Leon Fleisher, has received international acclaim for his musicianship, touring Africa, Asia, Japan, and Afghanistan. He has performed concerts in New York, Moscow, Paris, Geneva, Helsinki, Australia, North Korea, and the Bahamas. His lecture recitals featuring French and American music illustrated with relevant art are particularly engaging to lovers of music. He is comfortable as soloist, accompanist, chamber musician, organist, conductor, and teacher. After a 35-year teaching career at Wheaton College, Phemister is now professor emeritus, still instructing, performing, and composing. His talents are perfectly complemented with those of his wife, Mary Anne. Born in China to missionary parents, she echoes Pearl Buck, who, when asked about home, replies, "I'm not quite at home anywhere and somewhat at home everywhere." After the publication of *32 Wheaton Notables: Their Stories and Where They Lived*, Mary Anne realized her deeply personal reason for writing: "It made me a kind of mini-expert in the town in which I have lived for the past 38 years. Finally, I had my own strong, settled sense of place." She relates the circumstances of her youth in *Lessons from a Broken Chapstick: A Memoir of a Peculiar Childhood.* Multitalented and venturesome, Mary Anne has enjoyed careers as a registered nurse, parent, and massage therapist, and now writes and edits. She volunteers at the Outreach Community Center in Carol Stream, where she tutors students. The Phemisters, aficionados of C.S. Lewis and the Inklings, frequently host guests in their spacious, relaxed Wheaton home; indeed, like J.R.R. Tolkien's Rivendell, it is "a perfect house, whether you like food or sleep or storytelling or singing, or just sitting and thinking best, or a pleasant mixture of them all." (Courtesy of Mary Anne Phemister.)

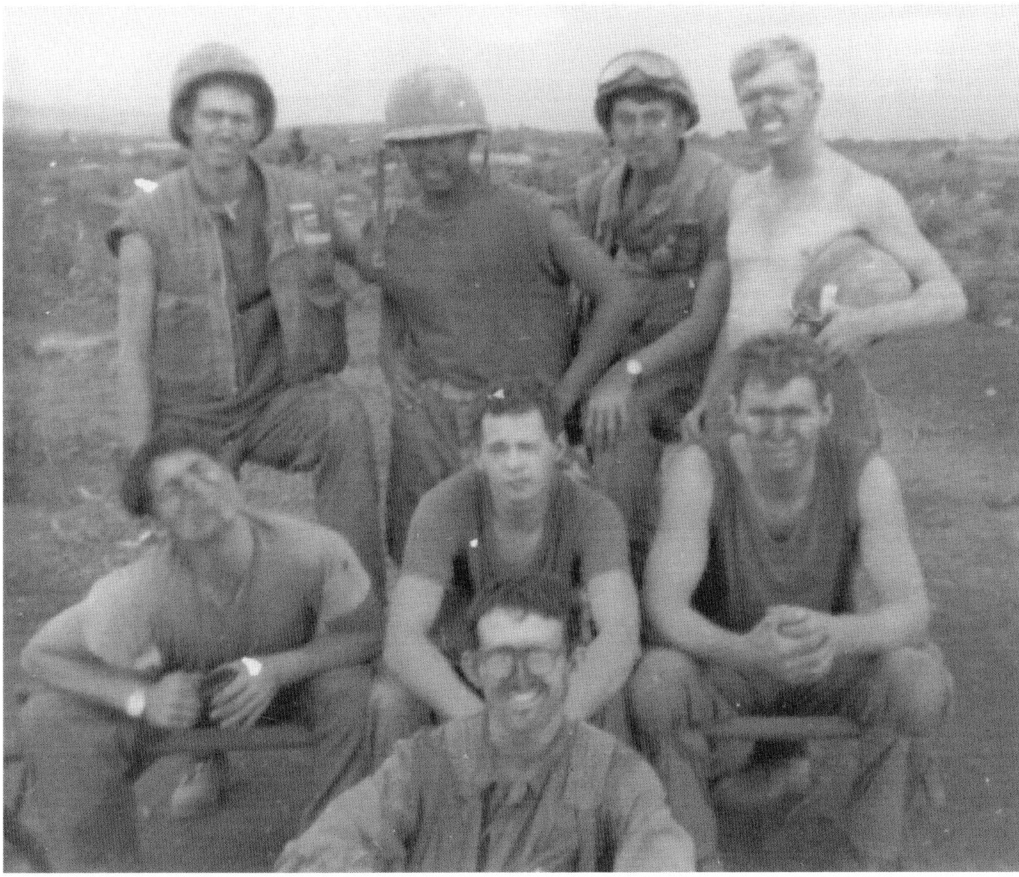

Midwest Shelter for Homeless Veterans
Robert M. Adams (bottom, center) poses with his squad in Vietnam, 1968, after enjoying their first bath in three months when, after a tank ride, they are splashed with mud. As a veteran, Adams is acquainted with the filth, confusion, and degradation of war. Through the years, he saw his comrades return to the United States from the horror of battle only to encounter scorn, addiction, and homelessness—conditions he found decidedly unacceptable. Quite simply, Adams believes that the men and women who have honorably served this country deserve a home. Founded and incorporated in 2000 by Adams, the Midwest Shelter for Homeless Veterans opened in 2007, offering a variety of independent living/transition housing services. Adams, a US Navy combat veteran of the Vietnam War and a licensed clinical social worker (LCSW) in private practice, has provided individual, group, and family therapy especially for veterans. As president, co-founder, and clinical director of the shelter, he specializes in the treatment of post-traumatic stress disorder. The shelter provides for five veterans of any era, offering opportunities for medical and psychological treatment, education, and job training. In DuPage County, one out of every three homeless is a veteran. In 2009, Adams was honored by the American Red Cross of Greater Chicago as a Military Hero, the award presented to an active, reserve, ROTC, or retired member(s) of the Armed Forces who acted above and beyond the call of duty. The Midwest Shelter for Homeless Veterans recently completed the purchase of a second property in downtown Wheaton, which will eventually provide affordable housing for six additional veterans and space for a female veteran. The shelter announced that the accommodations will honor the memory of Staff Sgt. Robert J. Miller, a Medal of Honor recipient and a graduate of Wheaton North High School. "What old warriors are supposed to be doing," says Adams, "is taking care of the younger ones." (Courtesy of Bob Adams.)

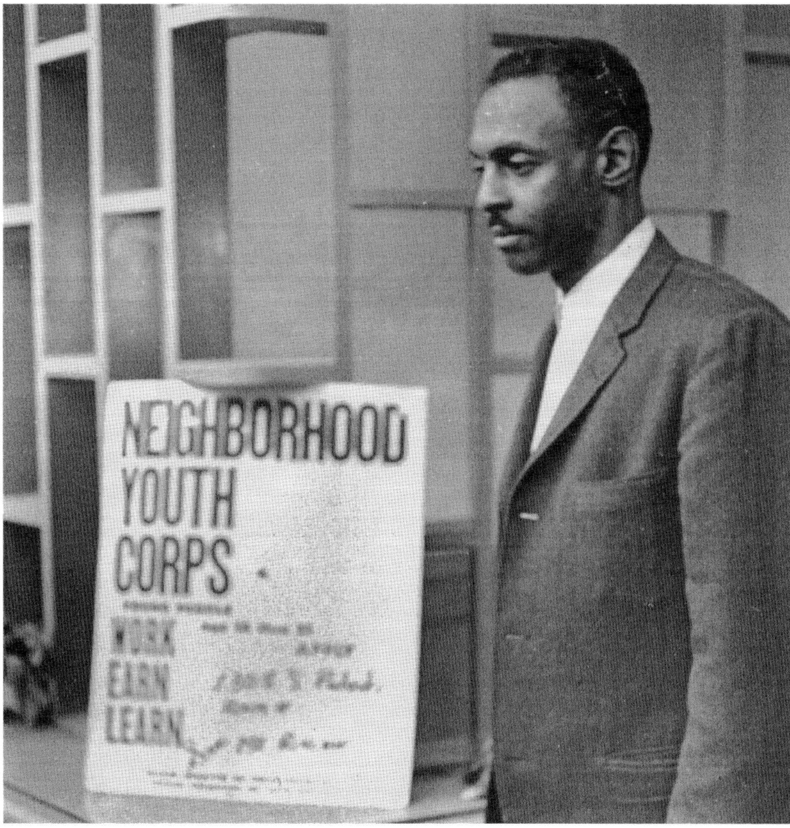

George Dryden

Announcing in 1967 that he was "The best street worker in the United States," Dryden was not bragging so much as simply stating the truth. Born in Wheaton in 1934, Dryden grew up in a strict, thrifty Baptist household, the youngest of four boys. A robustly athletic lad, he frequented the Physical Education Department at Wheaton College, befriending the coaches. Soon he was receiving friendly visits from Pres. V. Raymond Edman, who attempted to convince him to attend the school. Though Dryden had been offered scholarships from all Big Ten schools except Michigan, he finally surrendered to Edman's persuasion. Playing brilliantly, Dryden, slim and agile, was one of the first black athletes to wear the Crusaders football uniform. One coach was so fond of Dryden that he continually showcased his life to players as an example of sheer perseverance. After serving with distinction in the Air Force during the Korean War, Dryden returned to Chicago, gravitating to juvenile work, finding employment at the Sears Roebuck YMCA. Though he had initially desired to be a physical education director, YMCA executives wanted him as a "detached worker," sending him directly to the streets rather than administering activities from an office. Confident and charismatic, Dryden's natural abilities were perfectly suited for relating to gangs, quickly gaining their confidence and respect. He proved extraordinarily effective, often interceding with police and judges, if necessary. Slowed down in 1964 by tuberculosis, which confined him to a facility for two years, Dryden returned to work and often spoke to such groups as the Wheaton League of Women Voters and the Wheaton Lion's Club. Eventually he was hired by the City of Chicago Department of Education, and later employed by the board of education at the Illinois Juvenile Division Correctional School. Dryden's tuberculosis returned and for the final two years of his life he was hospitalized at the Municipal Tuberculosis Sanitarium in Chicago. He died at 62 in 1991. His funeral was conducted at the First Unity Missionary Baptist Church on the South Side of Chicago, of which he was a member. He is buried in Wheaton Cemetery.

CHAPTER FOUR

The Visionaries

The Honorable Michael Gresk, mayor of the City of Wheaton, speaking at the 2010 inauguration ceremony of Dr. Philip Ryken, eighth president of Wheaton College, rightly observes, "Mayor Warren Wheaton, first mayor of the city of Wheaton and President Jonathan Blanchard, first president of the College, were both men of vision—a shared vision of greatness for our town and for our community . . . The cooperative synergy we have enjoyed for 150 years has meant that both entities have not only survived, but we have prospered and we have thrived because of each other." From its inception as struggling prairie village to the present, Wheaton has hosted an extraordinary variety of visionaries, from those looking at religious, political, or scientific issues in the city, to those looking beyond its boundaries to the possibilities of space exploration, or backward down the corridors of time to the enigmas of history. Jonathan Blanchard, bull-headed and indignant, envisioned the abolition of slavery and hurled himself into that cause. Here Edwin Hubble set his eye to the stars, and here Grote Reber pressed his ear to the mountainside of space, listening to its weird, discordant music. Shannon Lucid, attending Wheaton College for two years, surpassed Hubble and Reber, actually traveling to space, orbiting Earth. Engineer John Belle designs aerospace technology. Dean Arnold, anthropologist, dedicated himself to solving the puzzle of Maya Blue, the mysterious pigment coloring ancient stoneware and murals. David Maas, historian, knew in his heart that the answer to the question of whether Wheaton was a stop on the Underground Railroad or not was out there . . . and he found it. Explorer David Fasold, examining ancient texts, believed that he discovered the ruins of Noah's Ark. Theologian Robert E. Webber changed the way many evangelicals worship, examining the past while partnering it with the present. Kay McKeen harbored a vision for sustainability and now heads an international organization dedicated to recycling. The "cooperative synergy" of which Gresk eloquently speaks nourishes not only the city, but the world.

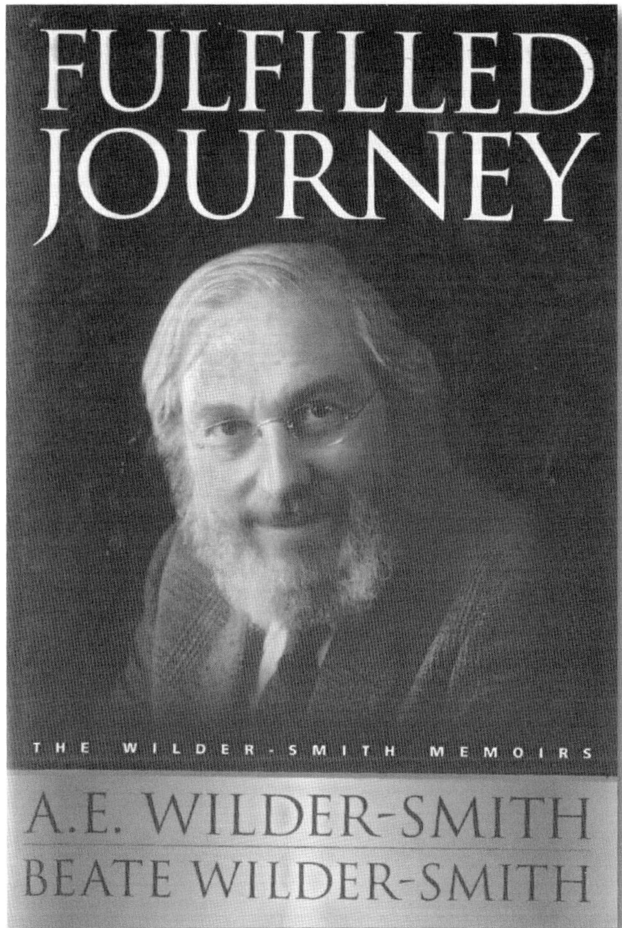

A.E. Wilder-Smith

A proper English gentleman, educated at Oxford and the University of Geneva, the soft-spoken but razor-sharp pharmacologist Arthur Ernest Wilder-Smith addressed students on campuses worldwide, calmly challenging with courtesy and impeccable academic credentials evolutionary theories and Old Earth Creationism. Employed for five years as professor of pharmacology at the University of Illinois (where he twice received the "Best Teacher of the Year" award), he writes in his autobiography, *Fulfilled Journey*, "we sought a house in Wheaton, a suburb about thirty miles from the center of Chicago . . . The church we attended in Wheaton was Bethany Chapel (a church of the Open Brethren) where I sometimes helped with the ministry on Sundays. We were very happy there . . ." Returning to Europe in 1969, Wilder-Smith served as consultant and drug advisor in the rank of three-star general for US NATO Forces in Europe in the Drug Abuse Program to officers and servicemen. Lecturing extensively, he was popular with students, scientists, laymen, and military personnel. He received three Golden Apple awards for the best course lectures, and four senior lecturer awards for the best series of senior-year lectures. His books include *Man's Origin, Man's Destiny*, *The Creation of Life* and *The Scientific Alternative to Neo-Darwinian Evolutionary Theory*. Many of his books are published by The Word for Today, an arm of Chuck Smith's Calvary Chapel denomination. William A. Dembski, mathematician, philosopher, and author of *Darwin's Black Box*, a foundational text in the Intelligent Design movement, cites Wilder-Smith as a major influence. His wife, Beate, completed his biography after his death in 1995. (Courtesy of the Word for Today.)

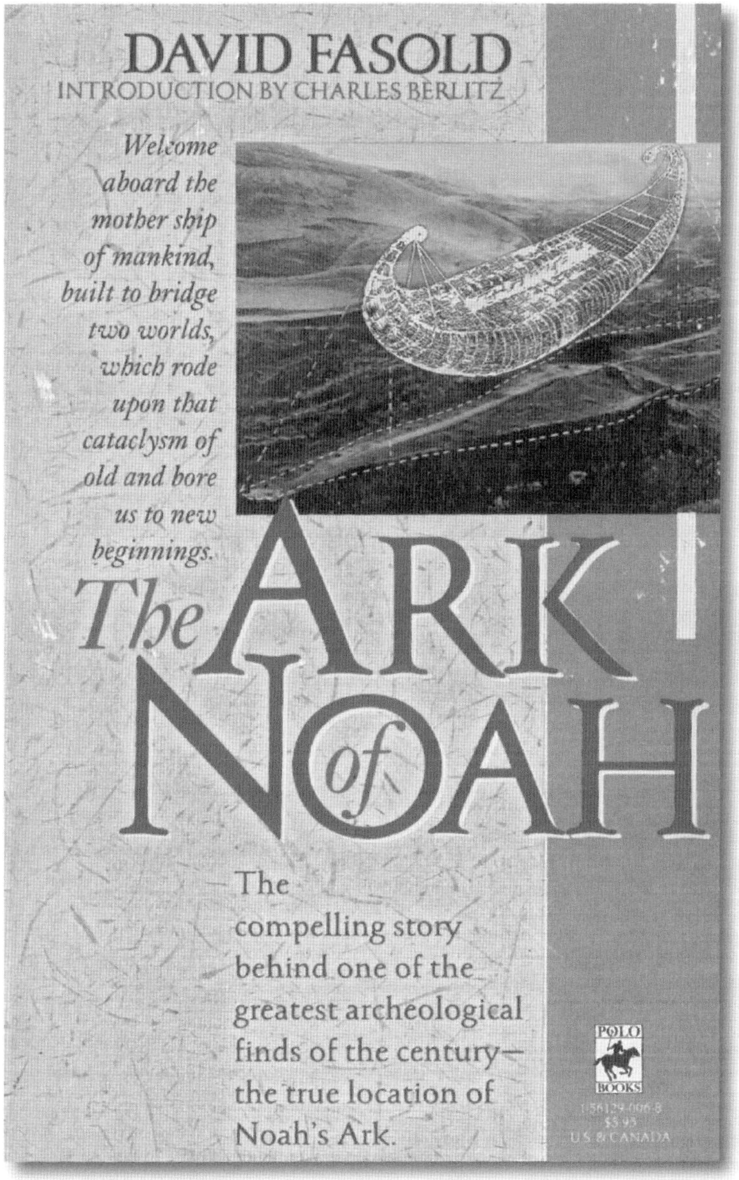

David Fasold

A self-described "Ark-ologist," Wheaton-raised David Fasold claimed to have discovered curious formations which he believed to be Noah's Ark on Mount Mahser Dagi, 17 miles from the traditional Mount Ararat. A former US Merchant Marine and salvage expert, Fasold proclaims in *The Ark of Noah*, "The search for the Ark is over. In June 1987, the Turkish ministers officiated . . . a blood sacrifice at the groundbreaking ceremony . . . The area is now a national park and under constant attention and guard." Fasold's findings generated some controversy among other adventurers searching for the famed relic. Others were solidly convinced. Larry King, the famed CNN interviewer, remarks, "Why isn't this front page of the *New York Times*? I mean, you would think that the discovery, the actual, factual discovery of Noah's Ark would be page one!" Fasold was a dedicated Young Earth Creationist who sought to permanently disprove Old Earth Creationism.

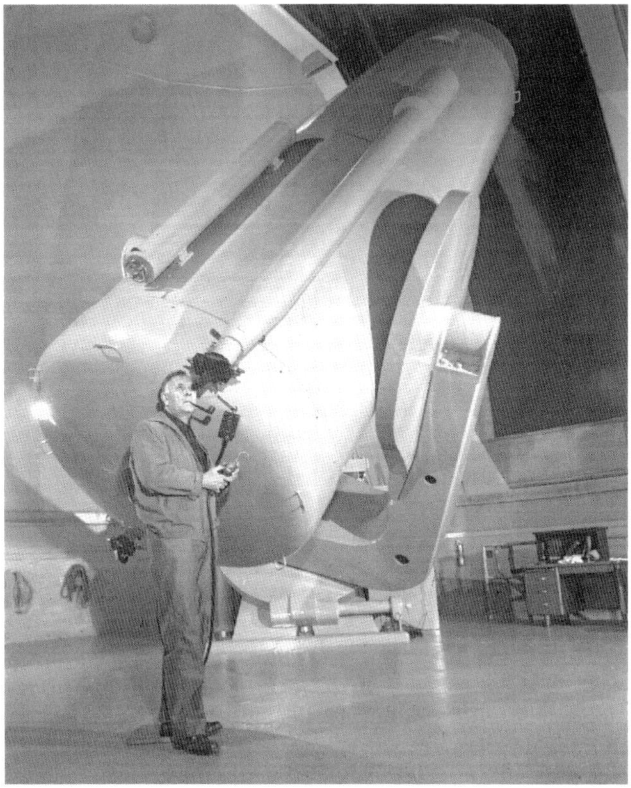

Edwin Hubble

A trusty English briar clenched between his teeth, astronomer Edwin Hubble serenely peers at celestial mysteries through the wide-angle lens of the 48-inch telescope at Mount Palomar Observatory. Born in Marshfield, Missouri, Hubble resided for several years with his family in Wheaton where he graduated from high school, distinguishing himself in athletics. Hubble then entered the University of Chicago, during which time he assisted at the Yerkes Observatory in Michigan, gazing at the heavens. During his senior year, he scored well on his competitive exam and won the right to represent Illinois as a Rhodes Scholar at Oxford University, studying law. After serving in World War II, Hubble moved to Mount Wilson Observatory in California, where he utilized its superb equipment to phenomenal advantage. In 1923, he published his explosive paper, "Island Universes," revealing his discoveries regarding "redshifts," the increased wavelengths of radiation emitted by a celestial object. Nebulae farther away, he observed, were receding at the fastest rate, indicating an expanding universe. His seminal work placed him on the cover of *Time* magazine in 1930. Residing near Hollywood, Hubble and his wife, Grace, enjoyed the camaraderie of Charlie Chaplin, the Marx Brothers, Helen Hayes, and Walt Disney. Another friend, Albert Einstein, modified his own equations on relativity to accommodate Hubble's research. *National Geographic* cites Hubble as possibly the most important astronomer since Galileo, and Stephen Hawking in *A Brief History of Time* writes that "Hubble's discovery that the Universe is expanding was one of the great intellectual revolutions of the 20th Century." Grote Reber's mother, a schoolteacher, stimulated her son's interest in science with articles written by Edwin, a former pupil. A middle school in Wheaton is named after Hubble, in addition to an orbiting telescope known for its spectacularly successful functionality as well as its occasional malfunctions. Struck with a cerebral thrombosis, Hubble departed Earth in 1953. He was cremated and his ashes placed in a copper box, buried in a secret place. As we observe with brilliant clarity the edge of the universe with its spinning planets and gorgeous, terrifying riddles, we thank Edwin Hubble.

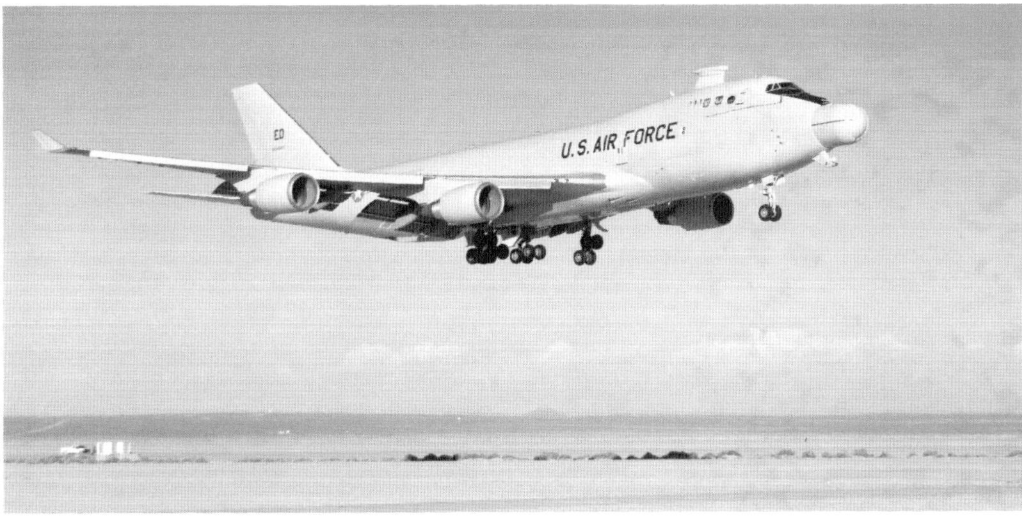

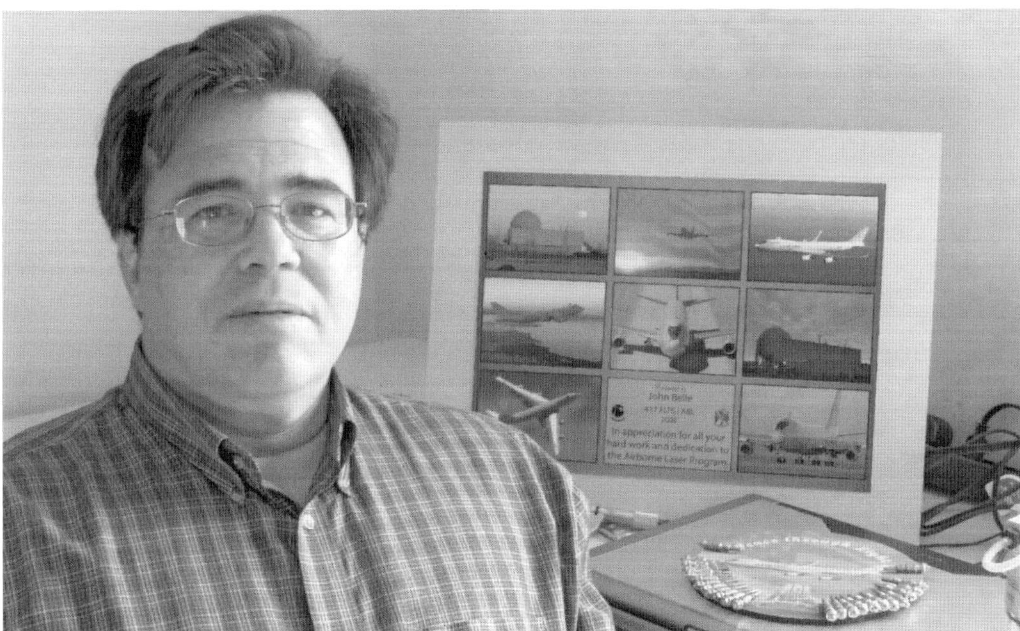

John Belle

If asked, Belle can honestly claim that he is a rocket scientist. For the past 28 years, he has worked as a structural mechanics engineer in advanced product development for the aerospace and medical industry. Belle began his education at College of DuPage and finished his undergraduate degree in mechanical/aerospace engineering at Illinois Institute of Technology. Significant projects he has worked on include: Airborne Laser Modules installation and flight structure repair of the YAL-1; dual speed centrifuge design for the AMICUS®, a continual process apheresis blood cell separator from Fenwal, Inc; primary support structure for the F-18E/F fighter 20mm Gatling gun; and of course rockets (Atlas, Centaur, Shuttle-Centaur, Trident II D-5 3rd Stage nozzle, Titan-IV Engines both solid and liquid, Shuttle RSRM, and the CrIS instrument of the NPOESS Satellite). Belle resides in Wheaton. (Courtesy of John Belle.)

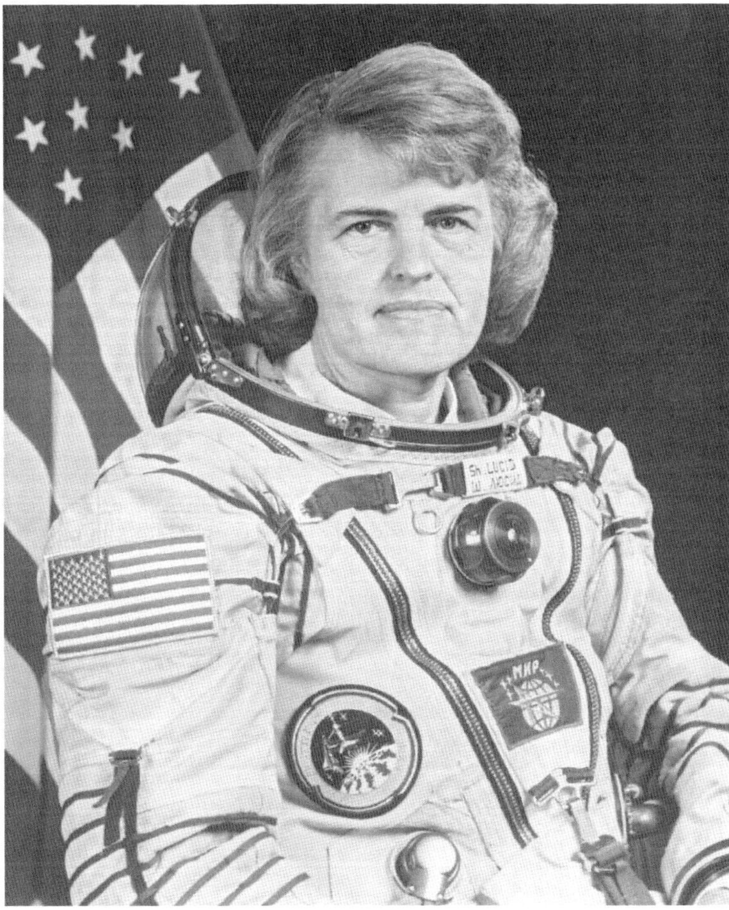

Shannon Lucid

Though the stars were her destination, Shannon (Wells) Lucid was born in the equally exotic but earthbound environs of Shanghai, China, her parents serving as Baptist missionaries with China Inland Mission. When she was six weeks old, her family was taken by the Japanese as prisoners of war. Incarcerated for one year in an internment camp, they were released in a prisoner exchange and returned to the United States. After the war, they returned to China. When the Communists took control and China closed its doors to missionaries, the Wells family moved to Bethany, Oklahoma. From 1960 to 1962, Lucid attended Wheaton College, but departed before completion due to tuition increases, finishing her education at the University of Oklahoma. In 1978, NASA selected her as the first American female astronaut for its Space Shuttle flight crew. Flying multiple missions, Lucid clinched the record for most hours in low-earth orbit of any woman, remaining for 188 days. However, her record was broken in 2002. She also held the United States single mission flight endurance record on the Russian space station Mir, until her record was surpassed by Sunita Williams on the International Space Station. "I really, truly enjoyed living in space for an extended period of time," she says. During one mission, Lucid famously craved M&M candies. To accommodate, President Clinton sent a 10-pound box from the White House to NASA, awaiting Lucid's return to *terra firma*. She has been awarded the Congressional Medal of Honor and the Russian Order of Friendship Medal. "We are building the infrastructure with the Shuttle and the International Space Station. We are learning how to live and work in space, learning what it takes so we will go back to the Moon on a fairly regular basis." (Courtesy of NASA.)

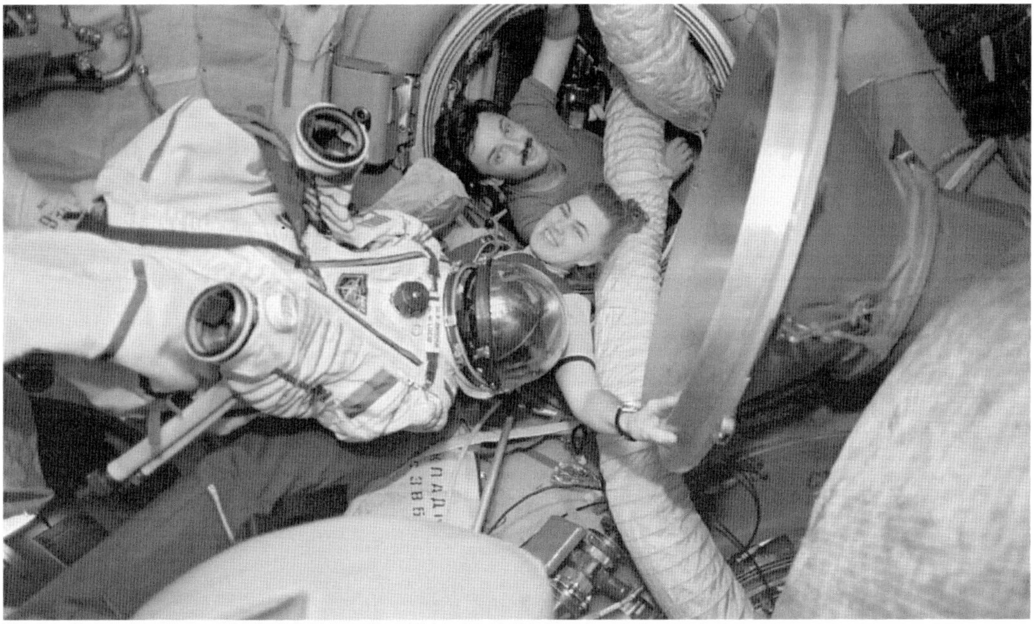

Lucid Aboard Mir

Lucid floats in zero-gravity with Russian cosmonaut Aleksandyr Kaleri aboard Mir. She is noted for her good humor and patience, qualities especially valued in the close-quarter environment of space exploration. Below: Earthside, the amiable astronaut sits at a control console at the Johnson Space Center in Houston. In 1994, she delivered a chapel address at Wheaton College. When asked by reporters if she found God in space, Lucid replies: "No. God found me years ago. *That* is your story." (Courtesy of NASA.)

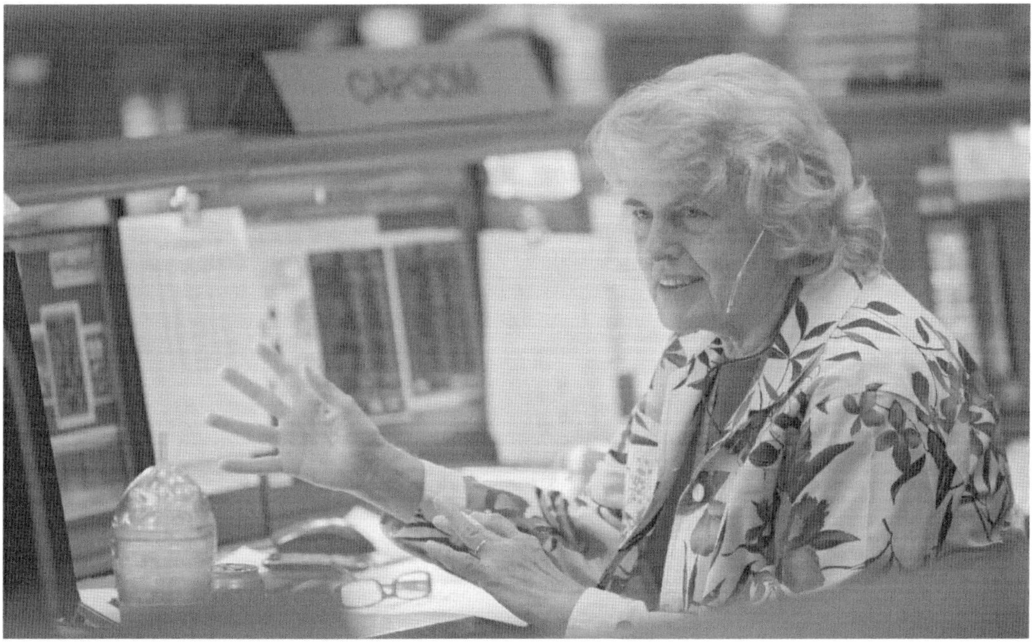

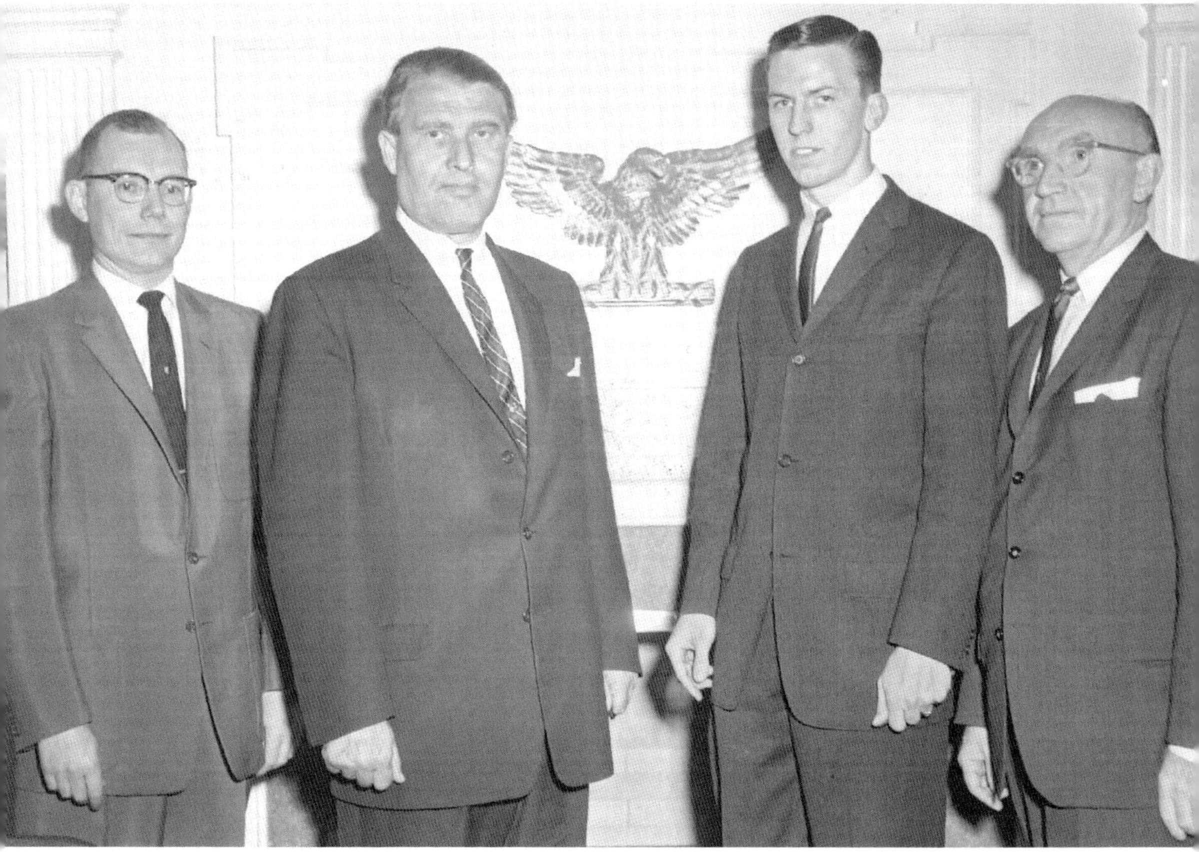

Wernher von Braun

From left to right, Dr. Stanley Parmerter, chairman of Division of Science, Wheaton College; Dr. Wernher von Braun; William C. Wood, chairman of Lyceum Union; and Capt. Bart J. Slattery Jr., chief of information, Marshall Space Flight Center, Huntsville, Alabama, pose for a photograph. In addition to theologians, pastors, and missionaries, Wheaton College during the 1960s invited an array of first-rate speakers from the secular realm, notably Wernher von Braun, who lectured in 1961 during Shannon Lucid's years as a student (though she could not attend). His talk, entitled, "Why We Must Conquer Space," was accompanied by illustrations, and perhaps the Disney-produced *Man in Space* film. Right: Another outstanding visitor was Haile Selassie, emperor of Ethiopia, with whom the college enjoyed a friendly relationship. Here trustee Joseph Evans moves in for a handshake with the somewhat distracted nobleman.

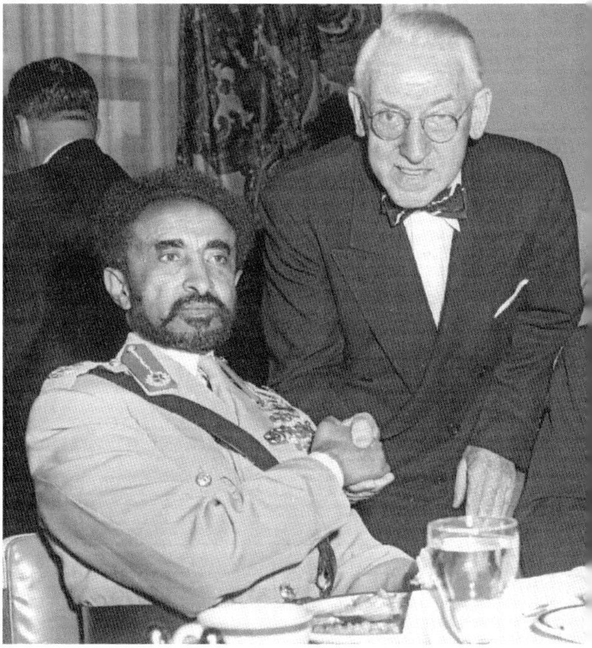

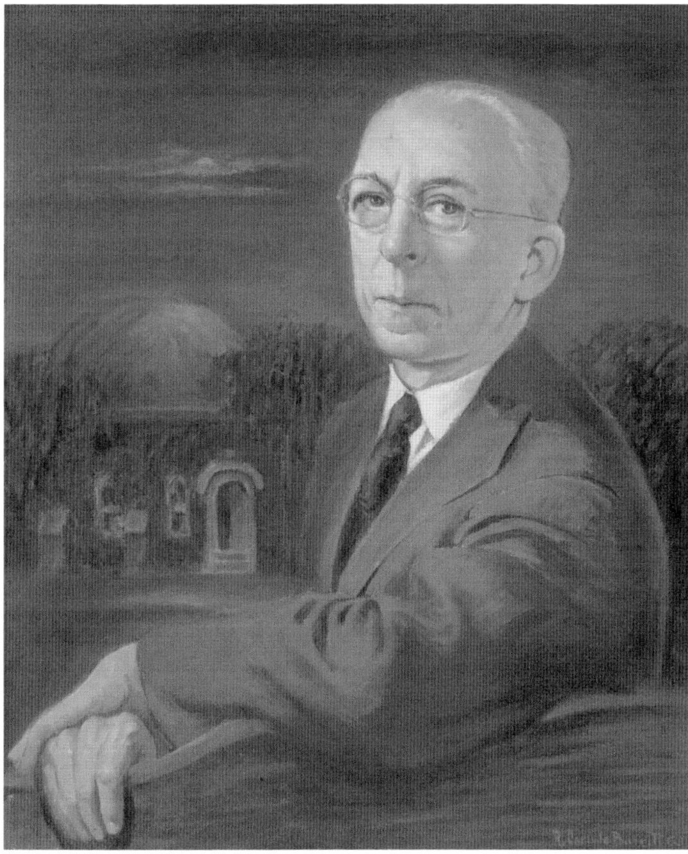

Harold Lee Alden

Born in Chicago, Alden graduated from Wheaton College in 1912. He acquired his master's degree from the University of Chicago in 1913, and his doctorate in astronomy from the University of Virginia where he studied the heavens at the McCormick Observatory, using its 26-inch telescope, one of the largest in the world. In 1925, Yale developed a new telescope and shipped it to Johannesburg, South Africa, to observe the clear southern skies. Alden, sent to direct the program, lived there with his family for 20 years. He thoroughly enjoyed South Africa, returning in 1945 to the States with some reluctance to the University of Virginia. Alden felt that he had accomplished more in South Africa with its agreeable climate and superior equipment in 20 years than had been done in the United States in 30 years. He served as professor of astronomy and director of the observatory until retiring in 1960. His name is starred in *American Men of Science*. He wrote, "Too large a proportion of astronomers are included in the starred group from which it follows that one should become an astronomer if he wants to have a star attached to his name. Or his name attached to a star if he discovers something unusual." Alden maintained a cordial relationship with Wheaton College, exchanging letters with Miss Julia Blanchard, school archivist. "I wonder what the Wheaton of today is like," he wrote in 1946. "I often recall the happy little family of 35 years ago when everyone knew everyone else and where each one had to make his contribution in order to carry on . . . When I visited Wheaton in 1932 I felt lost and doubted whether I would ever return again." After a long, distinguished career surveying the heavens, he died at 74. As one of 500 deceased men and women of science, including luminaries Jules Verne and H.G. Wells, Alden was honored to have a crater on the dark side of the moon named after him. (Courtesy of the Leander McCormick Observatory and Digital Curation Services of the University of Virginia Library.)

Paul W. Gast

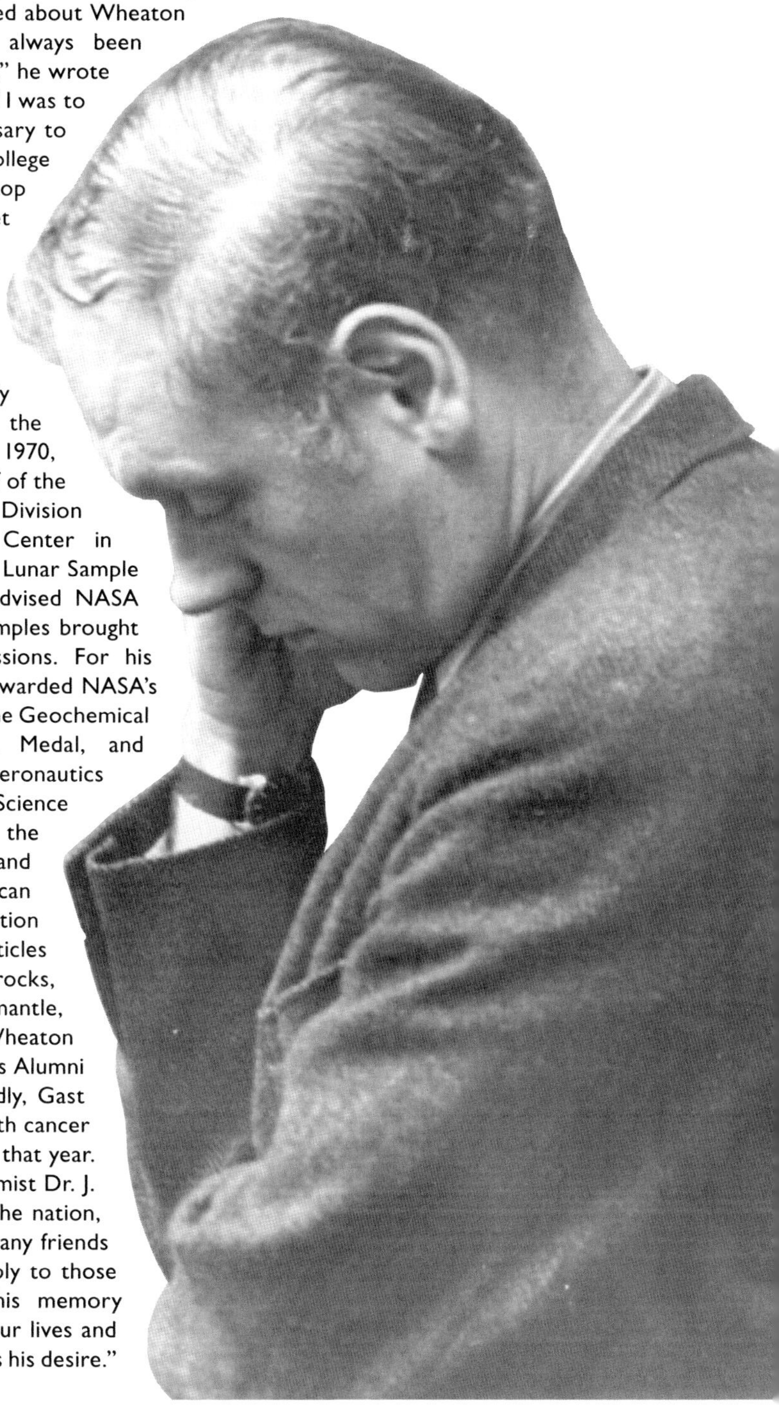

Listening to a speaker in 1971 at Houston's Lunar Science Institute, Gast is probably disagreeing. As a youngster in Chicago, Gast suffered poor health. Often staying home from school, he read books and magazines like *Moody Monthly*, published by Moody Bible Institute, from which he learned about Wheaton College. "My ambition has always been research and experimentation," he wrote on his application. "And I felt if I was to go into this field it was necessary to go to college." At Wheaton College where he was recognized as a top student in chemistry, Gast met his future wife, Joyce, with whom he would raise three children. Graduating in 1952, he pursued advanced education and taught at several universities, notably as professor of geology at the University of Minnesota. In 1970, he was hired by NASA as chief of the Planetary and Earth Sciences Division at the Manned Spacecraft Center in Houston. As a member of the Lunar Sample Analysis Planning Team, he advised NASA on the disposition of lunar samples brought to Earth by the Apollo missions. For his exemplary service, Gast was awarded NASA's Distinguished Service Medal, the Geochemical Society's V.M. Goldschmidt Medal, and the American Institute of Aeronautics and Astronautics Space Science Award. He was president of the Volcanology, Geochemistry, and Petrology Section of the American Geochemistry Union, in addition to publishing numerous articles detailing the origin of volcanic rocks, the chemistry of Earth's upper mantle, and geochronology. In 1973, Wheaton College recognized him with its Alumni Service to Society Award. Sadly, Gast had already been diagnosed with cancer and died at age 43 in March of that year. "His death," eulogized geochemist Dr. J. Lawrence Kulp, "is a loss to the nation, to science, to NASA, to his many friends and colleagues, but most deeply to those he loved—his family. May his memory strengthen us, may it enrich our lives and may it turn us to God. That was his desire." (Courtesy of Walter Gast.)

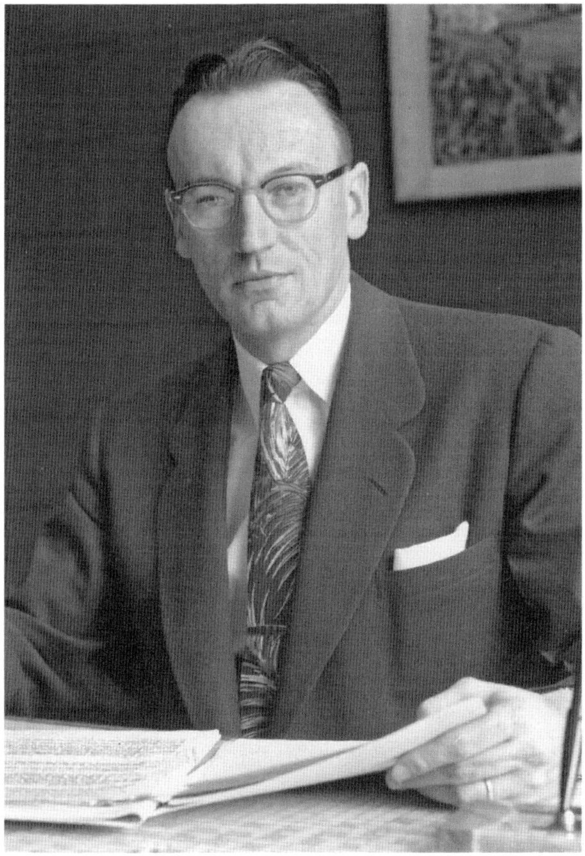

J. Lawrence Kulp

Kulp was born in New Jersey and raised as an Episcopalian. Educated at Drew University and Wheaton College, Kulp earned his PhD in geology from Princeton University. He was associate professor of geochemistry at Columbia University and director of the Lamont Geological Observatory at Columbia, serving between 1947 and 1965. He left the university to be vice president for research and development at Weyerhaeuser Company. Later in in his career, he involved himself with environmental and natural resource issues. Kulp was instrumental in developing radioactive carbon dating for rocks and fossils, studying for one month with Dr. Willard F. Libby at the University of Chicago. He was a member of President Eisenhower's "Atoms for Peace" delegation to Geneva, Switzerland, and served on the faculties of National Bible Institute and Nyack Missionary Training Institute, developing courses for integrating the Christian faith with modern science. Kulp investigated the amounts of strontium-90 that had infiltrated food supplies. He worked on the Manhattan Project during World War II. He was also on the council for the American Scientific Affiliation, a faith-based organization founded in 1941, dedicated to providing an open forum where scientific controversies can be discussed without fear of unjust condemnation. Kulp was largely responsible for leading segments of evangelicalism away from Young Earth Creationism to adopting Old Earth Creationism. During the 1980s, Kulp served as the director of the National Acid Precipitation Assessment Program. Findings were presented to the Ronald Reagan administration stating that the effects of acid rain on forests was not notably significant. As a geochemist, Kulp challenged "flood geology" and other positions advanced by Young Earth Creationism, feeling that such approaches by conservative Christians were pseudo-science at best. He was particularly critical of John C. Whitcomb's and Henry M. Morris's *The Genesis Flood*, which inaugurated the Young Earth Movement. Kulp died in 2006. He and his wife, Helen, had four children.

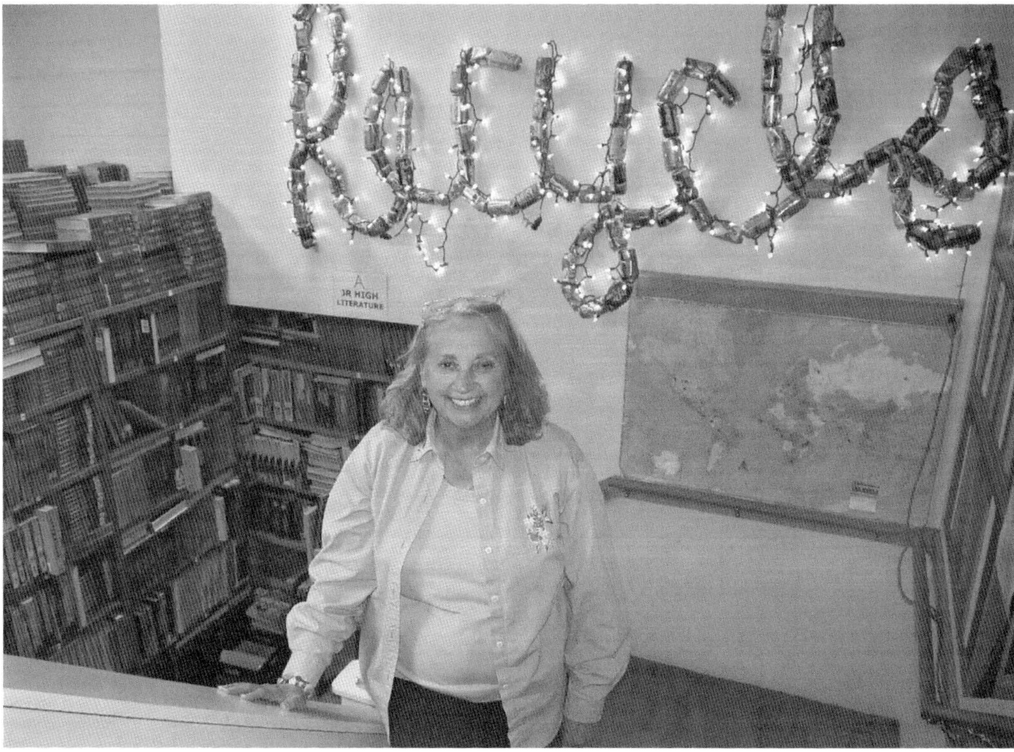

Kay McKeen

"I hate waste," says McKeen, founder and executive director of SCARCE (School and Community Assistance for Composting and Recycling Education). But she is infectiously passionate about continually recycling her vision for sustainability and creative reuse. While teaching about environmental issues in DuPage County educational institutions, McKeen realized that many schools possessed countless discarded textbooks occupying limited storage space. As the information was becoming obsolete, the books were taking up space in the schools, and it cost the schools money to send the books to the landfill. Consequently, in 1991 she started the Book Rescue with the idea of "rescuing" gently used books (text, reference, and library) from the Dumpster, instead placing these valuable resources into the hands of those needing it. Aside from book rescuing, SCARCE implements other programs to lend fresh life to exhausted material. For instance, worn-out, unwearable gym shoes are sent to Nike's Reuse-A-Shoe Program, which shreds the rubber, crafting it into new products like sports surfaces, playgrounds, carpet padding, insulation, basketballs, and Frisbees. Another program uses donated broken pieces of crayons from schools and residents to fashion "Super Crayons," in which volunteers peel, sort, and melt the petroleum bits using a crockpot and candle molds, forming large crayons to be used by children with special needs. SCARCE attempts to connect educators from around the world with one another, supplying classrooms with used furniture, musical instruments, or equipment that might otherwise be trashed. Through education, McKeen and SCARCE attempt to preserve and care for the Earth's natural resources while working to build sustainable communities. McKeen believes that all citizens of the Earth are able to contribute something positive toward a purer environment, an obligation to ourselves and those not yet born. The nonprofit organization has been featured on ABC News, WGN News, NBC World News, and in the *Daily Herald* and the *Chicago Tribune*. Recognition includes "10 Most Influential Environmentalists," the State of Illinois Hometown Hero Award, Educator of the Year Award, Role Model Program Award, Governor's Pollution Prevention Award, and the Illinois Recycling Association's Outstanding School Recycling and Reduction Education Program Award. (Courtesy of Kay McKeen.)

CELLS
ENGLISH

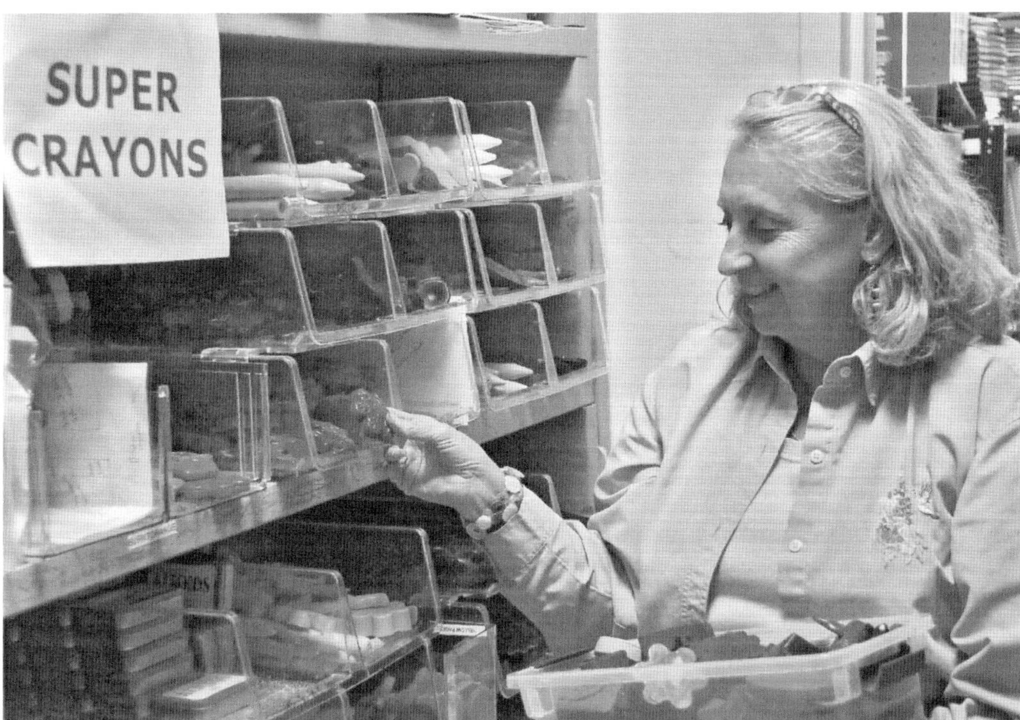
SUPER
CRAYONS

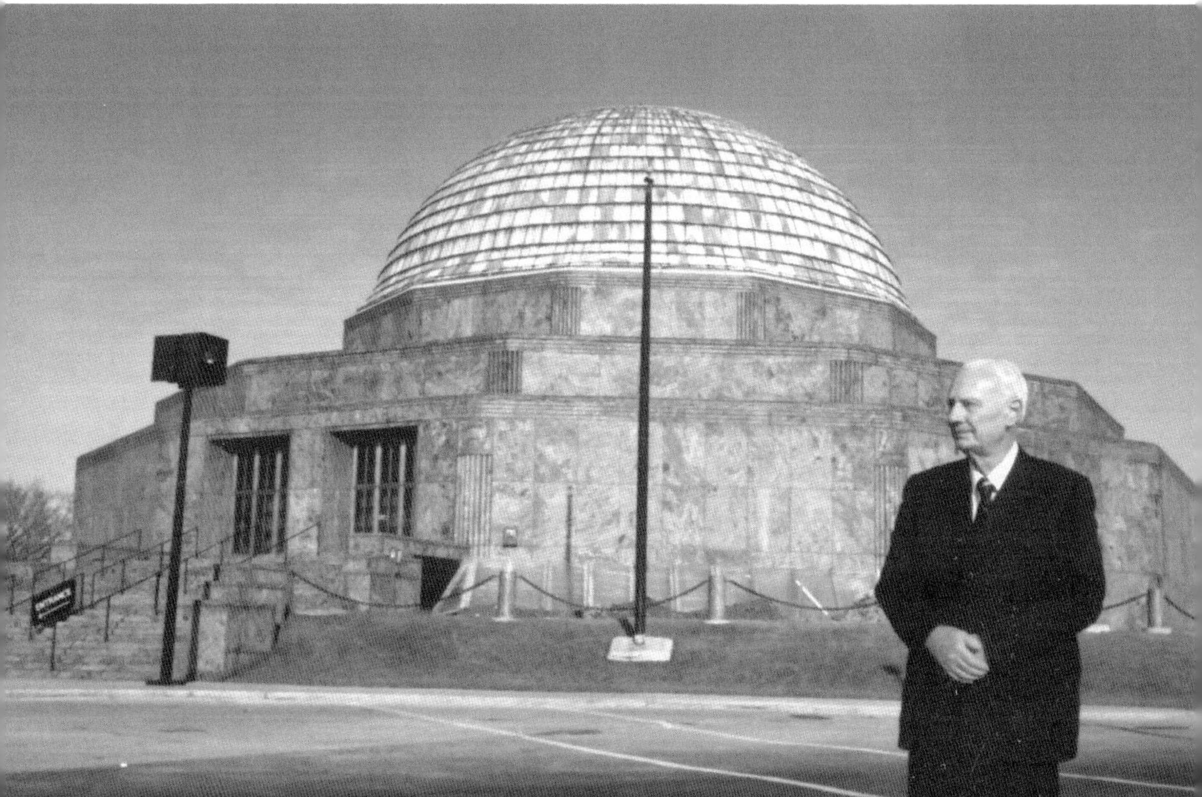

Grote Reber

Reber visits the Adler Planetarium, nestled on the shore of Lake Michigan in Chicago. Born in the Windy City in 1911, he spent the first 35 years of his life in Wheaton. Employed as an engineer at a Chicago station, Reber heard curious noises in radio transmissions. A Bell Labs engineer named K.G. Jansky had already noted this peculiarity, but Reber decided to further investigate. Using various parts acquired from the University of Chicago and elsewhere, he constructed in his Wheaton backyard a parabolic reflector used for cosmic radio reception. For 10 years he was the only active radio astronomer in the world, listening to the weak but constant static emanating throughout the solar system. In 1944, he published his discoveries on radio wave transmissions in the *Astrophysical Journal*. These discoveries allowed him to draw the first map of the galaxy charting sources of radio waves. In 1954, Reber moved to Bothwell, Tasmania, whose clear skies and peculiar atmospheric conditions allowed an uncluttered look, and here he built his own energy-efficient home as he continued mapping the radio spectrum. Reber's revolutionary research paved the way for satellite communications, AM and FM radio bands, and cell phones. Not limited to exploring outer space, he designed an electrically powered car called the Pixie. He was critical of scientists who will not take chances, but maintain the status quo to keep their jobs. When he returned to Wheaton for a visit in 1995, he was shocked at how large it had become since he lived there. Reber hoped to discredit the Big Bang Theory. "It's just another form of Creationism," he said. "Instead of being promoted by religious cranks it's being promoted by astronomical cranks . . ." Reber's radar dish was dismantled from its Wheaton location and shipped to Green Bank, West Virginia, where it is displayed on the grounds of the National Radio Astronomy Observatory. His home, which stood at 212 W. Seminary, is now a parking lot.

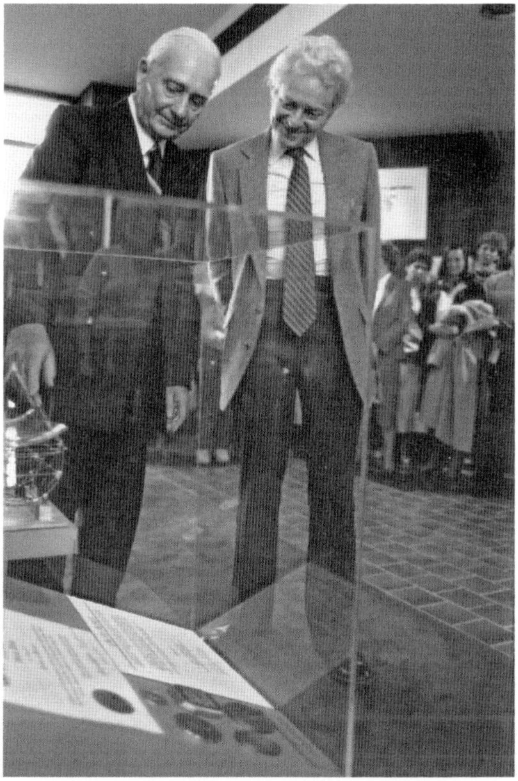

Reber Inducted into the DuPage Heritage Gallery

Touring exhibits at DuPage Heritage Gallery located in the atrium at the DuPage County Government Center, Reber explains a model of his radar dish to Leon Lederman, Nobel Prize winner in Physics and director emeritus of Fermilab in Batavia, Illinois. The gallery was dedicated in October 1980, with Gov. James R. Thompson presenting the main address. Below: Grote Reber poses with Kenneth Taylor, author, translator, and publisher of *The Living Bible*. Both were inducted into the DuPage Heritage Gallery, along with Harold "Red" Grange, Edwin Hubble, Joy Morton, Everett Mitchell, Elbert Gary, John W. Gates, Billy Graham, Robert McCormick, and Margaret Landon.

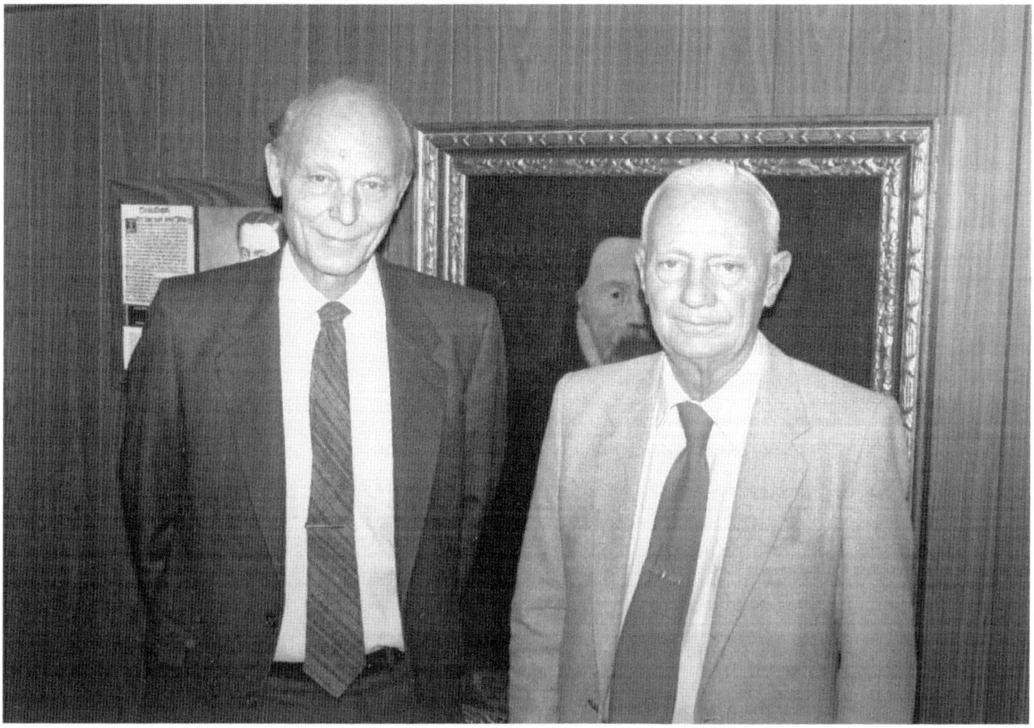

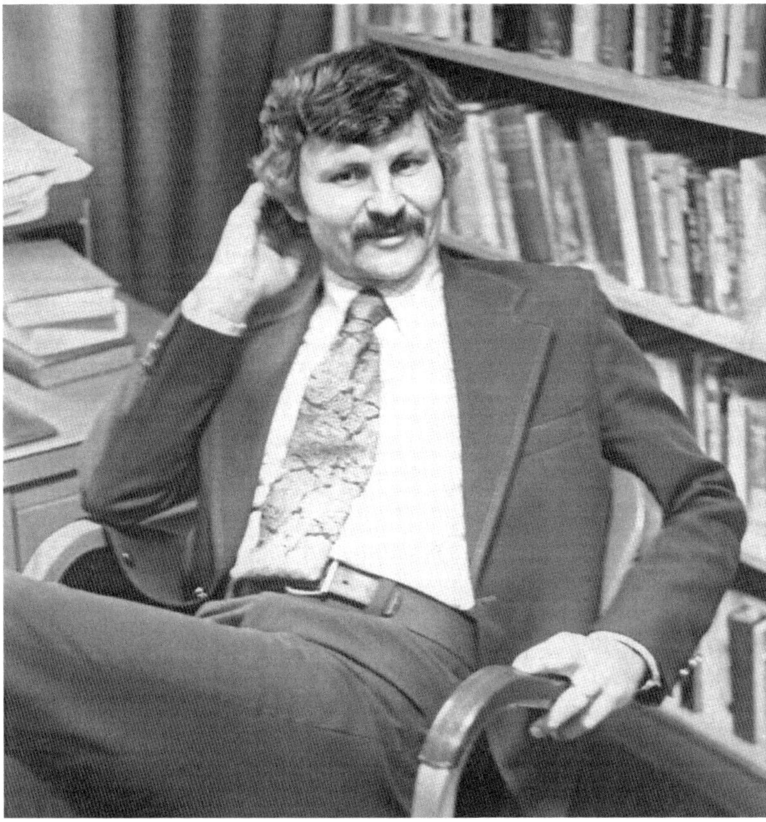

Robert E. Webber

One of the more controversial professors at Wheaton College, Webber influenced a generation of students and a large segment of evangelicalism. Raised in a Baptist church in Pennsylvania, he attended Bob Jones University in the late 1950s before enrolling at Reformed Episcopal Seminary, in 1960 finishing his graduate education at Covenant Theological Seminary. He began teaching theology at Wheaton College in 1968. Youthful, energetic, and sympathetic to the concerns of students, he was a popular and effective lecturer. As he studied ecclesiastical history, its variable trends and moods, Webber perceived that vital practices had been ignored or recklessly tossed aside during the Reformation. In 1978, he published *Evangelicals on the Canterbury Trail*, a collection of autobiographical essays by Webber and former evangelicals who gradually adopted Anglo-Catholic or Catholic forms of worship. When released, the book generated considerable heat among evangelicals who felt that Webber had betrayed the Protestant faith. Eventually, however, it was recognized that his pioneering research opened doors for fresh approaches to church life, whether liturgical expressions were adopted or not. Closely studying the permutations of Christian worship, Webber wrote or edited several additional books dealing with the history and function of liturgy, including *Worship Is a Verb*, *Blended Worship*, and the seven-volume *Complete Library of Christian Worship*. During his later career, he concentrated on the Church Fathers, attempting to draw from their treatises insights for contemporary contexts. His interest is expressed in the introduction to *Journey to Jesus*: "The model of evangelism proposed in this book is a resurrection of the seeker model . . . that originated in the third century . . . It speaks particularly to the current search for an effective style of evangelism in a world dominated by postmodern thought, a church living in a post-Constantinian society, and the challenge to overcome the resurgence of pagan values." Webber was director of the Institute for Worship Studies. At the time of his death in 2007, he was the William R. and Geraldyn B. Myers Professor of Ministry at Northern Seminary in Lombard, Illinois.

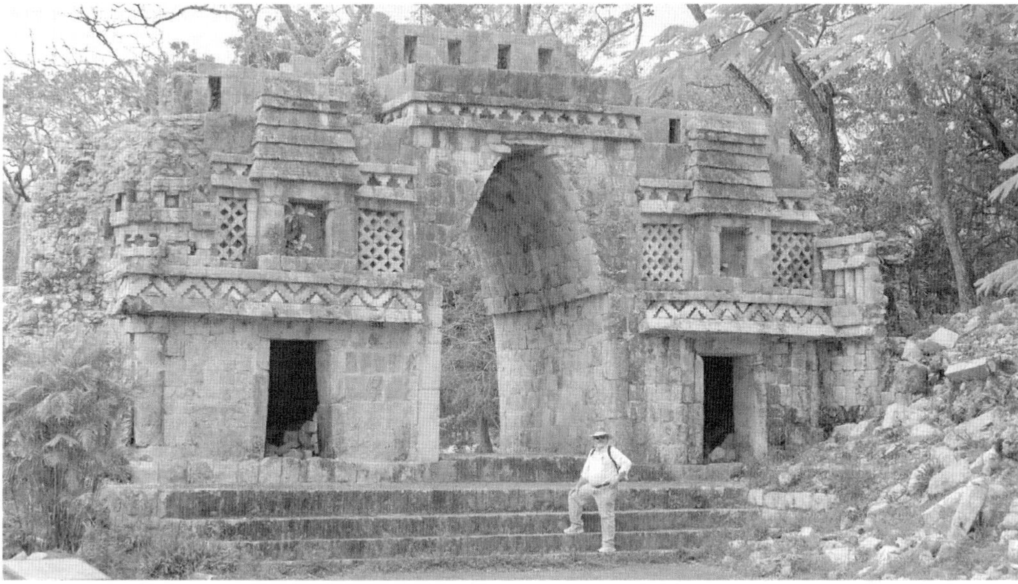

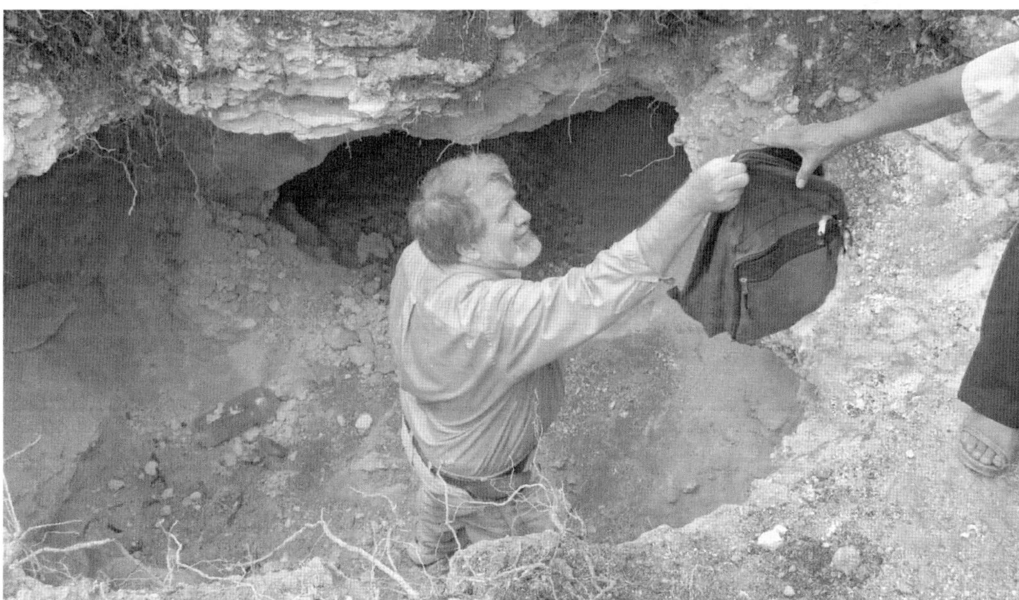

Dean Arnold

For much of his career, anthropologist Dean Arnold had investigated the composition of Maya Blue, the unique azure pigment manufactured by Meso-American cultures. Traces are still found on murals and pottery, but the production technique was long lost. Sorting through artifacts on the field and at the Field Museum in Chicago, Arnold and his team examined remnants on a ceremonial bowl, discovered over 100 years ago in a sinkhole at the Mayan site of Chichén Itzá, containing palygorskite, indigo, and copal incense, a tree sap believed to hold healing properties and burned as an offering to the deities. Arnold surmised that the mystical Maya Blue was likely generated during the sacrificial ritual itself, created through the heat of the burning copal. *Archaeology* magazine cited his finding as one of the "Top 10 Discoveries of 2008." (Courtesy of Dean Arnold.)

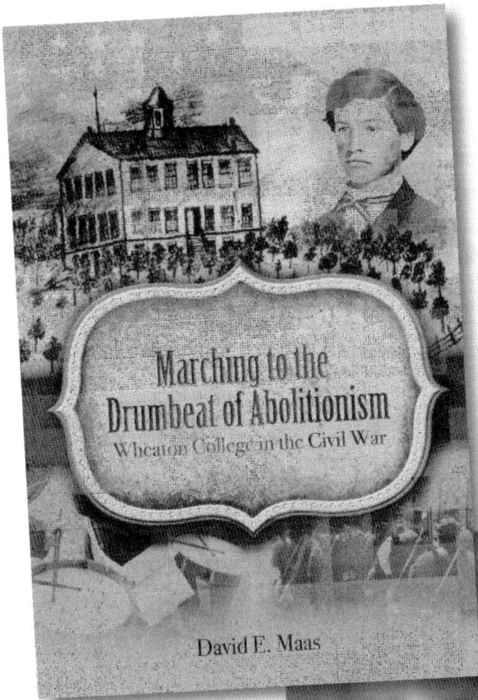

Marching to the Drumbeat of Abolitionism

Maas traces the history of Wheaton College's involvement in abolition, including its contribution to the Civil War and its aftermath, in *Marching to the Drumbeat of Abolitionism* (2010). Beginning with Wheaton's predecessor, the Illinois Institute, he investigates Pres. Jonathan Blanchard's interaction with Abraham Lincoln, Frederick Douglass, and other national figures, emphasizing his pivotal involvement with the antislavery effort. At least 298 Wheaton students fought for the Union and 26 died.

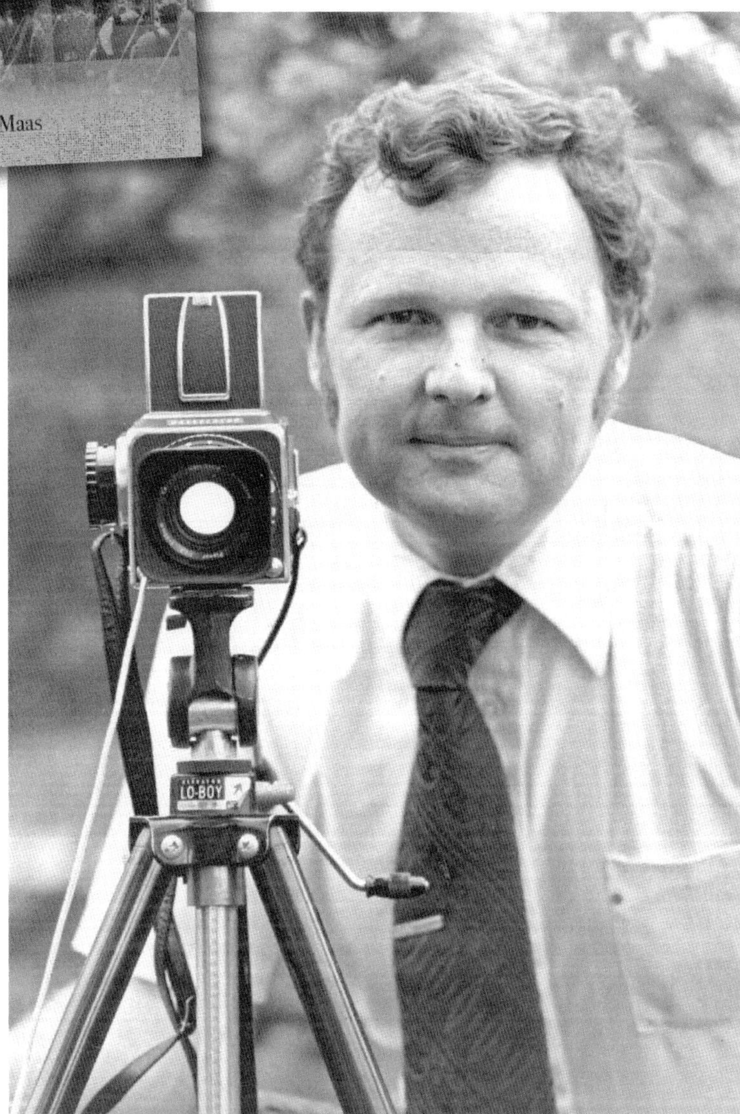

David Maas

Since the Civil War, rumors had floated about in DuPage County that Wheaton College was a station on the Underground Railroad, but no documentation ever surfaced. Historian David Maas, however, researching information relating to abolition in the *Thirty-ninth Regiment of the Illinois Volunteer Infantry*, discovered a reliable account proving that the college was indeed a stopover to freedom. Runaway slaves walked without hindrance on campus and worshipped in its chapel.

INDEX